To my five

Reginald Dickens

To my friend Paul Tierney

Larry Simon ☺

MW01253952

African Ambit

African Ambit

Reginald Dickenson

The Pentland Press
Edinburgh – Cambridge – Durham – USA

© Reginald Dickenson, 1995

First published in 1995
by The Pentland Press Ltd
1 Hutton Close
South Church
Bishop Auckland
Durham

All rights reserved.
Unauthorised duplication
contravenes existing laws.

British Library
Cataloguing-in-Publication Data

A catalogue record for this book
is available from the British Library

ISBN 1–85821-244-8

Cover illustrations are from two oil paintings by the author.
Photographs are from the author's collection, and include three photographs taken by the
Federation Information Department and one Jamaican press picture.

Typeset by Carnegie Publishing Ltd., 18 Maynard St., Preston
Printed and bound by Antony Rowe Ltd., Chippenham

To Doc, who knew so much about Africa but would not write it, and who loved to lead me on to express my own opinions and then confound me with the wealth of his experience, knowledge and wisdom.

The views expressed in this book are my own and do not necessarily reflect those of my former employers.

Acknowledgements

With acknowledgements to:

All those people who have written papers, articles and books which have provided the information and helped formulate the ideas set out in this book.

The Colonial Office, Jamaica Telephone Coy and World Bank, for employing me in positions which enabled me to see so much of the developing world.

My wife.
Frankie experienced it all with me and never lost her love of Africa and her sense of humour.

The late Sir Roy Welensky KCMG, prime minister of the then Federation of the Rhodesias and Nyasaland.
Sir Roy arranged for his office to review the original manuscript and confirm that I had made no major political gaffes.

Lt Col. Charles Royal Dickenson CMG, ICD, OLM.
My brother Roy provided useful criticism and gave a great deal of help in giving me information about the Federation after I had left Africa. He also pointed out a number of errors.

Mr Ton Schippers.

Ton made some useful comments. He also sent me his copy of Chief Areoye Oyebola's book *Black Man's Dilemma.*

Chief Areoye Oyebola.

Chief Oyebola has written the most objective book I have ever read about the problems of Africa as seen from the African viewpoint. I am grateful to Chief Oyeobola and his publishers for allowing me to include extracts from *Black Man's Dilemma* in this book.

Mr Ken Davies.

Ken worked with me in Germany, joined us in Nyasaland and contributed substantially to the development programme, kept me in touch with things Malawi and helped me find a publisher.

Mr D. H. Beal.

Dick helped me in a number of ways and encouraged me in thinking the book might have some educational value and readership in the United States.

Mrs Robin C. Brown.

Although changes to the subject matter were avoided, Jan made me adopt a more orderly format and eliminate much of the duplication. She made the book much more readable, and the reader owes her a great deal.

Mrs M. Breckenridge.

Margie corrected my computer's bad spelling and punctuation.

Contents

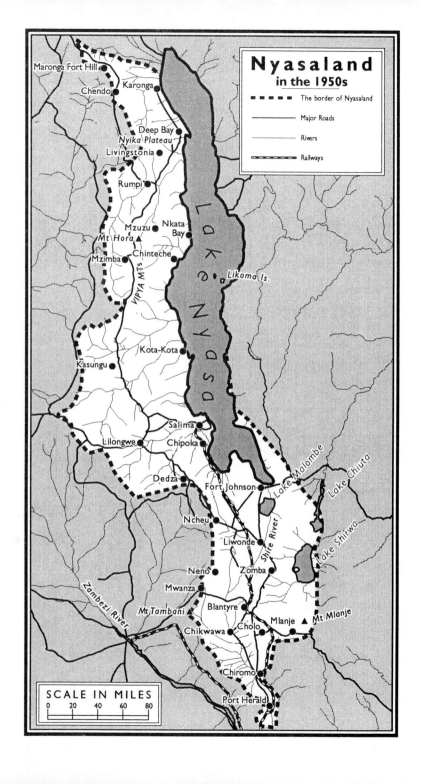

Nyasaland
in the 1950s

- - - - The border of Nyasaland

——— Major Roads

——— Rivers

╪╪╪╪ Railways

Maronga Fort Hill
Chendo
Karonga
Deep Bay
Nyika Plateau
Livingstonia
Rumpi
Mzuzu
Nkata Bay
Mt Hora
Chinteche
Mzimba
VIPYA Mts
Likoma Is.
Kota-Kota
Kasungu
Salima
Lilongwe
Chipoka
Dedza
Fort Johnson
Lake Malombe
Lake Chiuta
Ncheu
Liwonde
Shire River
Lake Shirwa
Neno
Zomba
Mwanza
Mt Tambani
Blantyre
Mlanje
Mt Mlanje
Chikwawa
Cholo
Zambezi River
Chiromo
Port Herald
Lake Nyasa

SCALE IN MILES
0   20   40   60   80

NYASALAND, THE FEDERATION AND SURROUNDING COUNTRIES

*If the names of countries have changed, the modern name is shown in **Bold***

Prologue

Florida 1993

The main chapters of this book were written in Jamaica during the period 1957/59. They were based on notes and diaries I had kept in Nyasaland. After producing a reasonably clean draft, with a view to possible publication, I reached the conclusion that the book would have greater interest if its scope was expanded to cover my experiences in Jamaica.

I started preparing notes covering the Jamaican section but realized that, although I had already been in Jamaica for nearly three years, I had still much to learn about the different racial relations and the many contrasts with Africa which I wished to feature in my expanded book. This became, therefore, something of a longer term project.

In 1960, I was appointed managing director of my company and found that, with my additional commitments, I was unlikely to be able to complete the book I had planned. I decided to keep the manuscript of the African section as a personal record and put it away until I gave up consultancy work in 1986.

*　　*　　*

During my many visits to Africa over the years, I have become increasingly concerned about the deteriorating situation there. I have also noted the almost constant criticism of the colonial system, which is blamed for most of the present problems in independent Africa. There seems to be an abysmal lack of appreciation of what was achieved under colonial rule and the dedication of most colonial officers.

I see black, and some white, students in the USA sporting medallions of red, green and gold, which they say stand for the bloodshed, land theft and stolen resources resulting from colonialism. These medallions might more appropriately stand for the blood saved through the suppression of tribal wars, the reduction in impoverishment and devastation of the land brought about through the introduction of better agricultural practices, and the national wealth created through agriculture, industry and mining.

Within the present-day context, it may be difficult to make a case for colonialism. It is, however, obvious to those colonials who went through the experience that conditions would almost certainly have been worse without it.

One of my friends who recently read my manuscript felt strongly that a case should be made for what we did in Nyasaland under colonial rule and what positive results were obtained. These factors led me to wonder if it was still not too late to try to publish a book setting out my experience and impressions during the colonial period.

*   *   *

Although I may now disagree with some of my previous conclusions, the subject matter in the main chapters has largely been left in its original form as an expression and outline of my ideas and experiences at the time. The manuscript has been subject to only minor alteration but with some rearrangement and a few notes and additions shown in italics. I have made tense changes to the past tense for what were at the time current events and circumstances. Features which have not been subject to change have been left in the present tense. I apologize to American readers for the British word usage and spelling.

I have generally avoided naming actual persons in the book. This has been done to preserve the privacy of the individuals concerned and their families. Some Christian names have been changed to protect the guilty.

An epilogue has been added at the end of the book and covers some of my experiences since leaving Nyasaland, and my changes in opinion over the last thirty years. In writing this section, it has been salutary to note my mistakes. However, I believe events have shown how right I was on many issues.

Please remember that, except for this prologue, the epilogue and the few notes and additions, the remaining parts of this book were written in the late 1950s.

Chapter 1

The How, Why and Wherefore

Jamaica, 1959

Seven is a number normally associated with wisdom, woes and wonders. The following chapters present a very incomplete story of some of my experiences and ideas while I was in Central Africa from 1950 until 1957. For me, these were years of endeavour, physical progress and development of both ideas and understanding. Often, they were frustrating; sometimes, they were times of defeat and negation. Overall, they were years of achievement and of hope for the future.

*   *   *

What was my background before going to Nyasaland?

I had worked hard at school and technical college to obtain the qualifications necessary for a career in telecommunications. In the depressed economy which existed in the late 1920s, the civil service offered reasonable prospects for a safe, interesting and rewarding job. It also offered employment directly related to my personal interest in radio technology. It is not generally known that the British Post Office and Admiralty were closely associated with Marconi's early experiments.

I joined the British Post Office engineering department as a trainee.

On completion of my training, I advanced through competitive examination to an executive position.

As gliding was one of my hobbies, I tried, at the outbreak of the second world war, to get released for service in the RAF. This was refused, owing to the shortage of communication specialists. Instead, I found myself in charge of the communications network in the Channel Islands, including the British forces' rear line of communications to Rennes in western France.

When the Germans broke through the Allied lines, it was decided that the Channel Islands could not be defended. I returned to England with my staff and what equipment we could recover. This was some two weeks after the Dunkirk evacuation. Although not as arduous an undertaking, ours was probably equally dangerous, as some six thousand of us, mainly British troops, made the crossing in a cross Channel ferry without naval escort or air cover.

After my return to England, I spent most of the rest of the war dodging enemy bombs and trying to organize the provision and maintenance of communications for the public and the forces in the Southampton and surrounding areas. In addition, I was appointed communications liaison officer to RAF Maintenance Command for the whole of England. This was a time of sixteen hours a day work, with interrupted sleep due to bombing, and ending with a crescendo of work at the time of operation Overlord.

Following the Allied invasion of France, there was some relief from years of overwork, strain and lack of sleep. I badly needed a change and in 1945 I joined the Foreign Office German Section.

In Germany, I became controller of postal and telecommunication services in North Rhine Westphalia, the largest and most important Region in West Germany. I also served at British Zonal Headquarters, where I was given special responsibilities and had to deal with many of the communication problems when the Russians blockaded Berlin and cut the cables from Berlin to the West. I was also responsible for the cipher network and for some intelligence matters. My job in Germany involved extensive travel dealing with the administrations in adjoining countries, the Russians in Berlin and, shortly before I resigned, the special requirements for the North German Iron and Steel Control (later to become the European Common Market). I flew weekly into Berlin at the time of the airlift. Travel became something of a way of life but was also an education in European politics and economies.

In 1949, I was approached about taking a senior appointment at Foreign Office Headquarters, with world-wide communications, cipher and intelligence responsibilities. This involved special screening, and it was decided, in view of my possible marriage to a German national and the pressures which might be applied through my girl friend's parents, who were in Eastern Germany, that I would not be eligible for the appointment and should try to forget all I knew about our intelligence and cipher activities.

When my appointment with the British Foreign Office fell through my friend Harold Ellis, who had recently been appointed Postmaster General of Nyasaland, suggested that I join him. I arrived in the protectorate in 1950, about one year after Harold, and shortly afterwards took over the responsibility for providing a modern network within the country and linking it with the outside world.

The development of the protectorate's communications was my main interest for my first two years in the country, though by that time I had been first appointed chief engineer and then assistant PMG. I had then to act as PMG for some six months, while Harold was on home leave. This was followed almost immediately by my own home leave. A year later, Harold left to take up a senior appointment in Nigeria, and I had again to assume the PMG's duties and grudgingly relinquish my direct responsibilities for the development programme.

Following federation, I continued to work in Nyasaland for three years on secondment from the Colonial Office as Regional Controller of the Nyasaland Postal Region. I was then asked if I was willing to transfer to Salisbury as deputy PMG for the Federation. Also, the Colonial Office offered me the post of deputy director of posts and telecommunications in Nigeria. A third opportunity, offered by a private concern, was a management position with the Jamaica Telephone Company. Because of my love for the federal area, my interest in inter-racial development in my department and a friendly association with Sir Roy Welensky, my first inclination was to join the federal service. However, this involved a conflict in my official and family relations, and I finally decided against it. I discussed the Nigerian offer with friends who had served there. They told me of the graft and corruption in the country and the likely political problems. I therefore decided to retire from the colonial service and accept the Jamaican post.

* * *

During my time with the Nyasaland Post Office, the second-largest department in the country, I had to deal with large numbers of African civil servants who formed a considerable part of the educated African population. As one running a public service, I was in touch with all sections of the community. While travelling extensively throughout the country, I could see developments, and note changes of thought and sociological trends, over a considerable period.

How far did I travel in Africa? In Nyasaland to the remotest parts of that remote country. In South Africa and what were Southern and Northern Rhodesia fairly extensively; to a more limited extent through British East Africa and Portuguese East Africa.

* * *

It was probably truer of Africa and the Bantus than of any other continent and race that the only way to understand the people and the political, social and economic problems was to live there for a considerable period. However, those who had done so were very largely inarticulate.

The settlers, of whom the writer Elspeth Huxley was a remarkable exception, were preoccupied with their day-to-day problems, and as much out of touch with the Western world as that world was out of touch with them.

The missionaries faced the problem of all men being equal but some being more equal than others. The result was that many became supporters of the African nationalist movement. Others rendered unto Caesar the things which were Caesar's and devoted themselves to truly Christian rather than Marxist/Christian service.

The last group, the colonial servants, were restricted by their conditions of service until they retired and were then too frustrated and exhausted to worry overmuch about the Africa they had left behind them, with all its complexities and problems.

There were, of course, the experts on Africa, such as Margery Perham, who had studied the continent and had a considerable knowledge of the economic and social problems. Due to their expertise in a little-known area, most were encouraged to accept appointments at overseas universities and became out of touch with local conditions. Their continuing contact with Africa was usually through the eyes of Bantu students attending the universities. This seldom provided an objective and unbiased source of information.

Africa had not become front-page world news, and press and radio coverage was very limited. The available correspondents were usually editors and reporters of the local papers. These were generally under-staffed, and the people concerned had more than a job to do producing their papers. When they did report, they usually set a high standard of accuracy and integrity based on their local knowledge and experience.

At the time, I went there, Central Africa was virtually unknown to the average European or American and had its own almost unique complexities and peculiarities. It was within this context that I wrote this book and tried to outline my understanding of the conditions in, and problems of, Central Africa. While commenting on these, I tried to be objective and realistic and avoid personal interests. Most of the Bantu political leaders and racial, sectorial and political movements had no such reserves. Although the tribal chiefs usually had the best interests of their people and country at heart they were largely inarticulate.

*   *   *

During the 1950s, when I was in Nyasaland, both the British Government and the Colonial Service came in for considerable adverse comment by visiting journalists, clerics and left-wing politicians after short visits to the country – presumably because any potential trouble spot may prove to be a fertile ground for comment designed to create embarrassment to the administration in power, or to stir up trouble. These visitors usually arrived with preconceived opinions, largely wrong, gathered from European, Asian or African malcontents, some with criminal records, who had been expelled from, or found it convenient to leave, the country. I met many of these visitors from press, pulpit and parliament and never ceased to be astonished at their capacity for speaking and writing with assurance on the problems of Africa after a visit of a week or so.

The local research undertaken by most of these visitors was extremely superficial. They were not altogether to blame for this, as they faced a language problem in speaking to the Bantu chiefs and headmen. What contacts they had with the Bantu were through the left-wing intelligentsia. Contacts with the European and Asian members of the community were usually at cocktail parties or leaning against the bar of the local hotel. It was a tragedy for Africa that even those visitors who were well intentioned seldom overcame the problems of travel and language.

Perhaps, I am over-harsh in making these comments about our short-term visitors. But after seven years, during which Africa was my main interest, I felt I would never fully understand the multiplicity of the problems involved in multi-racial development in Africa. Issues which on the face of things appeared straightforward and clear-cut, had a habit of becoming highly complex when all the interests and factors were considered.

A major problem was the need to understand the other man's point of view in a society which, perhaps more than any other, was divided racially, culturally, religiously, politically and economically, and where the state of development reached by the various races ranged from the most primitive iron-age tribal society to a modern European community.

The complexity of the problems of the society was probably one of the reasons so few Europeans who worked in Africa have written about the Africa they knew during this period, the benefits British rule brought, and the altruistic and dedicated services provided by most colonial officers. Much has been written, on the other side, by racists, clerics and Marxists in support of African nationalism and an egalitarian society, without considering the differences among members of that society.

There seems to be an abysmal lack of understanding of the good side of colonial government and the dedication of most colonial officers. In the play *Julius Caesar* Shakespeare has Mark Antony say, "The evil that men do lives after them, the good is oft interred with their bones." Never has this been truer and more appropriate than in the case of the British colonial system in Africa.

A criticism of colonial rule that might justly be made is that a greater proportion of the benefits of European development should have been passed on to the local population.

*   *   *

Although Africa, as I saw it, had little order, I have divided my comments into chapters covering the various aspects of life and experience in Africa. I could not, however, from my limited viewpoint, present anything like a comprehensive picture, as none of us, whether white, black or coloured; animistic, Christian, Moslem, Hindu or Buddhist; capitalist, nationalist or communist; had a clear and complete understanding of the others' ways of life, cultures or thought processes.

My comments are those of a European and are related to a European viewpoint and background. I have, however, tried to be honest and consider all aspects of the controversial questions facing Central Africa at the time. My comments outline my impressions based on experience during a particular period in the political and physical development of British Central Africa.

Chapters of this book, except that on the historical background, are not sequential and consist largely of impressions, anecdotes and information obtained, when and where possible, as a result of personal experience and such research as proved possible. My investigations were restricted by the facilities and time available and my other commitments and interests. What I have written was based on a love of Nyasaland (which, since the break-up of the Federation, has become Malawi) and a respect for a large proportion of the population irrespective of race.

If my comments are contradictory, it is because the facts, as I saw them, were contradictory and the issues conflicting. It was, I felt, better not to try to over simplify the political, sociological and economic issues. Over-simplification usually results from an incomplete understanding and inadequate investigation. Equally dangerous are racial, political and religious bias.

My opportunities to obtain knowledge on the history, political background, tribal customs, and all the "ologies" from anthropology to zoology, were limited, but I did, while on *ulendo*, get to know the tribal African and something of the tribal system. I also met and knew most of the Nyasaland politicians, whether European, Asian or African.

I did not have the advantage, or suffer the disadvantage, of being in a function of government directly concerned with the country's administration. This was probably an advantage, as it resulted in people talking more freely with me than might otherwise have been the case.

I lived and worked in Nyasaland before the ill-fated Central African Federation came into being, and continued to do so for another three years. This was a most difficult and interesting period. During this time I had first-hand experience of the disturbances in which many of the African people became involved, partly as a result of political agitation but mainly due, I believe, to the failure to publicize and explain the aims and advantages of federation.

I knew not only most government officials but also members of the federal cabinet, including that great, honest and forceful man Roy Welensky, who was minister for my department for two years before becoming prime minister.

Such then was the context within which I saw Africa. These were also the reasons for recording a European point of view obtained during a period which gave an extensive opportunity for observation. The original manuscript was written shortly after I had left Africa when I could take a detached view, free of personal considerations.

At the time, I left Africa, I believed there was a chance for multi-racial understanding and cooperation. My time in Africa was, for me, far too short, and I left Nyasaland, and my friends of all colours, with regret.

Chapter 2

My Brother's Keeper

If one looked at a map of Africa in the 1950s, almost the whole of the south of the continent was coloured pink and presumably under British control. In fact, Great Britain had very little say over the policies adopted in South Africa, the trustee territory of South West Africa and the internally self-governing colony of Southern Rhodesia. In the remaining colonies and protectorates, Britain was subject to internal pressures in the countries themselves and considerable international pressure about its policies. In fact, all the colonial powers had to consider world opinion. Owing to its close association with the USA, Britain took particular notice of US public opinion.

Policies in the colonial territories of other countries differed from those in the British territories. Except for the Congo Basin Treaty which regulated customs, trading and certain common services, and had legally abolished the slave trade throughout the area, there was little common ground in the policies followed in Nyasaland compared with those in adjoining Portuguese East Africa and the Belgian Congo.

A vociferous section of the Bantu intelligentsia, largely indoctrinated in India or Russia, was already generating internal pressures for independence. The powers having the most influence on British policy in Africa were the United States of America, India and the Soviet Union, probably in that order. These powers acted individually and through the United Nations. India and the USSR also resorted to subversion and propaganda. South Africa, through its internal policies and its close association with Britain since the Boer War, provided a basis for propaganda against the British in Africa.

Opinion in the United States was largely governed by its own experience of colonialism influenced by its increasingly articulate Negro population. Neither the US government nor its people fully appreciated the benefits British colonial rule had brought to Africa. *Perhaps they now begin to understand some of the problems and benefits following their experience with tribalism in Somalia.*

* * *

It was an unfortunate fact that the Union of South Africa, which, before all other countries, should have led the way to enlightened development of its political structure and its human resources, did not do so. The nationalist, anti-British, white minority government was, through its apartheid policies, creating embarrassment and difficulty for all other European-led communities in Africa. In consequence South Africa was doing more to help Bantu nationalism and discredit European government than any other country.

* * *

The role of India was ambivalent. India respected what the British had achieved in unifying India, creating a central government structure and a supporting civil service. The subsequent division of the sub-continent was a ghastly mistake largely forced by the intransigence of Nehru and Jinnah, and the ambition of Lord Mountbatten to achieve a basis for independence while he was Vice Regent. The Cripps Commission had earlier proposed a more practical and realistic political structure for independence based on a single federated state. The decision to partition the sub-continent, with East and West Pakistan separated by one thousand miles of potentially hostile India, led to untold misery and loss of life during the ensuing population movements and wars.

The Indians were almost paranoid about the failure of South Africa to accept the part Asians had played in, and could contribute to, the future of South Africa. They justifiably hated that country's racial discrimination against coloured people. Despite its limited resources and need for outside aid, India was operating a major propaganda network in Africa and providing scholarships for many left-wing Bantu extremists.

*   *   *

The Russians, with their centre of African operations in Ethiopia, were following their usual line of creating mischief wherever they could. Their headquarters in Addis Ababa was outwardly an aid development and medical operation. However, its primary purpose was to deal with propaganda and subversion throughout Africa. It seemed incomprehensible that Haile Selassie, whom I had known many years before as an austere but very Christian gentleman, did not realize the danger of the Russians' nefarious under-cover activities. (As crown prince, Ras Tafari and his family lived for some months, in the late 1920s, near my home at Canford Cliffs in Dorset and attended our local parish church. I knew the children very well.)

*   *   *

Our greatest problem in Africa was American public opinion. Americans were usually the most rational of people, but any system based on colonialism started with an almost insurmountable disadvantage. American politicians and the American public also seemed unable to differentiate between British rule in Central Africa and the Afrikaner nationalist party policies of South Africa.

South African policies, although wrong, had historical parallels. The South Africans argued, with some justification, that there were similarities between the European settlement of the USA and that of South Africa. There was evidence to support this contention.

Van Riebeck started the first settlement in the Cape in 1652 (I know because I was in Cape Town at the time of the three hundredth anniversary celebrations). This was only a few years after the Pilgrim Fathers arrived in America. There were then no Negroes in what is now South Africa. It was about fifty years after Van Riebeck's settlement that the Bantu tribes crossed the Limpopo and started to drive southward into what became South Africa, treating the indigenous Bushmen with even less ceremony than they had received from the Dutch settlers and very similarly to the treatment of the native Indians in America at about the same time.

South Africa has always been considered a product of British imperialism, but the ancestors of the ruling Afrikaners fought a long and bitter war against Britain. The British minority in South Africa had, since independence, opposed the Boer mentality and the government's racial policies.

South African politicians frequently commented on the results of Bantu rule in Liberia. Liberia was under American influence, had a constitution similar to the USA's and used American currency. The corruption, dishonesty, absence of social services and poor educational standards in Liberia during the 1950s could be compared unfavourably with conditions existing in the rest of Africa or, perhaps, anywhere in the world. The Union of South Africa offered a great deal more in physical well-being and social services to its Bantu population and migrant workers.

Far be it from me to support the South African position. What I have been trying to show is the bias, weakness and fallacy of much of the American viewpoint. I include some ideas on how to correct this in later chapters.

South Africa is a lovely, temperate country, and, as a result of the efforts of the early settlers and the discovery of its mineral wealth, the standard of living enjoyed by the Europeans was very high indeed. Even in the Bantu areas some prosperity had been passed on, and living standards were higher than elsewhere in Africa. The black population was probably better off economically and had better social services than much of the Negro population of the USA.

Economic and social welfare were not the complete story. The Bantu needed acceptance in the community, as much as economic advancement and basic social services. One had only to contrast the morose, unhappy-looking, but well-dressed person one saw in the streets of the large South African cities with the laughing, joking, likeable but ragged individual living under primitive conditions in his home village.

The conditions existing in the South African cities were artificial, and the Bantu, many of whom were migrants, realized they were regarded as second-class citizens. The Bantu could not be expected to welcome the creation of separate isolated housing areas, though they replaced the slums and shanty towns of cities like Johannesburg. The special pass system, which by the way applied also to some Europeans including my wife, was bitterly resented.

Without his family and tribal life, the black African wanted to be accepted by, talk to, live in association with and, most of all, learn from the Europeans. To him, they were fascinating, strange and wonderful people, if not always admirable. Rejection and segregation were an insult to a likeable and gregarious race. Also the Bantu, if he was able, and many were extremely able, looked for equal opportunity in advancement. There was every justification for giving him this opportunity, as Africa could not afford to waste its human resources whatever their colour. I believed, therefore, that South Africa should urgently reconsider its policies, and I deal with this matter in my later chapters.

*   *   *

The activities of the Euro/Asiatics from Russia and the Asiatics from India were of concern to all Europeans living in Africa. There was no open association between India and Russia in their disruptive activities. However, the aim of both India and Russia might well have been the destruction of the order colonial rule had brought and the subjugation of all countries and races in Africa.

Through their medical units in Ethiopia, the Russians had established a widespread intelligence network throughout Africa. This was designed to corrupt and destroy rather than to extend, develop and democratize the society. The amount the Russians contributed to development of the infrastructure, social services and humanitarian aid was infinitesimal. Their contribution to unrest and disorder was inestimable. Their intelligence and propaganda networks were aided and abetted by the students trained at their universities. The whole purpose seemed to be to embarrass the colonial powers and create political unrest and disturbances wherever possible.

* * *

India's activities were equally disruptive. There was a sizable Indian population throughout eastern, central and southern Africa. Many Indians were brought in to help construct the railways and other infrastructure. They settled in the African countries and took to trade and commerce. They had shown a natural acumen and by hard work prospered and found a higher standard of living than in India. After they had established themselves, they were joined by their families, friends and relations and had taken over a great deal of the trade and industry throughout central, eastern and southern Africa. Their ethics in trading and dealing with the Bantu villagers were, however, highly questionable. Partly for this reason and partly because of their living styles, they had not been accepted into the European community.

The Indians strongly resented the efforts of the colonial governments to stop unfair trading practices and Indian exploitation of the Bantu. They also objected to the limitation placed on further migration from India. Coupled with the resentment about British rule and policies (particularly South African policies) and with a possible aim to use Africa as an area for settlement of its surplus population, India was attempting to sow dissent internally in Africa. India was also, through UN circles, trying to create as much difficulty as it could for both South Africa and British colonial rule in Africa.

The African nationalist leaders trained and supported by India and Russia were great admirers of the Russian and Indian systems.

Usually, they hated colonialism and with it the tribal system, which had been incorporated into the colonial administrative structure. This had led to contempt for their chiefs and their own people. It seemed that their aim was to replace the existing ordered governments by some form of communism or socialism, through the development of totalitarian states, with Indian and Russian aid. These dictatorships, supported by India and Russia, could bring the whole continent to ruin for all of us, whether Bantu, coloured or white.

Chapter 3

In the Beginning

The mysteries of the unknown are always intriguing, and the more inaccessible parts of Africa have frequently formed the setting for the stories of some of our more imaginative novelists. Have writers such as Rider Haggard the slightest justification for allowing the scope of their imagination to range over this wide and historically unknown continent, or has the interior been occupied by human beings only since comparatively recent times?

One pre-eminent factor is the size of Africa. Because of this, the relatively recent European exploration and the absence of written records, we still knew little of the continent's history, and our archaeological and anthropological research had been negligible. Even those discoveries which have been made were largely chance findings in connection with other activities. However, we could be certain that, while there might be no *She*s waiting to be discovered, there were some intriguing mysteries buried in the pre-history of the continent, mysteries that might include the evolution of the human race.

What justification had we for this conjecture? The original clue was the discovery in 1921, in a lead mine some sixty feet below ground at Broken Hill, Northern Rhodesia, of a fairly highly developed Pleistocene skull of from 250 to 500 thousand years ago (*Homo rhodesiensis*).

The accepted distinction between the higher apes and man is normally related to the development of tools and weapons. The remains of probably the oldest tool maker ever discovered were those of the Nut-Cracker man (*Zinjanthropus bosei*) discovered by Dr Leakey of the

Nairobi Museum in 1959. These were found in the lower Pleistocene layers of the Oldavai Gorge in Tanganyika and were dated to be between 600 and 700 thousand years old.

There are many traces of Stone Age settlement throughout the Rhodesias and Nyasaland dating from the upper Pleistocene period of from 50 to 100 thousand years ago. These had been related to what were termed the three Nachikufan periods of culture, the last of which was a community which developed pottery and was probably contemporary with the Iron Age in Europe. Mr Rodney Wood and Dr Desmond Clarke, curator of the Rhodes/Livingstone Museum of Northern Rhodesia, uncovered two interesting Nachikufan burials from this later period in a cave on Mount Hora, Nyasaland. These were of special interest, as the skull formations were neither Negro nor Bushman but Caucasoid and similar to those of African Mediterranean or Ethiopian origin.

One could also find evidence of Bushman existence throughout Central Africa ranging from Mesolithic times. The absence of early Negro remains would seem to show that the Bantu race developed elsewhere in Africa.

Field work and excavations by archaeologists and anthropologists had been extremely limited when related to the size of the country. There were several areas, such as the shores of Lake Nyasa and Mlanje Mountain (a source of many legends), which would probably be fertile fields for investigation.

There were certain other signs of prehistoric settlement throughout Nyasaland, which could be examined if one did not mind clambering over rocks, entering caves and taking a chance with snakes. These included pottery shards and wall paintings. Many of the paintings were unusual in that they were schematic in form and contained geometrical designs consisting of ladders, gridirons, stars and circles. Similar motifs were widespread throughout the Rhodesias. Overlaying certain of these paintings, and in some cases overlaid by them, were naturalistic Bushman drawings showing stylized animals. Sometimes, overlaying both, were drawings of more recent Bantu origin.

It appeared not unreasonable to assume that the geometric drawings were of Nachikufan origin and that the Nachikufan people were
the earlier inhabitants, in some cases contemporary with the Bushmen
and followed by the Bantus. In no case did the paintings I have seen
show the scope or merit of the Tassili cave paintings in Algeria (I have
only seen these in photographs); nor did they have the peculiar
interest of the prehistoric White Lady frieze discovered in the Brandburg
Mountain caves in South West Africa. The features of all the people in
the Brandburg paintings show Caucasian rather than Negroid characteristics. What is even more interesting is the portrayal of a white
woman amongst several brown coloured men.

Could it be that with the change in climatic conditions which resulted in the large desert areas in North Africa, there might have been
a general movement southwards of a race with Caucasian characteristics? Alternatively, it might have been possible that the Caucasian
race originated in Africa and migrated northward. Any remnants
remaining in southern Africa may have been exterminated by the
Bushmen, who in turn gave place to the negroid Bantus. *In the light of
more recent discoveries by Dr Leakey, his family and other anthropologists
in Kenya and Ethiopia, it appears likely that the latter hypothesis may be
correct.*

Possibly owing to the problems of the environment, none of the
central and southern African tribes appear to have developed civilizations comparable to those which developed in the Mediterranean area,
the Sudan, Ethiopia, the coastal area of Kenya and parts of west Africa.
There are, however, several fascinating and unexplained stone ruins
throughout Rhodesia, the largest and best known being Zimbabwe, in
the Mashonoland area of Southern Rhodesia. The origins of these
ruins are still obscure.

Zimbabwe consists of a series of impressive structures with massive
cut-stone walls. It includes an elliptical temple, with a major axis of
nearly one hundred yards. Several carved soap-stone birds were ex-
cavated in the vicinity. Without organic matter, it has been difficult to
date Zimbabwe's construction, and estimates of age range from 900 to

5,000 years. There are no inscriptions on the ruins and, to add to the mystery, no burial ground in the vicinity which might typify its builders. Possibly the builders cremated their dead, a practice foreign to the Bantu tribes.

Around Zimbabwe were traces of gold-mining activities including smelting crucibles, so it appeared likely that it was a centre for a people interested in extracting gold.

The name zimbabwe, meaning as it does the court of the chief, undoubtedly led to confusion in the interpretation of the early Portuguese records and the association of these ruins with the Mashona chief Monomatopa and his tribe. The ruins almost certainly pre-date him, and probably also the date of arrival of the Bantus in Central Africa.

The existence of pieces of Chinese ceramics at Zimbabwe might suggest a connection with a trading society such as that which constructed impressive stone buildings at Kilwa before the Arabs and Portuguese arrived there.

Although the country has now been renamed after these ruins, it seems doubtful whether they were of Bantu origin, as the ruins are different from anything constructed by the Bantus, or for that matter the Bushmen, elsewhere in Central Africa.

One of the reasons historical records were almost completely lacking throughout southern Africa was that no written language had been developed by any of the Bantu tribes or their predecessors. It was only after the arrival of the Europeans that dictionaries were compiled and tribal languages were recorded in a written form. Of the wars that resulted in the conquest and occupation of Central Africa by the Bantus we know almost nothing.

There is generally no evidence in the physiognomy of most Bantu tribes that might show the mixture of two or more races. It appeared likely that conquest was through wars of extermination or that the earlier population was a relatively small one. There were, however, two widely separated tribes in central and southern Africa which exhibited traces of other ancestry. These were the Hereros in South West Africa, who had almost Mediterranean features and when born were quite light in colour, and the Hima in the Ruwenzori district, some of whom had straight hair and European-type features. These people might be partly descended from an earlier race displaced from larger areas of Africa through the centuries by the Bushmen and Bantus. *I had read about the Hima tribe when in Nyasaland. During my subsequent travels in Africa I failed to find the tribe. However, a number of Watutsis had settled in south western Uganda near the borders of their homeland Rwanda. These people were a distinct ethnic group, very tall, often with European style features. They face extinction by the majority Hutus.*

The Bushmen existed in only a few isolated areas mainly in the Belgian Congo and the Kalahari Desert, and had been exterminated, absorbed or confined. The survivors were a pathetic remnant, living under conditions of considerable hardship.

While the Bushmen had almost vanished, there were still records, in Bantu folklore and myths, of the widespread existence of these little people and of the fear in which they were held. One story common amongst the Yao tribe in Nyasaland was that many years ago there were light-coloured little people who wandered about the country and were called Nlukuwewe. One seldom saw any women or children of these people, but they were extremely vain and dangerous. If you met one of their warriors you had to be very careful as he would point his spear at you and say, "Where do you see me?" The correct reply was "Over there, far away, but not so far, mighty warrior that you could not throw your spear and strike me down." If you made a mistake and said you saw him close by, he became annoyed that you knew how small he was, and you were in danger of losing your life. There was evidence of real fear in this story, such fear as would have resulted from a war of extermination with no quarter given on either side.

In the early days of my service in Nyasaland, I found that the Bantus disliked entering uninhabited areas such as the Nyika and the Mlanje Mountain Plateau, where the Nlukuwewe were still thought to exist. By 1957, following the establishment of forestry plantations in these two areas, this feeling had largely disappeared.

One interesting legend about the Nlukuwewe was that of Mwanyonga the Bantu hunter. Mwanyonga went into the forest looking for game. After he had travelled many days, into the more distant parts, he heard someone crying for help. He hurried to the place and found a leopard mauling one of the little people. Mwanyonga was a brave man, and, although he feared the little people, he attacked the leopard with his spear and finally drove it off. The little man was very grateful and said to Mwanyonga, "Come to my village, and I will give you something which will make you the greatest hunter of them all." Mwanyonga went with great fear, and the little man gave him a small box and explained how to use it. Mwanyonga returned to his village, and with the help of the small box he became famous for his hunting ability. When other members of the tribe could not find game, Mwanyonga could always make a kill and bring it back for the pot. He became a legend, but foolishly, as men do, he confided the secret to his wife.

Mwanyonga's wife was no different from other wives. Not much later she was telling her friends that Mwanyonga was not as clever as he thought he was. With the *mfiti* he had in his box any fool could go out and kill game. In fact, she could do it herself,

When next Mwanyonga was sleeping heavily after a beer drink, his wife took his little box and went into the forest with her friends. Now the secret was there were two flies in the box and you must only let one out. It would then fly and bite an animal, which would die. The fly then returned, because the other fly in the box was the only one in existence of the opposite sex. Unfortunately, Mwanyonga's wife allowed both flies to escape, and they were never seen again – or perhaps they bred and were seen too often as the tsetse fly, which became the scourge of cattle in Africa.

It was only in comparatively recent years that we realized that trypanosomiasis resulted from the bite of the tsetse fly. One wonders whether the African races had learned this at a much earlier date.

Without written records the date of the arrival of the Bantus in Nyasaland and the Rhodesias was hard to establish. It was, in all probability, between the eleventh and thirteenth centuries. We were also not sure where they came from, but it seems likely to have been from the Congo area. Successive waves passed southwards and, we know, reached the Limpopo about the time that European settlement of the Cape was taking place (1652).

Until the Europeans arrived, the Bantu way of life was a nomadic one of movement and conquest. Shelter was obtained by building simple mud and grass huts. Clearing and cultivation were by burning off the ground. Overcropping and soil impoverishment was the rule. The plough was unknown, and ground was broken for planting using Stone and Iron Age implements. The rule of the chiefs and witch doctors was one of tyranny, fear, sorcery and black magic. Tribal law was inflexible in its operation and was based on witchcraft, necromancy and communion with primeval tribal spirits.

Outside his capacity to conquer and destroy, the Bantu had failed to meet the challenge of his environment. The nomadic existence and the constant internecine tribal wars obviously played their part in this, as must also the absence of permanent written records of tribal culture, which had to be passed on, from generation to generation, by word of mouth. Before the arrival of the Europeans, the Bantu record in central and southern Africa was one of extermination of his fellow men and devastation of the soil on which life depended.

Chapter 4

The Outsiders

While the Bantu tribal wars and migrations were going on in the interior, Asian and European settlement of the coastal areas of Africa was beginning to take place. The Arabs had first migrated down the east coast of Africa and established the sultanates of Zanzibar and Zinj. The first written evidence of itinerant penetration into the interior is contained in the writings of El Wardi and later Ibn Batuta, who visited Zinj in 1330. It is likely that the slave routes used in the nineteenth century between Nyasaland and the slave centres at Kilwa (Zinj) and Zanzibar followed the line of earlier routes taken by the Arabs, who almost certainly were the first to reach Lake Nyasa.

Vasco da Gama had rounded the Cape and entered the Indian Ocean toward the end of the fifteenth century and had started a period of Portuguese settlement and colonization of the East Coast. For the next three and a half centuries this area was given little attention other than by the Arabs and Portuguese.

The Dutch settlement of the Cape Province of South Africa under Van Riebeck commenced in 1652.

One of the major Portuguese settlements in East Africa was at Sofala, near the mouth of the Zambezi. This was established in 1505 to exploit the gold trade. We know that Portuguese penetration from there to Mashonaland took place and there was considerable traffic in this metal with the Mashonas. According to early Portuguese records, the journey from Sofala to the zimbabwe of Monomatopa, which was probably, from the details given, in the region of Mount Darwin, took twenty-four days.

Portuguese penetration up the Zambezi River resulted in the setting up of stockaded forts at Tete and Masaha. Portuguese explorers almost certainly reached the southern part of Lake Nyasa during the sixteenth century.

Dos Santos' *Ethiopia Orientale*, published in 1609, probably contains the earliest written reference to Lake Nyasa and calls it "the great river". It seems likely that Gaspar Bocarro visited the lake in 1616 on a journey from Tete to Kilwa, which had been captured by the Portuguese from the Arabs. Bocarro in his description of this journey said that he crossed the Chiri (Shire) near the great river Manganja, which looks like the sea and from which issues the river Chiri, which flows into the Zambezi below Sena. The direct line for Bocarro's journey would take him via a point where the outlet of the lake flows into the Shire River.

To the British, Nyasaland is Livingstone's country, and we credit him with discovering Lake Nyasa on 16 September 1859. Before making this journey of discovery Livingstone said, "I return to Africa to try to open a path for commerce and Christianity." This association between the practical and idealistic was significant, although not perhaps as some detractors would have us see it, with the early missionaries holding a Bible in one hand and an order book in the other. The introduction of normal commerce and trading was essential to the elimination of the slave trade.

Following a speech by Livingstone at Cambridge in 1857, the university, and later the Church of Scotland, opened mission stations in the country. The University Mission party, accompanied by Livingstone, entered the country after a most difficult and dangerous journey up the Zambezi and Shire rivers. It established itself in 1861 at an unhealthy site, chosen by Livingstone, near Magomera in the southern part of the country. The mission station was under the control of Bishop MacKenzie.

The whole country was in a state of chaos and confusion. The warlike Ngoni, who had fled north to escape Shaka and his Zulus, were again migrating southward through Nyasaland and preying on another wave of invaders, the Yao. The Yaos, who were being forced southwards, carried out raids on the more peaceful Chewa/Nyanjas. The Ngonis sold captured Yaos as slaves, and the Yaos captured Ngonis and Chewa.

Bishop MacKenzie's station was in constant danger from the raiding tribes. In addition, repeated bouts of fever and shortage of supplies resulted in the deaths of many missionaries. In 1862 Bishop MacKenzie died in the lower river valley where he had gone to keep a rendezvous with Livingstone, greet arriving missionaries and obtain supplies; and the decision was taken to withdraw the mission. Nothing remained of the church and stockaded mission station in my time. The only surviving sign of its location and the end of the first, and unsuccessful, attempt to civilize Nyasaland through Christianity was a cross which marked the grave of Reverend de Wint Burrop.

After its withdrawal from Nyasaland, the University Mission set up a base on Zanzibar in 1864.

In 1875 the Church of Scotland established missions at Blantyre in the southern province and at Cape Maclear, called Livingstonia at the time. After many vicissitudes, the Blantyre mission settled down to a period of progress which continued up to the time this book was written. The mission's founder, Heatherwick, in addition to his other mission activities, produced the first Nyanja dictionary.

The mission at Cape Maclear ran into difficulties like those experienced by the University Mission at Magomera. At the rear of the old Cape Maclear hotel, abandoned in 1955, were several graves of the early missionaries: a reminder of how unhealthy central Africa once was. The Cape Maclear mission, headed by Dr Laws, was first removed to Bandawe at the north of the lake and later to Livingstonia, a higher and more healthy location on top of the escarpment overlooking the lake.

The Church of Scotland Mission obtained commercial assistance through the setting up of the African Lakes Company. This company was formed in 1878 to deal with transport and trading activities in association with the mission. The original heads of this company were the brothers Moir. The company took its commonly used name Mandala from the name given by the natives to the spectacles worn by one of the brothers.

In 1883, at the request of the missions, Her Majesty's consuls Foote and Hawes were appointed to Blantyre and Zomba respectively.

The effects on the slave trade resulting from other trade activities became apparent in 1888 when the Arab, half-caste and Bantu slave traders, who by this time were mainly operating from the north end of the lake, started what can only be termed a war against the African Lakes Company. Things might have gone hard for the company but for the intervention of Cecil Rhodes who provided the funds necessary to purchase arms and undertake punitive action against the slavers.

In the meantime, the University Mission, wishing to recommence its activities in Nyasaland, had in 1879 made an unsuccessful attempt to reach the lake overland from Zanzibar. A further expedition under Archdeacon Johnstone reached the lake at a point near Likoma Island in 1882 and, in 1886, finally established a mission station on the island. This station was still the headquarters of the University Mission and the seat of a bishop.

In 1885, a treaty was signed in Berlin affecting the future of all colonial territories in Africa. This was the Congo Basin Treaty, which removed preferential tariffs, established the equality of all nations in trade and development, and technically abolished the slave trade.

Another significant development having a bearing on the future of Nyasaland then took place. A Portuguese expedition under Major Serpa Pinto entered the south of the country. To stop the threatened Portuguese territorial expansion, the acting British consul, a planter settler named Buchanan acting on his own initiative, declared protection over the country on 21 September 1889. It is unlikely that such action would ever have been taken if communication facilities had been available to consult the British government in advance.

Despite Great Britain's reluctance to accept any addition to its overseas commitments, and considerable contention from the Portuguese, a proclamation was published in 1891 incorporating the protectorate in the British Empire. Sir Harry Johnstone became the first British commissioner.

Johnstone took energetic steps to suppress the remnants of the slave trade which were still operating in the northern part of the country. Using a contingent of Sikh troops brought from India, he attacked the Yao and Ngoni raiders and the Arab and half-caste agents and purveyors. These military actions culminated in the hanging of the half-caste Mlozi, whose stockade, when forced, was found to contain nearly 1,200 slaves.

Slavery was one of the great evils resulting from conquest and subjugation and had existed at some stage in most societies, continuing in Africa into the nineteenth century, when more enlightened thought led to the end of trading and emancipation of the slave populations in the Western world. Britain had abolished slave trading in 1807. Its interests in Central Africa dated from the latter part of the nineteenth century, so it had not been directly involved in slave trading in that area.

It is interesting, within the Central African context, to examine who was primarily responsible for this shameful trade in human beings. Slave trading in Central Africa was a commercial development of the tribal wars. Before the trade developed, tribal Africans had followed the practice of exterminating most of their captives. When they found there was a ready market for these unfortunate individuals, they turned to selling them to Arab and Portuguese traders and their middlemen. Despite the evils of slavery, it offered an alternative to almost certain slaughter.

When Brazil outlawed the import of slaves into Brazil in 1853, the market provided by the Portuguese traders dried up, and the available supplies were almost wholly sold to the Arab and half-caste traders.

The effects of missionary penetration and normal trading were to seriously curtail inter-tribal wars and raids, and the Arabs had to resort to direct raiding to maintain their supplies. For this they organized what they termed Ruga bands. These operated with considerable efficiency and great brutality in northern Nyasaland and Tanganyika.

There is little doubt that slaving was as prevalent in Central Africa as in West Africa during most of the eighteenth and nineteenth centuries. Owing to Arab involvement and the problems of access, it was probably more brutal and decimating there than anywhere else in Africa. The lucky ones had been those sold to the Portuguese and used to provide labour for the plantations in its Brazilian empire. These have been integrated into the population of the Brazilian Republic.

The unfortunate individuals captured or bought by the Arab traders were marched to the slave markets in Zanzibar and Zinj, under conditions of extreme brutality and carrying loads of ivory and other trade goods. This resulted in the loss, or execution, of an estimated 60 per cent of the captives starting from Central Africa. Any sick or disabled slaves who could not keep up with the convoy were summarily executed, usually by decapitation in order to save ammunition. This also served to discourage malingering.

Considering the high Negro and part-Negro populations in the USA, Brazil and the Caribbean, it is interesting to consider what happened to the slaves falling into Arab hands and ask where their descendants are today? Firstly, the journey to the coast carrying trade goods, and the sea crossings to Zanzibar and Zinj, were extremely hazardous and resulted in great loss of what was considered an expendable commodity, which had negligible value until it reached the market. Secondly, as eunuchs had a higher trade value in the Eastern countries, the Arabs castrated most of the men. The women were sold as servants and into harems. Any progeny were of mixed race and were absorbed into the local societies. The main markets of the Arab traders were the Arab countries, Persia, Turkey, India and China.

On the walls of my office in Zomba I had the earliest document in the archives of the Nyasaland Post Office. It was signed by Mr Alfred Sharpe, as acting postmaster, at Tschilomo on 25 July 1891. Later, as

Sir Alfred Sharpe, the first postmaster became, in 1907, the first governor of the territory. With this appointment the name of the protectorate, which had been changed to British Central Africa in 1893, was changed back to Nyasaland by royal proclamation. Executive and legislative councils were set up as the start of a move to give the population a say in government.

The territory became British almost wholly due to the Christianizing efforts of the early missionaries, the decisiveness of Mr Buchanan, the integrating work of Sir Harry Johnstone and the financial aid and help of Cecil Rhodes and his British South Africa Company.

One magnificent conception on the part of Cecil Rhodes was a proposal to construct a telegraph line from the Cape to Cairo. The section linking Nyasaland to Southern Rhodesia was completed in 1894, and in 1901 the line was extended northwards to Tanganyika. Owing to German reluctance, it was not extended further northward although a section was later constructed into Northern Rhodesia. The construction of this line through the bush was a considerable engineering achievement. During my time in Africa, many sections were in almost as good condition as when they were built.

*   *   *

The period from 1907 to 1914 was one of progressive development of mission and trading activities and the extension of planting activities by European settlers. These at the outset were mainly centred on coffee and tobacco, which had been introduced by the Buchanan brothers in the 1890s.

In 1914, owing to its common frontier with what was then German East Africa (Tanganyika), Nyasaland was in some danger of attack by German forces, including the German gun-boat *Hermann von Wiesmann* which was being reconditioned at Manda on Lake Nyasa. Owing to better communications, the British were able to land at Manda and disable this ship before the German captain knew war had been declared. During the war there was only one serious land action, when

German forces advanced into the country but withdrew after an action near Karonga.

Although there were no other attacks by German forces, an internal rising led by John Chelembwe took place at Magomera. Chilembwe was a Nguru from neighbouring Portuguese territory who had been missionary-trained and attended university in the USA, where he developed a hatred of white people. On his return to Nyasaland, he formed a neo-Christian sect which had as one of its aims the elimination of Europeans from Central Africa. In the initial phase of his planned uprising, he and his followers killed three Europeans and held a Thanksgiving service in his mission with the heads of the slaughtered victims on the altar. Rapid counter measures were taken, but Chilembwe, who deserted his followers, escaped. He was finally killed when resisting arrest on the Portuguese border.

* * *

Transport had always been a major problem in Nyasaland owing to the difficult nature of the terrain, the absence of an adequate road network and the impracticability of using horses in the tsetse-infested areas. While the lake was available for water transport in the central and northern areas, overland movement was largely by foot with the Europeans sometimes being carried in Machilas. Terrific problems were involved in the movement of produce and commercial items. In one year the number of head loads carried from Blantyre to Fort Jameson was more than 10,000. Similar large quantities were carried on the old Stevenson track from the upper end of the lake at Karonga to Abercorn in Northern Rhodesia.

The parts for the early steamships, the first of which was the *Pioneer* launched in 1892, had to be carried by porters from the limit of navigability of the lower Shire River, bypassing the Livingstone and Murchison falls, to a point where they could again be transported by water along the upper Shire River to Lake Nyasa.

At the outbreak of the 1914–1918 war, mechanized transport

consisted of two cars and one truck, used exclusively in the southern province, and a number of bicycles. As is so often the case, war provided the spur for development and resulted in a considerable extension of the road network and increased use of motor transport.

*   *   *

Following the 1914–1918 war, Nyasaland again became an almost forgotten country due probably to the difficulty of access and the absence of significant mineral deposits. However, there was some development of commercial planting activities, not only on European-owned estates, but also on small Bantu farms, with the commercial exploitation of tea, tung and tobacco.

Nyasaland's position during the 1939–1945 war was much easier than in the previous war, although many Nyasalanders, both European and Bantu, served with the forces in Ethiopia and Burma. Progress since the war had been considerable, with fairly extensive development of social services, education, public utilities, other infrastructure and agriculture.

Political development which started with the creation of a legislature in 1893 culminated in setting up the Federation of the Rhodesias and Nyasaland on 3 September 1953.

*   *   *

Before leaving my brief summary of the history of Nyasaland, it is appropriate to analyse the results of a hundred years of British influence and rule in Nyasaland. Starting with the Christian exploratory crusades of Dr Livingstone, there followed the peaceful penetration by the early missionaries, whose lives, which were pitifully short without our present knowledge of tropical medicine, were dedicated to civilization through Christianity at a time when the area was an arena of warring tribes, slaughter and slave trading.

It was largely due to the presence of the missionaries that the first consular representatives of the Crown were appointed to the chieftains of Central Africa. The development of trading activities, accompanied by limited but settled agricultural development by a relatively few European planters, also took place. (They were, incidentally, not all from Great Britain.) These planters have since been criticized and their rights of ownership challenged for acquiring land in exchange for small quantities of trade goods. The ethics of these purchases should be considered in relation to conditions at the time, the uncertainty of the future and the Bantu's absence of pride in, or care for, the land. They were certainly no worse than the Manhattan Island deal. The settler's method of acquisition would also better stand up to examination than the means normally adopted by the Bantu tribes of acquisition through tribal war and slaughter of the previous occupants.

It was only under the threat of occupation by another power that a British protectorate was proclaimed over the country. British rule had been enlightened throughout. The suppression of inter-tribal wars and slave trading, and the introduction of health and hygiene services, with the importation of food in times of famine, had resulted in the population increasing from about 700,000 at the turn of the century to 2,750,000 in the 1950s. However, the population included an estimated 400,000 Nguru who had migrated from Portuguese East Africa, presumably because of their preference for British rule. The figures show the benefits of British colonial rule and stand up well against some anti-colonial power's treatment of an indigenous population.

British colonial government has been criticized because greater efforts were not made to encourage development within the country. Gainful employment opportunities within the country were limited, and large numbers of the male population left the territory to obtain work in the Rhodesias and South Africa. Some criticism is justified, but it must be appreciated that Nyasaland was a small country with almost no mineral resources and, during the period of British rule, had become much more heavily populated than adjoining areas. The ratio of population per square mile compared to Portuguese East Africa was about six to one. Again, European settlement, which might have produced greater agricultural and industrial development, had been restricted to protect the interests of the indigenous population. Less than 3 per cent of the land was European-owned. Before federation, the social services were subject to British subsidization, and at no stage had the economy become self-supporting, nor was it likely to do so in the foreseeable future.

Chapter 5

The Country

Nyasaland is a very green and in many parts beautiful country, with a variety of scenery seldom found in an African territory. The country lies between 10 and 18 degrees south of the equator and between 33 and 36 degrees east of Greenwich and is, of course, tropical. It is landlocked and situated between Portuguese East Africa, Tanganyika and Northern Rhodesia. Its nearest point is a hundred miles from the Indian Ocean. Nevertheless, it has a shoreline of over four hundred miles on Lake Nyasa – a fantastic and very beautiful sheet of water which is over twice the size of Wales and lies in the trough of that major geological fault, the Great Rift Valley. The country is extremely mountainous having a number of massifs such as Mount Mlanje, which is 9,840 feet high and towers over the Shire highlands. Also rising above the Shire Highlands Plateau is Zomba mountain, which is more than 7,000 feet high.

The Port Herald, Chiromo and Chikwawa districts in the extreme south of the country, below the Murchison and Livingston falls, are only 100 to 200 feet above sea level and are extremely hot and humid although, thanks to tropical medicine, not as unhealthy as they were in the times of the early missionaries. Considerable quantities of cotton were grown in this region, which is watered by the Shire and Rua rivers and during the rainy season can be subject to severe and sometimes disastrous flooding. There was one such disaster in 1956 when, in addition to the usual flooding, the railway embankment had

Lower Shire River. Stern Wheelers.

Lower Shire River. 1956 floods.
"Too bad the bucket's got a hole in it. Now we can't buy no more beer."

been washed away and Nyasaland cut off from its seaport of Beira (and its beer supplies) for nearly two months.

Rising from the lower river valley is the Shire Highland Plateau, which ranges from 2,000 to 4,000 feet above sea level and is temperate and healthy. This had been the main area of European settlement and was the most highly developed area in the country. It included the twin commercial towns of Blantyre/Limbe, the tea-growing areas of Cholo and Mlanje, and the capital city of Zomba on the slopes of Zomba mountain. *Zomba is no longer the capital, which has now been removed to Lilongwe in the centre of the country.*

Zomba, with its flowering trees, waterfalls, and views of the sunset over the Mlanje mountains, had the reputation of being the most beautiful capital in the British Empire.

Large quantities of tea were grown on the slopes of the Mlanje and Cholo mountains, and tobacco and tung were produced around Zomba and Lilongwe.

To the north west of the Shire highlands is the upper Shire River Valley, through which the Shire River flows from Lake Nyasa and then drops down through the Murchison and Livingstone falls to the low-lying area around Chiromo. To the west of the Shire highlands, the land rises to the Kirk range of mountains which extend along the western frontier of Nyasaland, with Portuguese East Africa between Ncheu in the north and Mwanza in the south. This beautiful range consists of rolling grass-covered hills on which large quantities of wheat and other cereals were grown. The Kirk range has an altitude of from 4,000 to 6,000 feet.

North of Ncheu is another plateau, with Dedza mountain standing out as the main landmark. This plateau included the tobacco-growing areas of Kasungu and Lilongwe and ranges in height from 2,500 to 3,500 feet with certain isolated mountains such as Dowa rising to more than 5,000 feet. Further to the north is the plateau on which Mzimba and Mzuzu are located. Above these two towns tower the Vipya mountains, with altitudes up to 6,000 feet. One rocky outcrop north of Mzimba is Mount Hora, which was of considerable archaeological

Mount Mlanje.

Mount Hora.

interest with its caves and human remains. This was the scene of the slaughter by the Ngoni of many thousand Tumbuku who had taken refuge on its summit.

The Vipya is a very attractive range similar to the Kirk range. It was being developed as a forestry project. Tung was also being grown on its northern slopes around Mzuzu. (Tung trees produce nuts from which are extracted an oil used in the original Chinese lacquers and later in high-quality paints. The trees almost show their Chinese origin in appearance and looked quite foreign in the African landscape.)

North of Mzuzu the countryside first falls to the valley of the Rukuru River and then rises to the Nyika Plateau, probably, at the time, one of the least known parts of the earth's surface. This area was the subject of planting experiments with a view to possible afforestation. It was one of the most fascinating parts of Nyasaland and Northern Rhodesia. It consisted of an area of 1,400 square miles of undulating grassland at an altitude of between 6,000 and 8,000 feet. Until the forestry experiment, the high plateau was unpopulated, although the Apoko tribe lived on its slopes. The Apoko were largely cave dwellers and were seldom seen in the valleys below the Nyika except when they came down to sell the wild honey they collected.

It is hard to describe the interest and beauty of the Nyika, the rolling downlands, the wild flowers, the butterflies, the birds and the game. Unfortunately, with increased human penetration, large areas had been devastated as a result of fires. In the 1950s, the game to be seen on the plateau included impala, roan antelope, warthogs, zebra, lion and many kinds of extremely rare birds including Crawshay's frankolin and Stanley's bustard.

Probably the first European to visit the Nyika was Richard Crawshaw, a government official, who crossed the plateau in 1893. Frequent visits also were made by the Reverend Young of the Livingstonia mission between 1930 and 1938. Many of the missionaries had continued since then to take leave on the plateau.

One interesting feature of the Nyika was Kaulima's Pond, which

Nyika.

had been formed by a natural dam of the Rukuru River, which rises on the plateau. This pond was the watering hole for most of the game on the plateau. It was therefore possible, in the evening, to watch many types of game from a hide near the pond.

Another interesting feature of the plateau was an isolated pocket of juniper trees, some of which were more than 100 feet high. It is probable that large areas of the Nyika at one time were covered by juniper trees, which may have been destroyed by bush fires.

From the extreme south east escarpment of the plateau you could look down an almost sheer drop of some 6,000 feet to Lake Nyasa, with the Livingstonia mission standing out to the side on the ridge of Mount Lawes.

North of the Nyika the land falls to the Karonga Plain, which is broken only by the Misuku Hill area. This had become the centre of a coffee-growing cooperative project which had proved highly profitable to local farmers. I was most amused on one occasion, when

invited to visit this project, to
be taken into a room where
some old crones were industri-
ously biting the berries off the
beans and spitting the residue
sideways. The Nyasaland coffee producers said their coffee
had a unique flavour. Perhaps,
in the circumstances, not altogether surprising.

Karonga, at the north end of
the lake, had the distinction of
being the only battleground
with the German forces in the
First World War. There were
still some bullet holes in an
old baobab tree. I always
found Karonga rather flat and

*Karonga: baobab tree
with World War I bullet holes.*

War Memorial, Zomba

uninteresting country. Even the lake had not the scenic beauty of its lower reaches. It was also a devil of a drive to get there.

*　　*　　*

I have briefly described the country passing northward and to the west of Lake Nyasa but largely avoided reference to the lake itself, which is the outstanding feature of Nyasaland scenery and life. The lake takes up more than a quarter of the total area of the country and has an expanse of 10,000 square miles. It is 380 miles long and, at its widest, 50 miles wide. Its surface lies 1,550 feet above sea level, but its maximum depth is more than 3,000 feet, Facts cannot adequately convey the beauty of Lake Nyasa, with its wonderful clear blue water, which one could drink without hesitation, the beautiful beaches, rocky headlands and surrounding mountains.

The lake had recently been the subject of an hydrological survey, but we still had a lot to learn about it. Certain of the changes in its level were unpredictable. The old banks indicated that perhaps some 50,000 years ago its level was about 30 feet higher than the level in the 1950s. Actual records of levels dated only from the early part of the century, and even these were not complete and reliable. In 1914, the level was so low that it was impossible to use the main port at Fort Johnson. However, in 1924 the Liwonde road bridge some thirty miles downstream, on the Shire River, was flooded and washed away.

It appeared that the level of the lake followed an eleven-year cycle which might be linked to the sunspot cycle. Outside the periodic variations over the years there was an annual variation of about six feet. This was caused partly by evaporation, as the water flowing down the Shire River only accounted for part of the water loss. Sudden and inexplicable variations in the lake level had been seen. One interesting theory suggested by a geological friend of mine was that these variations were caused by a subterranean loss of water into the Indian Ocean, where variations in the salinity of the water off the coast of Mozambique had been noted.

In addition to the longer-term variations there are *seiches* (tides) of a few inches with a periodicity of about six hours. Because the lake lies in a geological fault, fluctuations have been noted when earthquake or volcanic action has taken place considerable distances away.

In the light of these factors efforts to control the level of the lake had proved difficult. (The Liwonde barrage constructed at considerable cost in 1956 had later to be breached owing to an abnormal rise in lake level.)

At certain times of the year when the Mwera was blowing, and the wind was channelled between the mountains, very rough seas could develop. One of the most dangerous aspects of this was the rapidity with which a storm could develop, due possibly to the depth of the water and its low specific gravity. The lake's record of boat losses and drownings was frightening. Every year there were fatalities affecting small-boat users. As early as 1895, Bishop Chauncy Maples was drowned when going to his seat at Likoma Island. In more recent years (1944) the *Vypia*, a sea-going vessel of 200 tons displacement, capsized on its fourth voyage with a loss of nearly 150 people.

There were many differences in character between the various parts of the lake. The lower arms were more river-like and could, at certain seasons, be covered by algae and sudd. These were some of the shallower parts of the lake and were full of hippo and crocodile. They could be dangerous. I was once following, and trying to photograph, a hippo when it surfaced under the stern of my small boat and nearly capsized me. This was some distance from the shore and amongst many crocodiles.

Farther up the lake one came to the wider and deeper sections, with the broken hills of the Cape Maclear Peninsula and Salima with its wonderful beaches made up of carborundum, ruby and garnet grains. Farther north still was the Nyika Plateau rising more than 6,000 feet above the surface of the lake, and finally the Karonga area more reminiscent of the lower sections of the lake. Near to the Tanganyika shore about halfway up the lake was Likoma Island, a rocky but fertile island with its mission settlement and large cathedral.

In many of the inlets and rivers feeding the lake you could see large

Lake Nyasa, Nkata Bay. With Nkungu fly.

numbers of hippo and crocodiles. Some of the latter were monsters growing to more than thirty feet in length. Fortunately, crocodiles seldom attack in clear water, and their presence did not prevent bathing from the beaches. There had, however, been cases of attack at night, even close to the beaches of the tourist hotels.

There was a story of a district commissioner who hatched a crocodile egg and kept it in his bath until it was over three feet long. One presumes he was so preoccupied with his study of the saurian that he had no time to take a bath.

There was a market for crocodile skins, and professional hunters were operating successfully on the lake. The belly skin, which is the usable part, is of no use if the crocodile is poisoned, so the difficult and expensive process of shooting, with some penning in river estuaries, had to be adopted.

The lake abounded in many types of fish, including some unique species, and supported two commercial fishing operations. The most valuable, and one of the most common fish, was the tilapia, or African perch, which has been used to stock ponds and lakes all over the world and is particularly suited for fish farming. Tilapia taken from its native haunt in this lovely clear water was one of the finest eating fish I have ever tried.

Another common fish in the lake was the African barbel, which has an enormous head, whiskers and a long slim body and may grow up to thirty or forty pounds. There were many other types of tropical fish, some as highly coloured as those in the tropical oceans. It had also been discovered that eels existed in the lake. This raised the interesting question as to where they bred, as it seemed unlikely that they could migrate to their normal breeding grounds in the southern Atlantic Ocean.

One of the most fascinating and interesting fauna peculiar to the African lakes was the Nkungu fly. This insect is so small that it can pass through the mesh of a mosquito net. Frequently when one was travelling on the lake, or on its shores, you saw what seemed to be columns of water spouts rising from the surface of the lake to heights of two or three thousand feet. These were in fact originally taken by the early missionaries to be water spouts but were actually composed of dense masses of Nkungu flies on their mating flight. There is a period of about one month between successive cycles of columns forming. Very little was known about the fly's life cycle, although it was thought that the Nkungu bred in the depths of the lake and that when the eggs hatched the larvae came to the surface, metamorphosed into flies and formed their column.

The columns were so dense that there were recorded instances of people being suffocated when the columns had blown onshore. A friend piloting a small aircraft once flew through a column at 2,000 feet and lost power for about a minute. Fortunately few flies got inside the aircraft. I have calculated the number of flies in each column as several hundred million. You could usually see seven or eight columns in only one area of the lake when they were swarming.

At the south end of Lake Nyasa, almost as a continuation of it formed by the widening of the Shire River, is Lake Malombe. This is a shallow and not very interesting or attractive sheet of water surrounded by reed-covered banks and swampy areas. It had a large population of crocodile and hippo, and mosquitoes made life almost unbearable.

There are two other sizable lakes in Nyasaland. Lake Chiuta on the Portuguese border forms the headwaters of the Lugenda River, which flows into the Indian Ocean, and Lake Shirwa. Lake Shirwa, close to Zomba, has low banks and although large is very shallow. It attracted many water birds, had some fish but contained no crocodiles. This was almost inexplicable, and it had been suggested that it might be due to chemical or radioactive conditions. Python Island, the one island in the lake, was infested by many of the more unpleasant types of snake.

*   *   *

The country was one offering many contrasts and having the sombre brooding grandeur of its mountains, the life and humour of its waterfalls and the colour of its lake with many-hued sands. Perhaps what made Nyasaland so fascinating was that, though for Africa it was a highly populated territory, there was an easy escape to a wilder, lesser-known world which existed in the mountains and on the high plateau. But one had always to remember that it could be wildest Africa; and, during the progress of a walk, you might surprise a leopard or, perhaps more frighteningly, a mamba.

Besides the fauna there were other factors to beware of. When one was climbing, particularly on Mlanje, the Chiperoni mist, named after the Chiperoni mountains in Portuguese East Africa, might descend and limit visibility to a yard or so. The maps were also in some cases inaccurate and misleading, and it was not difficult to get lost.

Chapter 6

The Wildlife

Most people who had not visited Africa thought of the continent as one over which large numbers of wild animals roamed and life was hazardous, with people in constant danger of being chased and eaten by lions, or attacked by other predatory beasts or reptiles. In fact, as a result of the population density and the widespread issue of gun permits to the African villagers so they might protect their crops, it was unusual to see most of the larger animals. The game population was much less than in British and Portuguese East Africa, and the only area with any major concentration was the Nyika Plateau. One other factor which had reduced the wild life population was the systematic clearing of game in certain areas to limit tsetse fly infestation.

The tsetse fly had always been the major factor in restricting cattle farming in Africa. Early hopes of curing trypanosomiasis using antricide had not confirmed their initial promise, because the parasite had developed a resistance to the drug. For this reason clearing of game was still prevalent in many areas.

The tsetse fly is similar to an ordinary house fly, and only a small percentage carry the parasite. Its bite, as I know from personal experience, was painful, and you faced the unpleasant prospect that you might develop sleeping sickness, a frequently incurable disease.

It was important to ensure that vehicles leaving a tsetse-infested area were sprayed to make sure any flies in the vehicle were killed. However, this was Africa, and you sometimes arrived at a tsetse post to find the staff missing or fast asleep. It was then up to the conscience of the traveller to see that the necessary attention was given.

The greatest danger to all of us in Africa was not from the lions and larger mammals but from one of the smallest creatures, the anopheles mosquito. Malaria was endemic, and despite the advances in tropical medicine and the use of prophylactics you were always likely to go down with malaria when you stopped taking these drugs. This might happen years later in an area not subject to malaria.

In my experience, the most aggressive creature was the driver, or soldier, ant, followed closely by the black mamba. The soldier ant was feared by every animal and reptile, as well as man. This was another species where the female was more deadly than the male, which was a harmless creature looking something like a wasp. The female developed in several ways. The worker was an insignificant-looking ant, but another form, the soldier, was a large ant, with the heaviest and most formidable mandible of any insect. Stories of driver ants were legion; they were carnivorous and sent out scouts exploring the way ahead for possible food supplies. Once they started to move in on a quarry, nothing would stop them.

On one occasion, some friends found that driver ants were advancing on their house. They tried to halt the advance using boiling water, the servants lighted fires, and I hurried to assist with a blow torch. While we must have killed millions, the more we slaughtered, the more poured into the attack. Finally, our friends had to leave their house to the ants. In the morning there was not an ant to be seen, nor was there any living thing in the house. Every bat, cockroach, snake etc. had gone. Anyone who stayed would have been eaten alive by ants. This has happened to children and invalids.

One horrid feature of this insect was that it first attacked the eyes, blinding the victim. In the case of a large animal, the ants surrounded it, in millions, before attacking and smothering it. When you saw driver ants, the wise thing to do was to leave rapidly. This was true for all creatures, including lions and elephants.

I had one interesting experience with driver ants. At the time, our governor was a very able, but also very austere, man who was a stickler for protocol. I had been showing His Excellency a radio station on the top of Mpingwe mountain, and he expressed a wish to look at the view from a ridge some little distance away. We had to walk there through rather high grass and did not notice that a column of driver ants, which normally avoid sunshine, was also moving through the grass.

His Excellency must have put his foot in it literally (for once), and a number of ants started to march up his legs and bite him in the tenderest of places. At this stage most ordinary persons would have been doing a very good imitation of a tribal dance, war cries and all. As Her Majesty's accredited representative, HE was made of sterner stuff, and he suffered in silence until he had been badly bitten and was in such pain that he had to bring his quandary to the notice of lesser persons, such as his ADC and me. Fortunately, the ants had not done any lasting damage to his nether regions. *Sic transit gloria mundi.*

The Bantus sometimes used the soldier ants in a primitive form of surgery. The ant was placed with its mandibles across the cut, and when it clamped these tightly the body was cut off. You could therefore close a wound with twenty soldier ants instead of twenty stitches.

The termite was another formidable enemy of man in Africa. This is called the white ant although not entomologically a true ant. Termites are probably the most intelligent and highly organized of the social insects. They are also the only creatures which can feed on pure cellulose. This is possible because they have protozoa in their stomachs, a symbiotic parasite which breaks the cellulose down into protein.

The termite will attack and destroy most timbers in a relatively short time. Normally, it builds up a mortar wall covering its operations, but in occupied premises it often goes under cover, and frequently the first sign of termite activity was when you tried to open a door, and the door, frame and all, collapsed into a pile of paint flakes and a few splinters of wood.

In 1950, we had an unfortunate example of termite activity at our headquarters. The termites managed to enter one of our strong rooms and, before they were noticed, destroyed nearly the whole of the written records of the department. The total paper mass had amounted to about two tons. It has been suggested that one of the main reasons a more advanced civilization did not develop in Africa was that termites would have destroyed anything which might have formed a permanent written record.

During the early part of the rainy season the termite mating flights took place. At these times the termitaries were like huge bonfires with a smoke column of flying ants rising from the top. On such occasions flying ants, or the wings they shed, were everywhere. They were on your food, in your bed, on the furniture, in your hair and on the ground chasing each other. They were ubiquitous and annoying in their fecundity and apparently senseless and profligate reproduction.

The percentage of new colonies formed by these mating flights must have been very small indeed as predators were taking their toll everywhere. Many termites were taken in the air by birds. Every verandah had several frogs, with their tongues shooting out like whips collecting them. The lizards were also busy. The Bantu collected them for what they called African sardines.

The termites were not normally eaten by the Europeans; but I recall one story of a lady who served a caviar-like dish which was much enjoyed by all until she informed them that it was made out of the egg sack of a queen termite. At this stage many of the guests turned rather green and hurriedly left the room.

I once saw a termite queen which had been dug out of a termitary. It was virtually an egg laying machine. The fore-part had a normal-sized head and body; however, this was attached to an egg sack five to six inches long and about an inch in diameter. The queen lays about an egg a second for the whole of her life. With the workers carrying away and tending the eggs, this is probably one of the most efficient production lines that has ever evolved.

*   *   *

Our major sources of danger in Nyasaland were the parasitic diseases carried by insect and other hosts. Malaria and sleeping sickness have already been mentioned as major scourges. An equally dangerous and most objectionable disease was bilharzia, which was present in most stagnant water.

Bilharzia has a life cycle which is so complex that it seems a wonder that it can continue to exist. The parasite, at the stage it infects a human being, has the form of a delicate filament which is easily broken and destroyed. So one cannot be infected in rapidly flowing streams or where there is wave motion. Consequently, Lake Nyasa is only dangerous at the river mouths and estuaries. The filaria penetrates the human body through the skin, then passes through the blood stream into the liver, kidneys and bladder. Here, it develops and breeds. After reproduction, the eggs pass out of the body through urination. The next stage of existence, before the filaria can again be produced, is that these eggs must be absorbed into the body of a secondary host, a type of snail present in most rivers. It will hatch only when this has taken place. The disease was a most unpleasant one, debilitating and sometimes fatal.

A most frightening disease carried by many animal hosts, and very prevalent in Nyasaland, was rabies. The course of this disease, which is fatal if inoculations are not given quickly, is well known. I can assure readers, from personal experience, that even the inoculations against it were not to be taken lightly.

Turning next to the reptiles, the crocodile was a voracious and most unattractive inhabitant of most of the lakes and rivers in Central Africa. It is a cautious beast and does not like entering shallow, clear water. But if the water is murky, it will attack in quite shallow streams. It is also semi-nocturnal, and for this reason it was dangerous to bathe, or even wade, in any water after dusk. While I was in Nyasaland, seldom a week passed without someone being taken by a crocodile, usually a woman who had gone to a river to collect water. On one occasion one of our linesmen, who was crossing a river in a canoe, was thrown into the water and taken.

The crocodile does not normally eat its prey immediately but stores it for a period in a hole, or under an eroded river bank, until it has decayed. For this reason, one needed a very strong stomach when hunting crocodiles, as the stench of the creature's breath was overpowering.

Nyasaland had more than its fair share of dangerous snakes, including the mamba, puff adder and spitting cobra. These included both the snakes whose venom coagulates the blood and those attacking the nervous system. However, the most feared snake was probably mythical and, in a rather free translation, was known as the crowing crested cobra.

An area near Nkata Bay in the northern province had an extremely bad reputation for fatal snake bites. Our linesmen hated patrolling the section of the old Cecil Rhode's line which passed through this district, which was the reputed habitat of the crowing crested cobra. The snake was believed by most Africans, and some Europeans, to have a red head, live in trees, sing like a bird and possibly fly, or at least launch itself on the unwary traveller below.

Was there such a reptile? I very much doubt it, although many people believed there might be an undiscovered species of mamba living in this district. I think it was probably the black or green mamba, which frequently lives in trees and will attack, without hesitation, when its nest is approached. The explanation of the red head: probably one of the red-headed lizards had been seen just before an attack. The bird song might have been that of birds almost certain to have been in the tree. Nevertheless, the crowing crested cobra was very much alive in the minds of people who had to travel through this district. I had qualms myself when walking through the bush in that area.

The most dangerous African snake, perhaps the most dangerous snake in the world, is the black mamba. This reptile is unpredictable and differs from other snakes in that it frequently attacks even though not disturbed. Most other snakes beat a retreat on the approach of a human being. The mamba, as often as not, came for you; and, as it could move more rapidly than any other reptile and carried a most virulent poison in its fangs, it was extremely dangerous. It has been estimated that a mamba can travel for short distances at forty miles per hour. Cases have occurred of it biting galloping horses.

I have on two occasions encountered a black mamba, which, by the way, is not black but dark brown. It is a slender but beautifully proportioned snake. On the first occasion, I was fortunately in my car, and the mamba, which was travelling about as fast as I was, hit the door with its biting stroke. My second experience was on a small island in the Zambezi. When I first saw the snake it was lying on a rock. It saw me and suddenly launched itself in my direction and appeared to travel almost as if a stone were thrown along the ground. Fortunately, it passed me at a distance of about a yard. The method of progression seemed to be by the contraction and expansion of rings along the body, with the snake stretched out in a straight line and the head lifted above the ground ready to strike. The mamba is such a wild creature that it cannot be kept in captivity and dies almost immediately if penned in.

The spitting cobra appeared to differ from the well-known cobras of Asia in being able to spit, accurately, at the eyes of its intended victim.

If the mamba and cobra have attractive forms, the puff adder is singularly unattractive with its flat repulsive head, its thick, slug-like body and little tail on the end. The puff adder usually left you alone unless you were unfortunate enough to tread on it. Its bite is, however, dangerous even when the snake is very young; as one of the leading authorities on snakes involved in the production of snake bite serum at Port Elizabeth snake park discovered. He was working in his laboratory and picked up a newly born puff-adder not more than three inches long. In view of its size, he handled it carelessly, and it turned and sank its fangs into his thumb. He was not unduly troubled, as he thought the bite from such a small snake was unlikely to be dangerous. However, a few minutes later he staggered into the street and collapsed. He was taken to hospital, where it was suspected that he was the victim of a heart attack. His condition was critical, and the hospital searched through his papers and discovered his identity. As he was a leading authority in his field they then realized he was probably suffering from snake bite. Following an injection of anti-venom he recovered from what might have been a fatal bite from a newly born snake.

Snake anti-venom was a horse serum to which some people had a violent reaction. I carried the two types of serum whenever I was trekking in the African bush. In 1958, shortly after I arrived in Jamaica, I required an anti-tetanus shot. As this was also a horse serum, my doctor made the usual routine check and found I had a violent reaction. I told him about the snake anti-venom and he told me that if I had used it in the bush I would have killed myself.

I remember two rather lighter experiences with snakes. The first involved a new arrival who came out to join us and live in a bachelor mess where I was staying. The toilets, or *chimbuzies* in Chinyanja, in most of the older houses were located outside the main house. They consisted of a small hut containing a seat with a hole in it. Below the seat and at the rear was a trap-door through which one of the house boys put in dry grass which absorbed the moisture and excrement. He removed this daily for disposal.

When you went to the *chimbuzi* you usually passed members of the domestic staff, who would sit around in quiet meditation, wondering when they might have to do some work and in the meantime contemplating the comings and goings of the mad Europeans in whom they took a considerable interest. It was not, therefore, unusual for them to comment on a person being in the *chimbuzi*, sometimes to a large gathering.

On this occasion, we were having a party and were not unduly concerned when my head boy arrived and informed the company that Bwana Adrian was making much noise in the *chimbuzi*; most of us suffered from a local complaint known as Zomba tummy when we arrived in Nyasaland. Shortly afterward the second house boy arrived to say Adrian was having much trouble. He was followed by our cook who said Adrian was making even more noise in the *chimbuzi*. My friend Ted said, "What's wrong with the man? He must be blasting his tail off."

It was only after a protracted absence that we felt we should investigate. We discovered the unfortunate Adrian standing on the *chimbuzi* seat, with his trousers round his ankles, and still shouting weakly. As we opened the door, a rather inoffensive-looking and equally scared grass snake glided off into the night. I later heard Adrian telling the story of how, on his first day in the country, he was attacked by a black mamba and bravely managed to protect himself and drive it away.

The second story was of a friend of my wife's and also related to a *chimbuzi*. In this instance, the boys had cleaned out the *chimbuzi* and put in new straw. Unfortunately, they forgot to close the trap-door. One of the local chickens was passing by and thought this an ideal place to nest. Some time later Frankie's friend went to the toilet, and the chicken then found itself being rained on from above. It decided to attack the source of its discomfort, and the lady took off shouting that she had been bitten by a snake. I gather that afterward she used to regale her morning coffee parties with the story of how she had nearly suffered mortal injury by the beak of a wild chicken.

*   *   *

On the road between Fort Johnson and Monkey Bay was a sign: "Beware of elephants on this road." The only places I have seen African elephants were in the Northern Rhodesian and East African game parks. At one time large herds of elephants roamed Nyasaland; but, owing to the increase in human population, the activities of ivory hunters and the reduction in available feeding areas, these no longer existed, although periodically a herd entered the country from the less populated areas of Mozambique.

The African elephant is a much more dangerous and unpredictable creature than the Indian and differs in appearance in having much larger ears. It is extremely intelligent and very rapid-moving. When angered, it takes its place, with the cape buffalo, as the most dangerous of the larger animals. The African elephant had not been successfully domesticated, although some attempts at training had been made in the Belgian Congo.

There used to be a large lion population in Nyasaland, and some prides still existed in the mountain areas, descending periodically to create a

Beware of Elephants.

little excitement in the villages and European settlements. My first
week in the country, a lioness and her cubs came down from Zomba
mountain into the town and created considerable alarm and despondency until, shamefully, they were shot in the garden of our chief
accountant. The only lion I ever saw in the Zomba area was standing
at the roadside as I motored out for dinner at a friend's house.

There were records of large numbers of lions roaming the country
until about the 1930s. One settler claimed to have shot eight within
300 yards of one another. One lovely story of the early days was of a
settler in the lower river valley who was returning home in his *machila*
after a convivial evening with friends. He found his progress halted
by what he took to be a herd of donkeys on the track. Having urged
his boys to get their friends out of the way, he took a hand himself by
trying to twist the animals' tails only to realize, to his horror, that the
tails had the hairy protuberance at their ends that is common only to
the lion. He hurriedly returned to his *machila* until the lions dispersed.
His bearers had wisely disappeared into the bush.

Come twist my tail.

There was yet another lion story in Nyasaland which bore some resemblance to the stories of leopard men in West Africa. This case also occurred in the Fort Manning area, and was about a man-eating lion which was never seen but which killed old men, women and children when they were alone. The villagers firmly believed the lion changed itself into a human being after a kill. The local district commissioner, when called to a kill near to his *boma*, had the unnerving experience, on following the spoor, to find that it suddenly disappeared and was replaced by human tracks travelling in the same direction. The footprints were followed, but they faded out in rocky ground. The lion continued to terrorize the neighbourhood until its victims numbered more than seventy. It was finally shot by one of the district's settlers, destroying the myth.

If lions had become scarce, except on the high plateau and in the mountain ranges, the leopard, which was the symbol of Nyasaland, was still very common. I have seen them many times, sometimes as close as a few yards. The leopard is a beautiful animal, and fortunately it seldom becomes a man-eater, unless injured or too old to hunt its normal prey. It has gained a taste for dogs, and many pets were taken in the Zomba area. My wife was always terrified when our cocker spaniel took off on one of his jaunts.

Two animals one seldom saw, but often heard at night, were the jackal and hyena. These are usually nocturnal and timid although the hyena has been known to attack an injured or sleeping person and inflict frightful injuries, such as taking off a leg. In an instance shortly before we left Zomba, a hyena bit off the face of an African asleep in his hut. The hyena is a very ugly creature, having heavy forequarters, a massive head, and a very rough and untidy coat. The jackal looks rather like a large dog and was more to be feared for the rabies it frequently carried (it became much more aggressive when rabid) than for any normal likelihood of attack.

The most ubiquitous animal in the country was the baboon. This animal is intelligent and cunning and caused a tremendous amount of damage to native crops. For this reason, guns had been made available to the Bantu to protect crops. Unfortunately, the guns were used to shoot game for the pot, hence the virtual extermination of many species. The baboon with its natural cunning continued to flourish.

It was difficult to approach a pack of baboons when carrying a gun. However, if you were unarmed, they approached you closely and barked defiance. The baboon could be a dangerous animal. They frequently attacked native dogs and tore them to pieces. They also would attack isolated and unarmed human beings. Most of such attacks were on the male sex, and the tribal Africans said that if a woman was alone and surrounded by baboons they would not attack if she lowered her robe and showed she was a woman.

These were the creatures common to our lives in Nyasaland. Sadly, you had to go to the high plateau and mountains to see many of the others common to other parts of Africa.

Chapter 7

The People

"For the sake of friendship be mine enemy"
– William Blake

A. The Bantu

The Bantu are generally defined as the African Negro peoples who speak the Bantu group of languages. There are many hundreds of Bantu tribes in the central and southern part of Africa. As indicated earlier, the Bantus probably originated in the Congo Valley area. All the tribes in Nyasaland were of Bantu origin.

Owing to the tribal wars of extermination which largely eliminated the Bushmen and earlier societies, there were few people of recognizable mixed race (half-caste) in Bantu-occupied areas although some individuals exhibited traces of Arab descent.

In 1957 the estimated population of Nyasaland consisted of 2,750,000 Bantu Africans, 11,000 Asiatics and 6,000 Europeans. For the Federation as a whole, the population was estimated at 6,750,000 Bantu Africans, 12,000 Asiatics and 250,000 Europeans. These figures show the greater degree of European settlement and the very small amount of Asian penetration into the Rhodesias. Given its much smaller area, Nyasaland differed from the rest of the Federation in being a densely populated and essentially Bantu African country. As it was also largely agricultural, with most of its area given up to tribal and African trust lands, it would, under Federation, remain a predominantly Bantu country. It is therefore proper to consider the Bantu first in any description of the people of the country.

Most Europeans who had lived in Africa had the warmest feelings of regard for the tribal Bantu, who had a terrific sense of humour and was generally a very friendly person who approached even the most menial task cheerfully. One should, however, discount the tradition of the "noble savage" which had caused considerable misconception amongst the people of Europe and America. The Bantu was likeable but not noble, and in considering the lighter side of Bantu character and culture, one should not overlook the darker side. This included the continuing belief in witchcraft and the ancestral tribal spirits.

Despite the efforts of the missionaries and the administration, the *mwabui* poison ordeal was still practised in some areas. Under this, all suspects were made to drink poison. Those who did not vomit the poison died and were presumed guilty. In some witchcraft rites necrophagy, which involved the digging up and eating of some organs of a recently buried body, was still practised. All too often tribal superstitions and rites had been grafted onto Christianity as in the case of John Chilembwe (mentioned in Chapter 4) and the more recent bestiality of the Mau Mau in East Africa.

Because of the different stages of development reached, the dissimilar nature of their culture and the wholly different historical and social background, which was based on a nomadic, warlike existence under conditions of considerable hardship, it was only to be expected that the Bantu's thought processes would differ from our own, although mental ability might be similar. People who had no first-hand experience of Africa found it hard to understand that you could both educate and convert the Bantu to Christianity (or a political ideology) without imparting the responsibilities basic to modern civilization. The Bantu culture had, however, developed the characteristics of loyalty, cheerfulness and an ability to stand up to hardship sometimes under almost intolerable conditions. Against this, there was often a lack of responsibility, and the veneer of civilization was still thin for most individuals.

One Bantu characteristic to be guarded against, possibly also related to the cultural background, was an unusual capacity in the dialectic. This was frequently used to avoid responsibility for past actions. Even an uneducated tribal African had the ability, in argument, to make black seem white and turn the most damning circumstances in his favour. Based on this, one could expect that they would make persuasive politicians, lawyers and evangelists.

In any appreciation of the Bantu one had to draw the distinction between the simple and contented villager and the intelligentsia who, although educated, were not accepted by the Europeans. This lack of acceptance, for which the Europeans were largely to blame, was undoubtedly one of the reasons many Bantu political leaders were so strongly opposed to European leadership.

Accompanied by a European friend, my wife and I once visited the home of the first Bantu assistant district commissioner. We were entertained with tea and scones in typical English fashion, and we all appreciated what had been done to entertain us and sensed our host's desire to be liked and accepted. To her credit, my wife was completely relaxed. In all honesty, I had qualms about accepting a social relationship which was completely foreign to my experience. My normally outgoing friend was even more uncomfortable and made a move to leave as soon as possible. It was essential that we should overcome these reserves to help understanding and cooperation under multiracial conditions.

One other problem with many educated Africans was that they had become detribalized and cut off from their own people. Too often they did not recognize the merits of the tribal system which had developed over hundreds of years as the basis for the communities' social and cultural systems.

It was hard for anyone who had not lived in Central Africa and had only heard the opinions of articulate but self-interested African political leaders, and the short-term visitors from press, pulpit and parliament, to have any idea just how primitive was the life of the bulk of the population. Also, how little such a person understood the economic and political problems facing the country and how unready most of the leaders were to take responsibility for the well-being of the community and the affairs of government at a national level.

Life in the villages, though primitive, was mostly pleasant, certainly better than in the pre-colonial days, when sudden death or enslavement was an ever present possibility, and the tribal laws and punishments were much harsher than those later introduced or permitted under colonial government. The abominations inflicted by the witch doctors had largely been ended. The constant threat of death by famine had been removed, and the health of the community improved by the introduction of medical services. While the overall position had improved, the African woman remained in a subservient position.

The *lobola*, or bride price, was still an essential element to tribal marriage in Africa, whether the tribe was patrilineal or matrilineal. This was a price paid for both the procreative powers of the woman and her services as a worker. In matrilineal societies descent was through the female blood line. Except for the Ngoni, most of the Nyasaland tribes were matrilineal. The bride price varied considerably and could be as little as a pound sterling or as much as several hundred pounds.

I remember two cases of bride purchase which came to my notice. The first was when one of our Bantu staff, on *ulendo* with a European engineer, wished to borrow four pounds to buy a wife. The lady was standing demurely by with her uncle while the loan was being discussed. When my engineer suggested he might buy the girl himself, she left rapidly. The other case was that of one of our postal agents in the Misuku area who borrowed three hundred pounds, from the till, to buy cattle to pay the bride price for the chief's daughter. We never recovered the cattle or the three hundred pounds from the chief, a wily old Tumbuku. His son-in-law had a curtailed honeymoon in the prison farm, looking after cattle. This seemed a fitting punishment.

The duties of a woman in tribal societies had remained unaltered and included all the domestic tasks of drawing water, tilling and planting the fields, pounding the grain and preparing the food; besides

Village Washday.

bearing children, usually carrying an infant on her back with several trailing behind her

With the end of tribal warfare, the man had become something of a displaced person and had little to occupy his mind or time. This had been a factor in the development of the major migration of labour.

Even in the more distant past, the Bantu were inveterate travellers, as we know from the early tribal movements. It was therefore the traditional love for change and movement, as well as underemployment and economic advantage, which had resulted in many tribal Africans taking employment in the mines of Northern Rhodesia and South Africa and on the farms of Southern Rhodesia. These migrations created serious social problems and were much disliked by the women, who remained at home with one of their essential functions interrupted. Childlessness or lack of fertility was regarded as a social stigma.

Reginald, one of our postmasters in the southern province, showed initiative in taking advantage of this situation. We first learned of this when we began to receive complaints that some of the girls visiting Reginald's post office found themselves in an interesting condition after returning home. We learned that they were the wives and daughters of migrant workers who had sent them money by postal order.

When they arrived at his post office, Reginald would tell them that he could not pay them that day, but if they came back in the morning he would be happy to do so. He would then suggest that if they had nowhere to stay overnight he would be pleased to accommodate them in the departmental house he occupied.

We stopped Reginald's social cum sexual activities, but he did not appreciate the gravity of his offence and pointed out that the ladies were lonely and were usually happier when they left in the morning. When we suggested that the husbands and other relatives might seek revenge and attack him with a *panga*, he said this did not trouble him. They would blame the Bwana Postmaster General, in whose house they were staying and who was also called Reginald. Incidentally, Reginald was the postmaster who, when we first introduced books of stamps, wrote me a plaintive little letter asking what to do with the empty books after he had sold all the stamps from them.

The large-scale migration of the Bantu workers had other serious aspects in addition to the loneliness of their wives in the villages. There was considerable homosexuality amongst the migrants, and prostitution was rampant, particularly in the mining areas. The social evils were in part balanced by the economic advantages to the families and to the country's economy. While I was in Nyasaland, the number of migrant workers approached 200,000. They sent more than one million pounds sterling annually to their families in Nyasaland, a considerable item in the country's economy.

The migrants were almost wholly transported by air and it was interesting, when visiting the airfields, to contrast those arriving from their villages, many of whom had never seen an aircraft and were mainly dressed in rags, with the returning workers brought in by the same plane and dressed in natty suiting, wearing trilby hats, carrying briefcases and with suitcases full of purchases and presents for their families.

*   *   *

The closest association many Europeans had with the Bantu population was through their domestic staffs. Conditions had remained virtually unchanged over the past fifty years, and it was common for a family of two people to have at least six employees. The families also lived on the compound, and with wives and children the community might total twenty to thirty people. This was, however, not a burden, and the little community existed very happily, side by side with the European family, in what was basically a feudal arrangement. A general impression of one's domestic staff was of cheerful, happy, loyal and improvident people who were always ready to take the new Bwana for a ride.

My first servant, whom I had before my wife arrived in the country, was an absolute paragon with the manners of a good English butler. He was also an excellent valet and, when I went on *ulendo*, a first-class cook. Unfortunately, as time went on, my colleagues started to lose things and blamed him for the losses. As he had proved to be completely loyal and scrupulously honest as far as I was concerned, I refused to accept that he was the thief.

After my wife arrived, and we set up our own establishment, it was rather disconcerting to find our guests also losing money and other possessions. I had a great liking for my major domo and appreciated all he had done to make me comfortable and ease my transition to a life in Africa. Rather than call in the police I had a talk with him and suggested that he might like to seek other employment. When he left us I missed him greatly.

For most of the time we were in Nyasaland, our staff consisted of Bita Saidi the cook, Wilson the number one house boy, Jamesie the second house boy, Dixon the gardener and two small assistants. Bita

Bita.

Jamesie.

Saidi was an excellent cook and could produce the most complex and difficult cakes and dishes on a primitive wood-burning stove. He was also without the most common failing of African cooks, who find cooking a very thirst-making business. Many of our friends, preparing for dinner parties, were consternated to find their cook paralytically drunk in the kitchen.

Cooks were full of idiosyncrasies, and frequent visits to the kitchen were desirable. On one occasion, all our food had a strange, fishy flavour. The cause proved to be that the pots had been used in the concoction of the local dish, known as African sardines, made from flying ants. A friend of ours found the cook making toast in front of the fire and putting it between his toes. He explained that he was only trying to keep it crisp.

The worst incident we had was that of the ubiquitous syringe. The house I had taken over a few days before my wife arrived had been occupied by a bachelor, whose girl friend had left a syringe in the bath room. Gingerly, I placed this in the waste-paper basket to be thrown out. I met my wife in Southern Rhodesia, and when we arrived back at the house all the European staff were hiding in the bedroom to welcome us and throw a party. Unfortunately, the syringe had been recovered by the boys and given a place of honour on the dressing table. The syringe was again thrown out, but both my staff and my wife regarded me with suspicion for some days.

About a month later, my wife made an inspection of the kitchen and discovered that the syringe had again been honourably resurrected for use in the kitchen. Bita was desolated at having to get rid of this useful culinary appliance, and I believe he sold it to one of the cooks at Government House.

Wilson, our number one boy, was a diffident, discreet and effeminate person. He was a good worker but above everything else loved arranging flowers. He was also the only Christian amongst a staff of Moslems.

Wilson's diffidence nearly led to his undoing. Zomba had suffered many burglaries, of which more later, and one night we were awakened by slight noises in the

Wilson.

Dixon.

adjoining room. This was actually Wilson who was trying to work up courage to wake me to take his wife to hospital for the usual delivery. We were only thinking of the burglar, however, and a very scared Wilson suddenly found the door jerked open and an automatic pistol jammed into his ribs.

Discretion was to be valued in one's African staff, as in its absence embarrassing circumstances could sometimes arise. A typical case of this occurred at a dinner party given by a farmer who supplied meat to the local market. On this occasion he was entertaining the medical officer of health, whose staff were responsible for meat inspection. A flock of sheep belonging to the farmer was suffering from some queer but fatal disease, and he had issued instructions to his shepherd about what to do if any sheep looked as if it might not last particularly long. You can imagine his consternation when the shepherd came into the dining room and said, "I am very sorry, Bwana, but two of the sheep died before I could kill them."

Jamesie, the second houseboy, was a hairy, husky and happy African of some eighteen years of age, whose wife had a habit of having fits and completely upsetting the whole compound, who believed she was possessed. The most notable thing about Jamesie himself was that he was an absolute Jehu on the roads. While most Africans on cycles had little road sense, Jamesie was an absolute menace. Repeatedly, my wife would ring me to say Jamesie had had another accident. His debt to me for bicycles and parts continued to rise, but he persisted in burning up the roads with the single-mindedness of Mr Toad.

I once saw one of Jamesie's accidents. Zomba is very hilly and coming down the hill outside the post office, at about fifty miles per hour, was an African cyclist. He was travelling too fast for me to see who it was, but I had a nasty suspicion who it might be. With mixed concern and amusement I watched him try to negotiate the bend at the bottom of the hill, to inevitably sail straight on, hit a series of rocks at the roadside and be thrown at least twenty feet into the air. By this time, I had realized that it must be Jamesie and rushed out to give first aid, only to find him uninjured but complaining he had hurt his bicycle a little bit. This must have been painful for the bicycle, which was a melange of mangled metal and tattered tyres.

You had to watch the health of your staff to safeguard your own health. This was brought home to us shortly after my wife arrived in Nyasaland. Frankie was German-born and spoke good English but sometimes had difficulty with the pronunciation. I returned home one afternoon to be greeted with the news that Bicycle, the second house boy, had cholera. None of us in Nyasaland had received shots against cholera, as the disease was not considered endemic in that part of the continent. My thoughts immediately turned to Axel Munthe and the Naples epidemic.

My curiosity was also aroused and I asked Frankie what Bicycle's symptoms were and was she sure it was cholera. She replied that he seemed OK but was limping badly. However, she had telephoned the African hospital and spoken to the medical officer, who had definitely confirmed that Bicycle had cholera. I was surprised that the medical people had not descended upon us and imposed strict quarantine.

We proceeded to disinfect the premises and later ourselves. By bedtime, when we had disposed of a bottle of whisky, we did not care if we were infected or not.

Before going to the office the next morning I telephoned the doctor Frankie had spoken to, and asked if it was safe to go to work. She replied, "Why not?" I tried again and said, "Surely cholera is most infectious and dangerous to everyone." This brought a fit of laughter and the doctor gasping out, "But it isn't cholera; it's gonorrhea." I should have realized that limping was unlikely to be a symptom of cholera.

While these comments give certain impressions of African domestic staff, it is only fair to also emphasize how likeable, loyal and interested in you they were, providing that you treated them reasonably and adopted a friendly and considerate attitude. They always appreciated the interest you took in them and their families.

The boys were something special in our lives. I hasten to add that "boys" is not used in any demeaning way but rather as my parents always referred to my brother and me as "the boys". Our domestic staff were in fact a very important part of the family. We lived together in our little community, of which Frankie and I were substantially in charge. Although we maintained, by African levels, a high standard of living, I do not think the boys were jealous.

We paid our staff at the high end of the going range, but it was a pitifully low wage, and they had always to borrow from us for any of the special things they wanted as a result of their contact with civilization. These included in particular small "saucepan" radios, gramophones and bicycles.They also received a *posho* or food allowance.

Fortunately, health services were not a problem and reasonably adequate, free services were available at the local African hospital. In an emergency, usually pregnancy, we took them, or their wives, by car to hospital. We saw that they took their medicines and followed prescribed treatment.

The boys wore a set garb, a khaki or white shirt and shorts. Each had his little house on the compound. These were very small but the boys and their families managed comfortably as the older children remained in the villages with their maternal grandmothers.

The boys were extremely proud of their adopted family. When I was promoted, they celebrated. When I returned from *ulendo*, they were all out to welcome me. If we were ill, they worried and fussed over us. If we took one of them on a *ulendo* trip, they always tried to look after our well-being and comfort. It was a poor employer who did not reciprocate and look after their welfare.

The boys particularly enjoyed our parties and would work to the limit in making them a success. They were always curious about the guest list and very proud when important people, or people they admired, were attending. In particular, they loved to see my friends Doc and the Bishop. Doc always encouraged them by greeting them in fluent Chinyanja, Chiyao or Chitumbuku and was a special favorite.

In their attempts to show the wealth and standing of the family, they could sometimes be embarrassing. We once went to the dinner table to find that Wilson had displayed Frankie's silver hair brush, comb and mirror in the centre of the table. Best of all they liked official functions and would carry out a sergeant major's examination of me in my uniform with topee and sword to see that everything was in order before they rushed to the parade. They were intensely curious about everything these crazy Europeans did and spent hours watching and listening to my amateur radio activities.

They were very clean and honest people, although they felt privileged, as part of the family, to help in the tea and sugar consumption. They were also proud of their own families and appreciated any interest you showed in them. Despite their poor wages, the families were clean and tidily dressed. Above all, they were usually happy and full of fun. Their humour was never malicious, although they might pull Dixon's leg about getting drunk and falling down at the KAR Mess or Jamesie about his cycling accidents. They had a natural camaraderie, although they usually deferred to Bita, whom they always called Babu.

One of the saddest things about finally leaving Africa was saying goodbye to our boys. When I wanted to take a photograph of them, they looked like a crowd at a funeral. Every attempt I made to get them to smile failed, although they were normally full of fun. Finally, Bita said, "How can we smile when you and the Donah are leaving us?" I regret that we did not keep in touch with them, but they were illiterate, and it would have been difficult to do so.

On a visit to Malawi in the early 1980s, I enquired about them. Bita had served honourably as a cook for many years and then retired to his village. Wilson had committed suicide after his wife betrayed him. Of the others I could discover nothing.

Although by American and European standards we led a very simple and modest life, we still look back with many regrets that we did not do more for the boys. They had so little, and we, in comparison, had so much.

*   *   *

Native craftsmanship had developed in Nyasaland, mainly the carving of ivory and wooden items. The centre for ivory carving was Kota Kota, and some of the workmanship was very fine indeed.

Most curios were sold by itinerant traders, who sometimes peddled items from as far away as British and Portuguese East Africa. Some traders also sold fruit and other produce. These traders would hawk their wares around the various offices, *bomas* and shops and were another main contact with the Europeans. Most were amusing characters, and some, complete rascals.

Ali Baba was an engaging villain who would appear every month or so, carrying a white calico sack containing his wares, with which he must have trudged many weary miles. My secretary fought long and wordy battles with him, but he knew me to be a compulsive buyer, and there was no way of keeping him out of my office. Once in, he would show all he had to sell, producing each item from his sack with a gesture and a smile, almost as a conjurer produces rabbits from a hat.

I shall never forget the time he staggered in almost bent double by the weight of the sack. Thrusting inside, he pulled out an enormous, and unbelievably ugly, ebony crocodile which he deposited in my unwilling arms describing volubly its beauty and merit as a carving, its size, the fineness of the wood, and all this for only five pounds. To get rid of him, I offered half a crown and after a lot of abuse finally got him out of the office. I fear, however, that no one else made any offer at all, and every few days he would again appear and display the monster. Gradually, the price came down by shillings as my offers went up by pence. After some weeks, I had reached ten shillings and still felt relatively safe. But then, in a moment of preoccupation, when I wanted to get rid of him quickly, I was foolish enough to say twelve shillings and sixpence. As he disappeared out of the door clutching the money, and I was left holding the monster, I persuaded myself that it might make a useful defensive weapon as well as a door stop. My wife's comments on first seeing the saurian threw some doubt on my sanity. Nevertheless, as years have passed, we have

Frankie with loot from Ali Baba.

grown reconciled to the beast and now regard him with affection and as a reminder of the wordy battles we fought with Ali Baba over many of the Nyasaland curios we have.

Yet another character was the deaf-and-dumb orange seller who traded on pity rather than the merit of his wares. He would appear in the office and put on a Karnoish act, starting by pointing at his mouth to show how hungry he was. After this, he would produce his small green oranges from a sack and hold up his fingers to show how much you should pay him. I am sure he was an utter rascal and had stolen the oranges from someone's tree long before they were ripe, as they were completely inedible. I was initially foolish enough to buy some and try to eat them. When he arrived the next time, I put on my own dumb-show act of eating an orange, then clutching my tummy and writhing. He was delighted with this and went happily on his way clutching his oranges and the tickey present I had given him.

Another itinerant trader I well remember was the egg man. What he could not sell he saved, and he would always try the next time to work off a few eggs of Chinese vintage on the unwary.

We had working for us, at the time, a Scottish woman called Margaret who had all the frugality of her race and used to hold long and amusing arguments with the egg man in a mixture of Scottish and Chinyanja. These touched on price and size, but were mainly directed against the eggs she bought which might better have been reserved for a political meeting. It was not long before she armed herself with a basin of water in which each egg was placed before being accepted.

My old friend Brian, who was in charge of Margaret's section, delighted in practical jokes and could not let this opportunity pass. Getting in early on egg day, he mixed a pound or so of salt in the basin of water Margaret used for her tests. The first eggs tested and rejected were regarded as the normal trial of strength, the seller knowing they were bad anyway. However, as egg followed egg floating halfway out of the water, a Scottish Bantu war seemed likely until a watching Brian burst out laughing.

*   *   *

An important and powerful section of the Bantu community, well to the fore in political matters, was that of the civil servants. Without any sizable professional or business groups, the civil servants, through their close association with the Europeans running the colonial serv-ice, had probably developed furthest toward an organized community based on European ideas and standards.

Many of the African civil servants, made up mostly of those who had advanced the hard way through honest endeavour and promo-tion, were reliable and efficient officers and men of principle, with an honest interest in their country's well-being and the work they per-formed. This sense of tradition and responsibility extended through all grades.

A typical example of dedication in the performance of his duties was that of Maccarani Msatilomo, our office messenger, who had previously been one of the old mail carriers. We achieved worldwide publicity on the retirement of Maccarani, who probably set an all-time record during his thirty years of mail carrying between the main centres of Blantyre and Zomba. A tiny man, he had been one of the armed carriers in the early days, when all kinds of perils had to be contended with and the carriers were armed with muzzle loaders. We calculated that during his service as a mail carrier he had carried 30 lbs of mail, on his head, for the equivalent of seven round-the-world journeys.

Maccarani Msatilomo. The seven times round the world mail carrier.

Unfortunately, this sense of dedication was not present in many of the better-educated, high school- and university-trained recruits who had no previous background in the service. These men frequently proved to be unreliable and untrustworthy, lacking dedication and, in some instances, honesty.

It would be wrong to assume that the high school- and university-educated African had not a responsible part to play in a properly organized civilized community. The danger was in accepting that passing examinations was all that was required. We tend to laugh at the tradition of the old school tie, and all too often we overlook our pride in honest craftsmanship in industry and husbandry in agriculture. These are, however, symptoms of community development over hundreds of years and had no parallel in Central Africa, where native ingenuity was often directed toward craftiness rather than craftsmanship.

There was almost a fetish amongst the younger, better-educated Bantus, who had obtained their general school certificate or gone to university, that any form of manual labour was not the thing for an educated gentleman but should be left to uneducated villagers. This attitude created problems in the technical branches of my department where we had the greatest difficulty in recruiting staff with the necessary educational qualifications to undertake any work which involved physical exertion or soiling their hands. When the work was of a sedentary nature, we had no difficulty in recruiting staff who met our educational requirements and took well to the work. Many of them also took anything they could lay their hands on.

Some apologists, including African political leaders, have tried to relate the high level of peculations by African staff to the low level of the salaries paid. Admittedly, African staff holding positions of responsibility were paid less than people holding equivalent positions in Europe. However, the adequacy of pay scales should be considered in relation to cost of living and the general living standards of the population. When considered on this basis, our staff were well off. It was also the case that increases in pay and upgrading of duties did little to resolve our theft problem.

The attitude of certain of the individuals involved was interesting. One "educated" postmaster, who stole thousands of pounds, was found guilty of theft and sentenced as a first offender. He protested indignantly that it had been unfair to penalize him as he had not taken a penny of post office funds but only stolen from the remittance letters of ignorant African villagers.

Sadly, it was my experience that a high proportion of our better-educated Bantu recruits were likely to finish at our prison farm. This augured poorly for the future of both the people and the economies of those African states which allowed these persons to have a major say in the rule of their countries. Some of our older staff also proved dishonest and finished in prison. The percentage was, however, much lower than for the younger educated staff.

Possibly because of the number of our staff who finished in the local prisons, I was appointed a visiting justice. Prisons are usually depressing places, and this was certainly true of our central prison. However, a visit to our prison farm, which was used for first offenders and occupied in the main by ex-post office staff, was not an altogether unpleasant experience. The farm was one of the best-run in the whole of the country and, besides making a profit from its milk and meat, supplied mainly to the hospitals, was also used to support the health services by producing lymph for vaccination against smallpox.

Whenever I visited the prison farm, I was likely to be greeted with a friendly "Hello, Bwana" from one of the older of our ex-postmasters. It was usually a pleasure to meet these old friends, who generally bore no malice and had considerable respect for the people they had worked with.

I first saw cashew nuts being grown at the prison farm and learned, from one of my old colleagues, the African explanation for this most peculiar nut. The cashew tree produces an attractive, highly coloured and shiny fruit, something like an apple in form but having a sweet if insipid flavour. The nut is attached as an appendage to the bottom of the fruit and looks completely out of place. The story, as told to me, was that, after God had created the universe, man and every living thing, man asked if he could be permitted to create something himself. God agreed, and man proceeded to make a tree and place attractive fruit on it. After he had finished God said, "Very nice, but surely you have forgotten something. How is it going to reproduce itself?" Man was discomfited, but God said, "It does not matter; we will just put seeds on the end of the fruit." That is how the fruit took its strange form.

On one occasion, I took my wife with me on a visit to the prison farm. She was particularly interested in the carpenters' shop, where six men were singing at their work and seemed a very happy bunch of people. After we left the shop she was curious about why such nice men should have finished in prison, even as first offenders, and asked the superintendent what crime they had committed. The reply, which I had no reason to doubt, was that they were all in prison for wife murder. A frequent excuse advanced for wife murder was that the wife had not kept the *posho* (corn porridge) warm. The illogical Bwana judge did not always accept this as an adequate justification for disposing of one's wife.

In contrast to the prison farm, the central prison was a most unhappy and foreboding place. While I believe in capital punishment as a necessary deterrent, it always depressed me to visit a place where executions were actually carried out. I always wondered if the inmates facing death really understood why they were being executed, since their culture had been based on war, slaughter and witchcraft. Also the prisoners were, in the main, people who had given up hope of ever having a normal place in society. Against this sombre background there was one rather amusing story which involved the central prison.

There had been a spate of burglaries in Zomba and the police, black and white, were completely defeated. The modus operandi of the thief was ingenious. Frequently, when entry was difficult, he used a long pole through the open window to hook up the items he was stealing. No one knew where the thief came from or returned to.

The thefts went on for months until an African constable saw a man carrying a sack and asked him what was inside. He found what seemed to be a quantity of stolen items and took the man to the police station for identification. When they identified the man from his fingerprints, they found, to their consternation, that he was an inmate of the central prison. Investigation showed that he was being let out each night by one of the warders, who shared the proceeds when he returned. It seems a pity that this ingenious thief was later executed following a prison riot in which warders were murdered.

Despite my comments on the irresponsibility of some African civil servants, I hope also that an impression of the likeability of the Bantus and their sense of fun, coupled with a natural dignity and humility in their normal environment, also will have emerged.

What the Bantu race had always failed to produce, above the clan or tribal level, was humane and responsible leadership. I believe that this was one of the reasons a more advanced Bantu civilization failed to emerge. There had been leaders in the past who achieved great power. However, it seemed that the more powerful these men were, the more despotic and bloodthirsty they became. Seldom did they have any real interest in the well-being of their subjects or other tribes.

In the short period of known African history there were many massacres throughout Bantu-occupied Africa. These ranged from the wholesale slaughter of over a million by Shaka's Impi hordes to the carnivals of sacrifice and banquets of human hearts in Benin Nigeria. In their bestiality these probably exceeded the greatest excesses of Tamerlene and Ghengis Khan in the Middle Ages, or Hitler in our century.

In common with the rest of Bantu Africa, Nyasaland had suffered from its own murderous leaders. Still lying at the foot of Mount Hora in Northern Nyasaland were the bones of some thousands of Tumbuku men, women and children driven, or thrown, over the precipitous side of the mountain by the Ngoni, who had at an earlier date been the subject of slaughter, pillage and rape by Shaka's Zulus. Even more recently we had experienced the Mau Mau atrocities although these were directed against the Europeans. However unpopular and unpleasant the comparisons might be, it was essential that future leadership should not follow the pattern of past history but be based on humane and democratic considerations with a respect for the rights of all races.

Perhaps the greatest problem facing us all in Central Africa was that of developing responsible Bantu leadership above the clan or tribal level. There would obviously be a need for such leadership whether within the federal structure or in the individual countries.

The chiefs and headmen had filled a special place in the society and had formed part of the colonial government structure. Largely uneducated, they were generally responsible and dedicated people. They had served the system of government well at local level. More recently, some had taken their place in district and provincial Councils and in the legislature. Their ability to govern at national level was, however, limited. I read a delightful entry in the *Hansard* for the Nyasaland legislative council in which one of the Bantu representatives suggested that Nyasaland should secede from the Federation, as weather conditions had deteriorated since the meteorological department had come under federal control.

Outside the existing government systems was the nationalist movement, largely organized through the African National Congress. This movement had no real say in either the colonial government system or the developing federal structure. Its membership was largely made up of the young intelligentsia who, while not accepted into the European community, had been welcomed and indoctrinated in anti-Western socialism and communism through scholarships provided by the Indian and Russian governments.

I had yet to find one of these nationalists who had any good to say about the tribal system of local government. The nationalists regarded most of the chiefs as the tools of British colonialism. (In all honesty, it must be admitted that the chiefs had been the channel through which British rule had been maintained.) The chiefs on their part, while generally for independence and, owing to the one-sided publicity, almost universally against federation, were not all supporters of the nationalists. I once heard a loyal and extremely intelligent chief describe them as *Wa Chabe Ndithu* – the worthless ones.

It was not surprising that educated Bantus might have wished to discard as unworthy and primitive the background and some institutions of their people. But the tribal society, however primitive it might have been, was the only wholly traditional Bantu institution. A system of rule by chiefs had existed for centuries, had developed naturally and suited what was still a primitive tribal society in the same way that the developed countries' systems had evolved to meet requirements in the more highly developed industrial societies. The dangers of destroying a tribal organization without anything to take its place were very real.

Most of the younger political intelligentsia were active in the African National Congress and supported communist ideals rather than having concern for the welfare of their fellow Africans. I met many of these people and became convinced that, although intelligent, there were amongst them unscrupulous men who were waiting impatiently to exploit their country's economies and people. These men took every advantage of the difficult racial position and were prepared to use racial issues as a means by which they hoped to get a universal franchise and be brought to power by the numerical superiority of the black African vote. They had little or no respect for what British rule had done to improve the lot of the Bantu masses and to provide the facilities which had enabled them, through education, to reach positions of influence.

Because of the lack of education and experience of the chiefs, and the racism, self-interest and political leanings of most of the nationalists, there were pitifully few African leaders at national level with both ability and integrity, certainly not nearly enough to fill the necessary executive functions of government. Many Bantu nationalists were corrupt careerists, and, for all my affection for their race, these were men to be feared. Unfortunately, there were men in this group who had considerable influence amongst the chiefs and tribal Africans.

We must accept a great deal of the responsibility for the nihilistic attitude adopted by many of the nationalists. A sense of inferiority had resulted from the Bantu's failure to develop an advanced civilization or culture. They tended to blame this on the tribal system. They had considerable admiration for, and wish to emulate, Western technical and economic advancement. However, they were full of an upside-down form of racial hatred, because by education and association the Europeans had made them unfit for a simple tribal existence amongst their own people but did not accept them as equals in a European society. This sense of not belonging, with the inevitable feeling of resentment, was a tragic aspect of educational advancement which was creating grave problems throughout Africa. Most of the nationalists I met were men without tradition or responsibility to any society and were ruled by envy of the Europeans and contempt for their own people. What was most worrying was their propaganda directed toward fostering hatred of the Europeans in Africa.

We should not forget the use by the Nazis of personalized daemons to build up hatred and place responsibility for the misfortunes of the German people on the Jews. I had attended some Nuremburg trials and become well acquainted with what had happened in Germany. It was symptomatic of Naziism, with its control of public opinion by propaganda, that one must appeal to feelings but never to reason. Truth, if against the regime, must be suppressed, and people made to believe what they were told. Hatred was the most effective force known against reason. In a totalitarian system reason must be destroyed at all cost, or the people might realize the true cause of their misfortunes and the failure of their own leaders.

The development of inter-racial feeling in Africa into inter-racial hatred could result in terrorism, with no mercy shown against hated racial groups.

It was to take place in Kenya, the Belgian Congo, Ruwanda, the Sudan and on an isolated basis in Zimbabwe. With inter-tribal rivalries, this was likely also to be progressively extended to the Bantus themselves. How true this became under the Idi Amin regime in Uganda, and in Angola, Mozambique, Liberia etc.

* * *

As part of our programme to advance Africans into management positions, we recruited a number of university and high school graduates. Amongst these were several active ANC supporters.

Although I did not know the full extent of the nationalists' political activity within the department, we had an indication that some of our staff were using our communications network for the transmission of nationalist/anti-federation information and propaganda. They were

The first Bantu woman in the Nyasaland Civil Service.

smart enough to use the teleprinter facilities, which offered some secrecy.

Despite the tense political situation, we tried to give our nationalist employees every opportunity to settle in, learn their jobs and advance through promotion.

Incidentally, at about this time, we recruited as a clerk the first black woman to join the Nyasaland civil service. She proved to be loyal and hard-working.

My contacts amongst the African nationalists were with the younger left-wing extremists, and I did not meet Dr Hastings Banda, who graduated from a local mission school, attended college in the USA and obtained his MD at Edinburgh University in the UK. He became a medical practitioner in the London area, where he practised for many years. Dr Banda, with the advantage of both American and British university education, had become a prominent and successful professional with a background which contrasted greatly from that of the left wing extremists.

Dr Banda differed from most of the nationalists in having been accepted as a valued member of a European society. He probably realized, from his own background and mission education in Nyasaland, the good that past British government had contributed to the advancement of his country and its people. He was also in his fifties and a person of considerable experience and discretion.

Dr Banda had almost messianic significance to his own people and had gained the respect of many British politicians, if not those in the Federation. (Lord Malvern had contrasted Dr Banda's bedside manner when talking to the British public with his inflammatory, anti-federation, speeches to his followers. These may have been political rhetoric influenced by the strong feelings against federation.)

These brief comments give some part of the picture I formed of the Bantu race: the simple villagers, domestic staff and manual workers, likeable with a great sense of humour and, on the whole honest, although not overly hard-working; the civil servants, professionals and more experienced leaders, in most cases good, intelligent, reliable and dedicated people. Unfortunately, many of the younger intelligentsia seemed to be self-seeking and lacking in responsibility to society, with little appreciation of the problems of the community, or wish to further the lot of their fellow Africans.

However desirable the aim of a universal franchise might be, I believed that it was in the interest of all concerned to proceed slowly and carefully. In the meantime, every effort should be made to encourage the development, through education and experience, of dedicated African leaders who were fitted to undertake a responsible part in the enlightened government of all races in Africa. These were substantially the aims of the Federation of the Rhodesias and Nyasaland.

B. The Arabs and Asians

An astonishing and perhaps significant factor in Central Africa, bearing in mind that the Arabs were, as far as we know, the first expatriates to have penetrated the interior of the continent in historical times, was the absence of any pure-bred, or half-caste, Arab people in Nyasaland. This has probably been because the Arabs located their settlements and families in the coastal areas, and journeys to the interior were only undertaken by the male explorers and slave traders. The Arabs had little colour consciousness and interbred freely with the Bantus, but because of their small numbers the children were absorbed in the various tribes. The only racial traces of Arab penetration were seen in the features and slightly lighter colour of some Africans in the lake shore area, where the slave trade was mainly centred.

The Arabs had left their mark in the predominance of the Islamic religion in many areas and the use of Arab words in many of the languages. It seems probable that the families operating the ivory-carving centre at Kota Kota were descended from Arab craftsmen who settled there centuries ago.

*   *   *

There were nearly twice as many Indians in Nyasaland as there were Europeans, and, with their very high birth rate, the Indian population was likely to grow far more rapidly than the European population. The Federation had, as yet, no Indian problem to the extent of that existing in East Africa.

While most of the Indian immigrants to Central Africa had been of low caste, they had tended to keep themselves apart from the Bantus and had either brought their families with them or sent for them later. There had, therefore, been little intermarriage. In the main, the Indians had been involved in trading activities, in which they showed considerable acumen. As a result, some had built up large fortunes, largely at the expense of the Bantu population.

Indian storekeepers were to be found at the main centres and in most villages. Sometimes they, and their large families, lived under almost indescribable conditions of discomfort and filth. Without competition, they overcharged and sold poor quality items and the commercial practices followed were often questionable.

The Indian traders also took every opportunity to trade on human weakness. If they had an efficient Bantu employee, it was not unusual to encourage that employee to get into debt. This debt was accompanied by such rates of interest that the employee could never free himself; thus, a new slave or caste system developed. One would see these employees working late into the night for Indians, a thing they would seldom do for a European employer. This re-introduction of slavery had been imported from India where, to the discredit of the Indian government, it was widespread.

In 1987, the Indian Government proposed to take legislative action to end the bonded labour/slavery system existing in India. Published data indicated there were between two and three million bonded labourers in India, many of them children.

From more recent press reports on the evils of child labour, the system was still common. It seems hypocritical that a government that had taken a hard line on apartheid and called for world action should permit a system involving much greater evils to persist in its own country.

It was not only the Indian trading methods which could be criticized, but also many of the things they were trading in. I had ample evidence of this. Every week, under our postal regulations, we confiscated large quantities of fake medicines, aphrodisiacs and charms. The last were claimed to make the wearer wealthy or give him power over women. These items were produced in India and widely advertised amongst the Bantus. The prices were high, much more than the gullible African could afford. Aside from the moral and ethical considerations, many were a danger to health. Some advertising leaflets were most amusing, although bawdy in the extreme,

A few better educated and higher caste Indians had also settled in Central Africa. This was the only Indian group which had any appreciable contact with the Europeans. They usually followed law, medicine or business activities as professions. Some were involved in political activities and perhaps understandably, given their Indian experience, were strong critics of the British colonial system. A number took part in the distribution of anti-colonial propaganda sent out from the Indian government's main centre in Nairobi.

C. The Europeans

The Europeans were the smallest group but perhaps, for the immediate future, could offer most to the development of Central Africa through maintenance of a viable economy and the improvement of the standard of living and way of life of the population as a whole.

The Europeans in most of Central and East Africa had acquired a reputation for peculiarity. This was often, but I think incorrectly, blamed on either the climate or the altitude.

In view of the dangers and discomforts, the early settlers must have had more than average courage and been unconventional in their outlook. In the case of the missionaries, there was also devotion to their faith and what they could do for the Bantu. Perhaps also the early government servants were in a special class driven by their traditional patriotism and the desire to spread the British way of life.

The living conditions – involving long periods of isolation without contact with other Europeans, the primitive facilities, the climate, the recurring bouts of fever and the local frustrations – must all have had a bearing on the evolution of individuals who had every excuse and justification for being different from the average European. Such was the diversity of human nature, and their experience in the country, that these old-timers seldom became typified and usually had considerable individuality. I was fortunate to be in time to know some old-timers. However, with improved social services, better living standards and more adequate transport and communication facilities, they had become a dying breed.

The old-timers I knew, and some became close friends, ranged from aesthetic but delightfully individualistic old gentlemen to old rascals who, even when over eighty, had an eye for a pretty girl and liked their glass of brandy or whisky before breakfast. On the female side, they consisted mainly of rather faded and dried-out old ladies. Here again there were exceptions, and I well remember a painted old lady of eighty from whom no man was safe from molestation. She once gave me a terrifying time in a taxi I was sharing with her, as she seemed to have more arms and hands than Vishnu.

With the development of more normal conditions, and improvements in hygiene and tropical medicine, life in Central Africa had become much more comparable with life in Europe, and more normal people were attracted to employment there. However, the effects of the environment were still present; living in Africa was to many an adventure, and the new generation still showed more individuality and personal idiosyncrasy than the average European.

Let us look at some modern counterparts of the "old-timers".

*   *   *

Sir Roy Welensky, as prime minister, was probably the most powerful person in the Central African Federation. He was also a man who looked the part. Born in 1907, he was of Polish/Jewish extraction. His parents were amongst the first trekkers into Southern Rhodesia. He came up the hard way, taking any job available, before joining the Rhodesian railways, where he became an engine driver. He graduated into politics through union activities, another tough school. As a politician, he became the most forceful, and probably most influential, unofficial member of Northern Rhodesia's legislative council. When the Federation was proposed, and after discussions with the Colonial Office, he decided to give it support and became the elected federal member of parliament for Broken Hill. He joined the federal cabinet

Sir Roy Welensky, Federal prime minister, and the author.

as minister of communications, later becoming deputy prime minister, and, on the retirement of Lord Malvern, in 1957, prime minister.

As the federal minister to whom I reported, I got to know him well. Although he did not drink or smoke, and kept to a strict diet, he was a massive individual whose aesthetic tastes were in direct contrast with his appearance. He gave an impression of great force of character, his most dominant feature being his piercing eyes below very heavy eyebrows. Probably owing to having to fight his way to the top, he had considerable sympathy with the underdog. He was slow-spoken but extremely quick-thinking and had a ready and comprehensive understanding of most problems, including technical ones. However, he was not a technocrat but chose his advisers wisely and made good use of their abilities. He was a person who did not suffer fools gladly, and he expected similar standards of integrity to his own from those who worked with him or with whom he had to deal.

Sir Roy's forthrightness, honesty and straightforward approach probably caused some of the difficulties which arose in his relationships with some African Nationalist leaders. He was accused of being pro-African by the European press in Southern Rhodesia: "We are being handed over to Welensky and his black friends" and being anti by the American press: "Welensky has small love for the Africans." This was probably a fair indication of his impartiality and his wish to do the best he could for all races in the Federation.

As an ex-heavyweight boxing champion of the Rhodesias, he was a keen follower of sports; he was also a lover of classical music, and he had a great concern for the environment, with a special interest in forestry.

Sir Roy always treated me as a friend and even after he became prime minister, expected to see me whenever he visited Nyasaland. Owing to a foul-up in secretariat, I failed on one occasion to meet him and I learned after his visit that he was annoyed. I wrote explaining the circumstances, and he replied, "I expect the reason you were told I had nothing to discuss with you was because I was not visiting any post offices but this still did not alter the fact that I should have liked to have seen you in your capacity as a friend of mine." When I decided to leave the Federation, he wrote saying how sorry he was to learn that I was leaving and hoped that I would continue to take an interest in it and perhaps return and settle there some day. When I last met him, he still regarded himself as an engine driver on unpaid leave from the railways. Following the breakup of the Federation, Sir Roy retired and settled in a small village in England a few miles from where I was born.

*   *   *

The governors under whom I served and whom I got to know were men of contrasting temperaments and styles, but extremely able people whom everyone respected. I also had three friends in the service who later became governors or high commissioners.

The original functions of the governor, in a colonial territory, were

HE the Governor at a mountain top radio station.

to act as Her Majesty's representative in all ceremonial matters and, as the head of the executive branch, to take a very active part in the government of the territory.

The governor's position was similar in some ways to that of the president of the USA, although on a much smaller scale. The governor would regularly chair executive council meetings. There were no cabinet ministers as such and heads of departments would report directly to the governor or executive council on major departmental policy issues. Routine matters would normally be dealt with through the chief secretary, or the appropriate department of the secretariat.

With the extension of the powers of the legislative assemblies, the position was changing rapidly, and the functions of Their Excellencies were being changed to the rather more mundane duties of looking after British interests, including those of British subjects, and dealing with aid and assistance grants and with the normal consular functions.

The average colonial governor was a person of ability, experience and integrity. He was usually appointed to governorship only for his last tour of service. This meant that he usually had some thirty years working experience in a colonial territory before his appointment, often starting as an assistant or district commissioner and ending as a provincial commissioner, or in another senior appointment. All the governors I knew were capable conscientious men with an almost unrivalled knowledge of their territory.

Governors came, however, in all shapes and sizes. They ranged from complete autocrats, who were sticklers for protocol and not very approachable, to very down-to-earth people who travelled without escort driving themselves in a Land Rover, were completely relaxed under all conditions and took care to put you at ease. In the case of the governors who stood on their dignity, I recall the canard about a rather snooty member of the legislative council that he only talked to the governor, who only talked to God. What however mattered was that the governors were all efficient and dedicated administrators.

Some governors had a sense of humour, others not. There was a story of one of the governors in East Africa who invited two Indian brothers, who had cornered trading activities in most parts of the country, to a cocktail party. Only one brother, who had a poor knowledge of English idiom, arrived at the party and said, "You must excuse my brother, but he is a very busy man as he has a finger in every tart in the country." His Excellency was a little taken aback but quickly countered, "He must be a very busy man indeed."

Socially, governors ranged from the extremely formal to those who were the life and soul of the party. One of my friends would torment us with his bagpipes, another was one of the best honky-tonk pianists I have ever heard. While dedicated to their work, they supported and did their utmost for the staff who had worked for them.

On my final journey home from Nyasaland, we travelled on an Italian liner which anchored offshore at Aden. The captain was surprised to see the governor's barge approaching and coming alongside. The governor was greeted with all due ceremony but he had only come to welcome my wife and me and take us on a tour of his colony.

Leaving aside their personal attributes, the governors I knew were people with initiative well-fitted to deal with exceptional conditions. This was certainly as well as far as Nyasaland was concerned, as the problems of the successive governors were considerable. Even in the 1880s Sir Harry Johnston was faced with the threat of Portuguese seizure of the territory, the problems of establishing a rule of law and order over the various tribes, of restricting the activities of the slave traders, of controlling and protecting the missions and introducing at least elementary social services. More recently the problems had covered such matters as population pressures, land settlement, introduction and extension of social services and communications, the building-up and extension of local and central government leading to federation and the subversive activities of the Russians, Indians and African nationalists.

*   *   *

My friend the Catholic Bishop was a character, a Yorkshire man with all the toughness and obstinacy of his native county tempered by a warmth and understanding of human nature unusual at such a senior level in his calling, where preferment based on political considerations seemed so often to replace human values. What was even more surprising was his capacity for achieving material results almost as outstanding as the spiritual effects of his ministry, and these were very impressive indeed. If he wanted a new school built, then the whole mission, including the students, was called on to help. If unwary callers arrived when he had work to do, they were also pressed into service. If you were wise you enquired in advance, from one of the fathers, what projects His Lordship had in hand before you paid the visit; otherwise you might find yourself helping to clean out septic tanks or mix cement.

The bishop was a master of improvisation and of doing things on a shoestring. If bricks and tiles were not available, or too costly, he would burn his own. If timber was required, he would buy a stand, cut it himself and set up his own sawmill, borrowing equipment he could not afford to buy. He had an outstanding knowledge of practical matters and of many engineering subjects. What he did not know he was not afraid to ask.

My friendship with the bishop started when we located our first training school at his mission. Later we had to enlarge the school and move it elsewhere, but he continued to use what technical knowledge I could provide whenever he needed it, and he was always a welcome guest at our home.

Emulating the pioneering spirits of the early missionaries, he laboured under the African sun for long hours each day supervising the work of the mission. He drove himself to the limit and had little patience with the indolent, to whom he gave an extremely hard time. To the white fathers, he was their spiritual leader and their driving force, and they loved and respected him. One of his theories (which he also tried to impress on me), based on his own dedication and the need he felt for continuity and understanding, was that no European should be recruited for service in Central Africa who was not prepared to sign a contract for a minimum of ten years service. His own fathers came out for life and never returned to their home countries.

While the bishop loved the Bantu, he nevertheless hated their short-comings, and he could sometimes be almost ruthless with them. He abhorred laziness and dishonesty. The students from his schools were much sought after, and in my experience their general standards of diligence and honesty exceeded those attained by the students from other missions.

Not only was the bishop's force of character and Christian dedication changing the countryside, as he constructed and developed his mission stations, but he also was achieving more in changing the minds and beliefs of the Bantu to Christian principles, the development of a sense of responsibility to one's fellow men and the community, and the acceptance of the need for honest work to achieve results than any other man in Nyasaland. In all his work there was a sense of urgency, and in talking to him you noted his sense of frustration and humility that so little had been achieved when so much needed to be done.

In spite of the dedicated work of my friend the bishop I worried about what was being done in Africa in the name of Christ by avowed Christians who were more interested in politics than Christian principles.

A pathetic contrast to the bishop was one of the Protestant missionaries. My immediate impression on meeting this man was of an apparent doubt about the purpose of his mission and a sense of apology for being in Africa at all. He had none of the driving force necessary to contend with an Africa which was still primeval, nor had he any conviction about the benefits the European had brought, and could still bring, toward solving the problems of Africa. He also appeared to be more than a little confused between the principles of Christianity and Marxism. This, not surprisingly, had led him to left-wing sympathies and an association with members of the nationalist movement. He seemed to have more interest in pamphlets than in progress, and in politics rather than Christian principles.

When Lord Fisher, the Archbishop of Canterbury, visited Nyasaland, we met at a party given by the governor. As my aunt was married to the brother of Lady Fisher, we exchanged family reminiscences. Our missionary friend was present and ever afterwards thought, wrongly, that I had influence with the church hierarchy. As a result, he always greeted me as a close friend and flooded me with his many publications and pamphlets, which he hoped I would distribute amongst our staff. These I religiously burnt, as a Christian service, before they could get into the wrong hands. Some more extreme ones, criticizing the British position in Africa, I sent to Police Special Branch for light reading but without saying from where they came.

Our missionary always had a tolerant and friendly approach to the mission's students and had the highest possible opinion of their abilities and character (even though they proved later to be utter rascals).

In visiting the mission school I always had the feeling that greater discipline was needed. In fairness, I must say that the students achieved reasonable educational levels but lacked the character and responsibility of those from the Catholic missions.

There appeared to be a lack of attention to the material needs of this mission, and the main headquarters gave an impression of decay. The missionary complained about the failure of the public to adequately support the mission and provide funds, instead of following the lead of the bishop and doing something himself to correct the material deficiencies.

To me, it was one of the tragedies of Central Africa that Protestant giants of the stature of Livingstone and Laws, who had done so much to open the territory and end slavery, should have to number amongst their persuasion someone who confused politics and Marxism with Christian teachings and was unable to meet the challenge and responsibilities of leadership based on centuries of Christian tradition.

*   *   *

As the head of a public service which suffered some interference and considerable pressure from the provincial and district administrations, which were rightly concerned with local interests, I might well have become critical of the provincial and district commissioners. I can, however, honestly say that I had only respect and admiration for these colonial servants who so ably filled their responsibilities to both their home government and the tribes for which they were responsible. The district commissioners, in particular, were living proof that conscientious and dedicated men could sometimes serve two masters.

All the district commissioners with whom I worked had an interest in the welfare and an affection for their "people" while also remaining completely loyal to the colonial service. Had British colonial government been less enlightened and concerned about the Bantu interests, the position of the district commissioner would have been much more difficult, if not impossible.

It was essential to the district commissioner's position that he should be beyond reproach in his personal integrity and behaviour. His duties were directly related to the welfare of the tribes in his district, and he was constantly working in their presence. In addition, his staff, except perhaps his assistant, were African. He literally lived and worked with his "people", and the slightest slip or indiscretion could be damaging to his prestige.

Something more than a punctilious figurehead was required. The district commissioner had to know the history, customs and traditions of his tribes and be aware of the characters, idiosyncrasies, feuds and sometimes sheer rascality of the chiefs and headmen. To achieve this he had to be a first-class linguist in perhaps several tribal languages. A knowledge of law was essential to the cases he had to try. He had also to be informed on economic issues, social matters, agriculture, soil preservation and any technical matters affecting the development of facilities important to the advancement of the standard of living and provision of social and other services.

At most stations the life of the district commissioner was an extremely simple and lonely one, often lacking even basic amenities. If he was lucky, he might have piped water and in a few cases water-borne sanitation. He seldom had electricity. Often, the only shop in the district was an Indian store catering for African villagers. The nearest club or centre where he and his wife could meet their fellow Europeans might be a hundred miles away over dirt roads which were often impassable during the rainy season. In any case, the district commissioner could seldom afford to leave his district for any considerable period.

You could well ask what type of men were attracted to such a job. The district commissioners could not be typified and were almost as varied in character as the districts in which they served. It is interesting to consider an individual case.

As soon as you got to know this district commissioner, you wondered what earthly reason there could be for him to be working in such a position. He had a good degree, as also had his wife, and their interests in literature, music and the theatre were, to say the least, seriously restricted in the small African village in which they lived. He came from a good family and was well connected, so other more gainful employment opportunities must have been available to him. Instead, he had chosen to bury himself in the wilds of Africa where after nearly twenty years' service his salary and his wife's small private income just enabled them to live modestly after they had met the costs of educating their two children overseas. There were, of course, no adequate educational facilities in their village, and after receiving their early education at home, from their mother, the children were sent away at a much earlier age than would have applied elsewhere.

Although debilitated, through years of tropical living and malaria, it was normal for this DC to spend one week in every month on ulendo with the tribes, sleeping in a tent, living out of tins and listening to, and adjudicating on, all the tribal problems that had arisen. During this time his wife stayed alone at home, with each worrying about the other, particularly at times of disturbance.

What compensating factors were there? First, I think, the knowledge that the job was important – a satisfying thought to any conscientious individual. Second, the interest and fascination of Africa experienced by all who have lived there.

Most of the DCs had, over a period, developed interests which could only be followed in Africa. Many had become authorities on such diverse subjects as native languages, customs, anthropology, and the flora and fauna. Africa offered a unique field for research, and once its claws were in you it was difficult to escape. Perhaps for these reasons the DCs, despite all their problems and discomforts, were happy people.

*   *   *

One of my good friends in secretariat was the financial secretary, who was appointed governor of another colony just before I left Central Africa. He was one of the best informed men in the country. Despite his extensive responsibilities, he always had time for anyone who

wanted to see or talk to him. It was only after we moved into the
adjoining house that I discovered that he left for his office at 4:30 each
morning and did his most effective work before anyone else arrived.

He must have had one of the capacities of genius – of managing with
very little sleep – as periodically we would be wakened very late at
night by the sound of his bagpipes, to which he was painfully addicted. This uncivilized sound, at an uncivilized hour in an uncivilized
country, was almost more than we could bear. His barbarian tendencies were restricted to this one vice, and he was otherwise a charming
and cultured individual, with a great sense of humour, and free of any
conceit about his ability or position. A most able administrator, he was
always ready to help and advise his juniors with a wisdom which
appeared unconsidered but was almost invariably the best advice
which could be given.

*   *   *

At the end of the second world war, and before the World Bank was
in a position to finance the development of the third world, the British
government had realized the need for a special effort to develop its
colonies, and the Colonial Development Corporation was set up. In
concept, this was an excellent idea, but in practice the corporation
proved initially to be a disaster, at least as far as Africa was concerned.

I believe the reasons for this were that many of the staff recruited
had little or no expertise in the areas in which they were operating,
and the local environmental and climatic problems had been almost
completely overlooked. There had also been little appreciation of
economic factors and the need for cost control.

Many of the staff recruited by the CDC were ex-army officers with
no business or agricultural background and with a wartime "spend all
you like" attitude. Stories were legion of requisitions for grand pianos,
billiard tables etc. to be sent to isolated locations in the bush; electric
appliances arrived where there was no electricity. Not surprisingly
results fell far short of expectations, and animals and poultry died of

queer African diseases. One lovely story was of a turkey raising project, which turned out to be a real turkey, as the birds flown at high cost from the USA were all males.

Finally, Lord Reith was appointed to sort the thing out. When visiting the Gambia egg project, he had an accountant friend of mine with him. Having done his research and gone through the project's accounts, my friend said he hoped Lord Reith had enjoyed his breakfast, as his morning egg had cost the British taxpayer more than one hundred pounds sterling.

We had several CDC projects in Nyasaland, and did our utmost in trying to provide adequate communications for their operations. During a *ulendo* trip I visited one of these projects and was invited to lunch by one of the senior staff. On our arrival at his home, he introduced, as his aunt, a very young and attractive woman. As he was a man in his fifties this appeared a little surprising, but he continued to address her as "Auntie" throughout the meal. We noticed that she became rather flushed but not more so than her nephew, who was literally and metaphorically in great spirits. However, the lady could finally take it no longer. She picked up her dessert, threw it at her "nephew" and, after shouting, "Not so much of the bloody aunt!" swept out of the room. Our friend, who seemed not at all taken aback, wiped the tropical fruit salad from his face and as a final surprise said, "You know, that lady is not really my aunt but my cousin." Some strange relationships existed in Africa, and, to this day, I do not know whether she was his cousin or not.

In fairness, the CDC did get its house in order, and at the time I left Nyasaland the few projects then operating were models of efficiency run by experts in forestry and agriculture.

* * *

Although a large part of the country was given up to African trust lands, European estates, of all sizes, existed throughout the protectorate. These, in the main, produced tea, tobacco, coffee and tung nuts.

A few settlers raised cattle. Estate sizes ranged from the very large
J. J. Lyons tea estate on the slopes of Mlanje mountain, extending over
many square miles, to those of a few hundred acres. The estate owners
were all hard-working, and, with their stake in the country, they were
an active political group.

Their leading spokesman owned a large tea estate in the Cholo area.
Handsome and in his mid-fifties he was typical of many big business
men to be found in any developed country. His estate and factory were
efficiently managed and a model for the country. Presumably they
were also highly profitable. He was also an enlightened employer,
with a personal interest in the housing and welfare of his Bantu
employees. He was thought to be a person of considerable wealth, but
he and his family lived in a modest style and were in no way ostentatious.

Having built up a successful estate and factory, he decided to seek
public office and entered politics through nomination from the local
planters' association. As a result of his ability and his extensive knowledge of one of the protectorate's most important agro-industries, he
achieved success in politics both in Nyasaland and at federal level. His
interests were, first and foremost, the interests of his country of
adoption, in which he had a considerable personal stake. He was
well-respected by the Europeans and by the Africans who worked for
him, but for the Bantu this was a local popularity, and, unlike the
African nationalists, he had little access to the population as a whole
or the appeal of the nationalists' Marxist propaganda and specious
promises. It was to be expected that this man's invaluable services to
the community would be rejected by a Bantu electorate.

*   *   *

In view of the subversive activities of many groups both inside and
outside the protectorate, mention should be made of the Police Special
Branch, which was known locally as MI4½. After the war, I had
worked closely with Intelligence in Germany and suspect that part of
their cover was to employ innocuous, and sometimes downright stupid,

people, to fool the enemy about the standard of British espionage. The key people were outstanding operatives with an extremely good cover. If I had not known otherwise, I would have assumed that the one with whom I was most closely associated was something in the city, bowler hat, furled umbrella and all.

An impression of ineptitude in security matters had also developed in Nyasaland – I am not sure whether accidental or deliberate – hence the common use of MI4½ when referring to Police Special Branch. The head of this branch was an ex-army major with toothbrush moustache and swagger stick. He gave the impression of being gullible, over-talkative and naive. This was probably a useful cover, as behind it all was an extremely intelligent, well-informed and hard-working individual. He may have even invented the MI4½ thing himself to lull the anti-establishment elements into a false sense of security.

When dealing with MI4½ I never ceased to be surprised at what he knew about our staff and their activities and of his contacts throughout the country. I believe that he served his country efficiently and well, and both the Colonial Office and the administration were very well-informed about subversive activities in the country.

* * *

At the time Sir Geoffrey Colby was appointed Governor of Nyasaland, the protectorate's telecommunications system mainly consisted of a telegraph land-line provided in 1896, which had formed part of Cecil Rhodes' concept of a line from the Cape to Cairo, supplemented by HF radio telegraph schedules to a few of the more important centres, and to Salisbury in Southern Rhodesia.

Telephone service was limited to small manual exchanges, with only nine hundred telephone subscribers in the whole country and with no international telephone service.

Adequate telecommunication facilities are vital to any organized society. Effective administration and social services depend on them. They are essential to public safety and security and provide the warning and information system at times of national disaster. They are cost-effective in saving transport and using available expertise to maximum efficiency. Agriculture, commerce, trade and professional services are heavily reliant on telecommunications for effective operation.

The importance of telecommunications in a developing economy is frequently underestimated. Often, because of the restricted transport facilities and limited expertise available, telecommunication facilities are even more vital in a developing country than elsewhere and should receive priority in any investment programme.

Seeing the pressing need for improved facilities, Sir Geoffrey recruited Colonel H. O. Ellis to take over control of Nyasaland's Post Office and initiate a telecommunications development programme. Harold Ellis was an outstanding engineer and executive and had been a colleague and friend for over fifteen years, during which we had served together in the UK and Germany.

Harold immediately set about designing a modern communications network and asked me to join him in this project. Although ambitious in concept the plan would only in part make good years of neglect. Also, because of limited funds and the competition for funding from other sectors, it needed to be super-cost-effective.

Until the telecommunications development programme came along, the postal and telegraph services provided most of the protectorate's communications. The European staff was small and these services had substantially been Africanized. They were nonetheless remarkably efficient (in fact, more efficient than those operating in many developed countries). The functions of the European postal and accounts officers were in maintaining the efficiency of the services, providing the department's link with the administration and the public, operating the department as a business, supervising the Bantu staff and, perhaps most importantly, training this staff. Almost without exception the European staff were outstanding people with a first-class knowledge of their jobs. When I took over the PMG's duties they did their utmost to help a mere engineer.

Shortly after my arrival in Nyasaland, I was given the task of carrying out Harold's programme. Fortunately, I had the support of very capable staff. These people were both able and dedicated and had a tremendous interest in their jobs. While united in their official aims, they were diverse in their private lives and included such characters as the diversity drinker, Pinocchio and the Laycock whom I describe elsewhere. Some came to us through the colonial service but most were recruited by Harold.

I should mention the rather special attributes necessary in our staff. Although a good theoretical knowledge was essential, a practical background and a capacity to improvise were also desirable. You had to be a good mentor to the African staff not only on the abstracts involved in theory and design but also the practicalities and complexities involved in the operation and maintenance of the equipment. Even in their personal lives, our staff had to know how to fix things, if they were to have a safe and comfortable existence.

In view of the high standards overall, it is unfair to mention actual individuals. But I find it difficult not to mention one person who perhaps best typified the special attributes needed. This outstanding member of our staff was my friend Ron. I first met Ron during the war when he was on the staff of the Post Office War Group. We later worked together and became good friends when we were with the Control Commission in Germany. Ron joined us as a senior engineer, some few months after I arrived in Nyasaland.

In addition to his executive ability Ron had an outstanding theoretical knowledge. He had worked on all types of telecommunications equipment and was the quintessential engineer who was never happier than when working with the staff with a screwdriver and wiring pliers in his hands and a wiring diagram under his arm.

The problem of so much which needed doing with only limited resources was always with me throughout the time I was in Nyasaland. To overcome this, we resorted to every possible means of reducing costs while maintaining service standards. Although our new main lines and telephone exchanges were state of the art, we purchased and modified war disposal equipment, at about a tenth of original cost, for

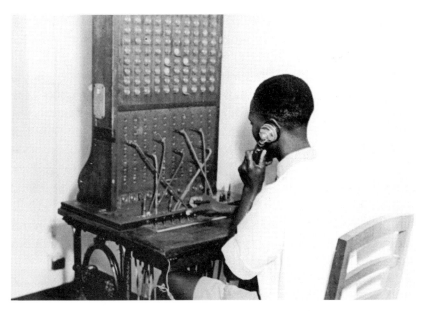

The old and new telephone exchanges in Zomba.

additional radio links. We used local timber for poles and fittings. We constructed many of our own buildings and built the mountain roads to our radio stations.

We used not only modern methods but also the knowledge of the local Africans. For example, in road construction large boulders were broken up by heating and pouring cold water on them, and water carried to building sites in open containers was prevented from slopping by using twigs to break up the wave motion.

Every project was examined in relation to possible cost savings. Ideas and suggestions were welcomed from all staff, European and Bantu. This staff participation and enthusiasm enabled us to achieve our objectives at unusually low cost. With a view to passing on our acquired knowledge and experience I wrote a thesis on some of our successful adaptations and methods during my first home leave.

Technical development of the telecommunications network was initially in the hands of the expatriate staff, but from the outset we used our Bantu staff to help in the work and as telegraphists, station attendants and telephone operators. With the recruitment of better-educated technical staff, and the output from our training school, local staff involvement was increasing in the more technical areas.

Our achievements in providing a modern telecommunications network for much of Nyasaland were substantially those of Harold, who conceived the programme, Ron who carried much of the burden, and the European and Bantu staff at all levels who carried out the work.

*   *   *

My old friend Doc was the person who had the greatest influence in educating me about the history of and early conditions in Central Africa. In this he helped me form my opinions, also paying me the compliment of not trying to override them from his position of greater knowledge and experience.

Despite Doc's influence on me, and my respect and admiration for him, I have left my comments about him until last. This was partly due to the difficulty of writing about a relationship that was both detached and personal but also to the complexity of our thoughts and discussions, which were wide-ranging to say the least. It was also partly due to his own reticence and because few of us knew much about his background and personal life outside the African experience.

We did know that Doc was a retired medical officer who had served in the protectorate from 1910 to the early thirties. After nearly two decades of retirement in the UK, he decided that he would return to Nyasaland and spend the rest of his life there. He bought some land on the side of Zomba mountain and built a magnificent house, doing the work himself with the help of African villagers. Here, he surrounded himself with domestic staff from the Yao tribe, mainly from families he had known during his earlier service in the protectorate. In effect, they became his family and he developed a great interest in their welfare.

In surveying possible locations for one of our radio stations we decided that a spur ridge from Zomba mountain was likely to be the most suitable location. The nearest point for access to this ridge was the road Doc had built to his house.

From local gossip, we had heard that Doc was a recluse who did not welcome visitors and wished to be left alone in his mountain fastness. Rumour also had it that he was a Moslem who had a greater community of interest with the Bantu than his fellow Europeans. Nonetheless, I decided that contact was desirable so that we could use his road for our initial survey. I set out to see him, taking with me the radio engineer who would be in charge of the project.

We were met by a tall, angular and very thin person in his late sixties or early seventies. After I had explained the purpose of our visit, we were asked in. As our discussions progressed, he invited us to have tea. It was immediately apparent that he was interested in our development plans, which would be of great benefit to the protectorate. He readily agreed to our use of his road.

Doc also volunteered to arrange for local villagers to extend one of

*Frankie and Nickie
on Doc's mountain road.*

the paths through the bush to our survey site and help in carrying the test equipment there. If our tests were satisfactory, he offered to undertake construction of a road to the station, providing we met the cost of labour and materials.

During our discussions, we uncovered some mutual interests, and our discussions were both long and animated. This was not the recluse we had been told to expect, and when we left, after an evening drink, I hoped that I could make a friend of this intellectual, informed and interesting man.

Over the succeeding years, my wife and I saw a great deal of Doc, at his house and our own. He attended our parties, despite his reputation for shunning European company, and was always the centre of discussion and interest. I believe he enjoyed the mixed company we usually provided. We also found that we were mutual friends of the bishop who was always a welcome guest at our house.

What did I learn about Doc? Of his family and background nothing whatsoever. Our discussions were however always rewarding and helped me formulate my opinions. Doc disagreed with me on many issues; in particular he had serious reserves about federation and its effects on the people and country he loved.

Doc was interested in Islam and Mohammed and was rumoured to have made the Haj to Mecca. He had also studied Buddhism and the writings of Confucius. His friendship with the bishop showed that he was not divorced from the teachings of Christianity. He also was friendly with the Anglican bishop. I think that his beliefs and ethics were based on a combination of religions leading into humanitarianism. Surprisingly, he did not seem to know the Kasidah, and I introduced this to him.

Doc was widely read in most of the published literature about the continent. This included not only history, natural history, anthropology, sociology and biography, but also included such far-fetched books as Rider Haggard's fantasies. Favourite authors whom he encouraged me to read were Margery Perham and Elspeth Huxley.

As a result of his reading, Doc had an almost encyclopedic knowledge of the continent as seen through other people's eyes. To this background, he had added his personal experience gained over thirty years in the colonial service. Even in this he had the advantage, over most of us, of being fluent in the three main tribal languages. He also appeared to have a good knowledge of Arabic.

Doc had developed a great affection for the Yao tribe and for the Bantu in general. Nonetheless, he fully appreciated their shortcomings, in particular the need to inculcate a greater sense of social and personal responsibility. In discussing the future of Bantu Africa, it was always doubly interesting if one could get into a joint session with both Doc and my friend the bishop.

Doc's relationship with the Bantu people, whatever their tribal background, was helped by his concern for their well-being and his ability to converse freely with them. They reciprocated with respect and even love for him. He had, I believe, a national identity amongst the Bantu and certainly amongst the Yao, while most Europeans regarded him as a rather eccentric recluse. I have noted elsewhere how our domestic staff always welcomed him as a father figure when he visited our home.

Doc loved to keep busy. After constructing our road to the radio station, he became so interested in road work that he undertook construction of another road along the side of Zomba mountain for the forestry department. This was a task which would have daunted many civil engineers, owing to the frequent gullies and streams. It was all done without any financial gain to Doc but purely to help development.

Another of Doc's interests, on which some stories in this book are based, was Bantu mythology, but he had yet to write anything about this, although he had a unique knowledge of the subject. He was working on what became the accepted dictionary of Chiyao based on notes he had collected during his thirty years of service as a medical officer.

Yet another of Doc's interests was needlework, and he produced the most beautiful and perfect embroidery. My friend the bishop made use of this for church vestments. One of the few places you could meet His Lordship without getting directly involved in one of his projects was Doc's house. You had, however, even to be careful there, or His Lordship would extract a promise of help of some kind or another.

Regrettably, I saw less of Doc as my responsibilities increased and I was tied to a desk in Zomba, but we still kept in touch when I could find time to visit him or during his visits to Zomba. These contacts became less frequent toward the end of my time in Nyasaland. He contracted shingles and spent a much greater part of his time at home, becoming largely the hermit he had earlier been reputed to be. About this time he decided to sell his house to the forestry department and move to the lake shore near Monkey Bay, about sixty miles from Zomba over dirt roads.

On my last *ulendo* I made a diversion to visit Doc and say goodbye. He was in considerable discomfort and very poor shape. To my even greater concern, I felt that he had lost much of the intellectual fire and superiority that had been present in our earlier conversations. However, I think he enjoyed talking of our association and our good mutual friends. He was probably too ill to reply to letters after I left the country.

One of the saddest things in life is that physical disability and loss of intellectual drive comes to most of us as we become older. Unfortunately, this affects even the most interesting and worthwhile people, with the loss to society of almost invaluable knowledge and wisdom. To preserve at least part of this I had frequently pressed Doc to write of his experiences and, in particular, what he knew of African mythology.

Chapter 8

Private Lives

We always called ourselves "The Working Class". However, people from all walks of life, and from all social and educational, levels were in the colonial service. There were very few whose primary interest was not their job.

The needs of the protectorate were so great and the resources available from the British government so limited that most branches of the service were understaffed, and however hard and long you worked there was always something waiting to be done. Most members of the service worked excessive hours and could not forget their jobs even when attending the frequent, interminable and usually boring cocktail parties at which one always met the same people drawn from the same levels of the service.

I believe that the reason these parties were so boring resulted from the reserve of the average Englishman and an inherent snobbishness which led people to restrict their invitation lists to those in similar or senior positions. This also encouraged people to talk mainly about their jobs. I always felt ashamed and annoyed when the wife of a senior friend and colleague referred, with pride, to a "top level" party they had attended or given. We found that when we invited people from all levels of the service, together with outsiders, the parties were much more enjoyable, though you might upset a few senior people who stood on their dignity. An addition of the bishop, Doc and a few commercial and estate people, together with more junior staff members, broadened the scope of conversation and resulted in the party being enjoyed by all.

If the colonial service officers were over-occupied, their wives had little to do, as they had more than sufficient domestic staff to perform the household chores. The wives' main recreation, other than to visit the club in the evening, was to take part in the ladies' tea parties.

It was not surprising that, as their husbands were preoccupied with their jobs, many wives frequently found consolation and amusement elsewhere. The chief source of temporarily unattached European men was the King's African Rifles, whose officers seemed to have as little to occupy their time as the colonial wives. We have an old English saying which refers to "the brutal and licentious soldiery". The KAR officers were not brutal, but they certainly provided solace to some bored and neglected wives. In a small community, nothing could be kept secret, and one of the main subjects of conversation at the women's tea parties was other women's affairs.

Besides gossip, we had our humour in the affairs of the heart. I shall not forget my consternation, at one of our parties, when a junior member of our staff, on being introduced to a senior official and his wife, said, "But this is not the Mrs. X I met you with in Germany." Fortunately, he had made a mistake, and the wife remembered the previous meeting. Sometimes there was also drama, as Frankie found when she was giving a tea party to introduce a new arrival, and the latter calmly said that she had come to the country to kill her husband, who had betrayed her. Her early pregnancy provided another solution.

*   *   *

Most things in Nyasaland ended by being discussed at the club, whether they related to the affairs or foibles of the individual or the future of the country. It was rumoured that both MI4½ and the African National Congress separately obtained their most up-to-date and reliable information from the waiters at the clubs.

The clubs of Nyasaland, and there was one at most centres of any size, were the focal point of European social activity and filled an essential function in the life of the community. The clubs' activities were designed, as far as possible, to meet the needs of their members but were limited by the size of their resources. At most centres, the club provided facilities for tennis, golf and the various field games. It was also, variously, the local pub, cinema, theatre, library, dance hall, church hall, parade ground, restaurant, barber's shop – in fact I can only think of one of the amenities of most cities which it did not openly provide.

Perhaps the most useful service of the clubs, despite the European membership, was in providing, on their playing fields and through the levelling influence of sport, a meeting place for people of all races. The clubs' sporting activities were multi-racial, and if the standards of play were not over-high the sportsmanship shown was first-class. The interest in any key match was considerable, and, when the game was between African and European teams, several thousand Bantu supporters would attend, some coming from quite distant villages. The crowd at these games was noisy and partisan but always good-tempered. Their greatest interest was in soccer, but rugby and cricket matches were also well attended and caused considerable excitement. The Africans invariably supported their own African team, but where the match was against the Indians, they always supported the Europeans.

The club playing fields were also used for ceremonial parades, such as that on the king's birthday. These were extremely colourful occasions and were attended by a large mixed audience of all races. The standard of drill and ceremonial set by the King's African Rifles compared favourably with that of a crack European regiment. The parades were one of the highlights of club activities, with His Excellency the governor and the KAR as the main performers in the pageantry. Also lined up self-consciously in the field would be the senior colonial officers in their white and gold musical comedy uniforms. I always felt that we looked rather like long-stemmed mushrooms under our topees and, as far as I personally was concerned, terrified of tripping over our swords. Although the ceremonies themselves were picturesque, the real colour was provided by the thousands of spectators dressed in a rainbow range of hues, under the tropical sun, adding a brilliant frame

The King's birthday parade.

Colonial Uniform.

for the parade ground. Supporting the pageantry and colour of the ceremony was the music of the combined police and KAR bands. Even today when I hear a military band my thoughts return to the Zomba parades.

The mention of the police band reminds me of another aspect of club activities, namely, the dances culminating with that on New Year's Eve. The police band always provided the music and managed to follow the melodies quite well. But they were a band trained to march time, and though you might start dancing a tango or waltz, it was inevitable, as they got into the swing of the music, that you would finish with a march. It was sometimes like trying to samba to Souza. You can imagine how confusing this was for even the best dancers. I was certainly not in that class.

The New Year's Eve Ball was always a command performance, and almost everyone attended. Normally, people were moderate in their drinking habits, but on New Year's Eve restraint disappeared, and amongst the headaches of the following morning would be at least one incident which was the subject of amused, or sometimes scandalized, comment. I was never sure whether to be proud or annoyed when one of our staff achieved notoriety.

One year one of our postal inspectors, a wee red-headed Scotsman disguised behind a Pinocchio nose, took possession of the stage and tried to demonstrate the Indian rope trick by climbing a bamboo held by two willing but inebriated assistants. The inevitable happened, and Pinocchio descended as a curse from Heaven upon the heads of his supporters below, swearing horribly in broad Aberdonian. His friends, having failed to revive him with another whisky, finally carried him away to the ambulance still wearing his false nose and muttering unintelligibly. Most people thought it was all part of a gag until he returned, an hour or so later, with his broken leg in plaster and a sailor's thirst.

Another year one of the local planters stole the show and achieved notoriety by borrowing his companion's lipstick and decorating the club's marble bust of Queen Victoria. When he had finished, she had red breasts and a clown's nose. On the dedication tablet, identifying the figure, another reveller had added in royal vernacular, "We are not amused." Although the planter undoubtedly added colour to a rather dull statue, the club committee was also not amused and requested the member concerned to apply his artistic talents elsewhere. Unfortunately, the lipstick must have contained a very fast-colour dye, as every known soap, detergent, dye remover and solvent failed to remove the desecration.

The matter became an issue of national concern and the subject of intense discussion at the bar, where it became known as "the titillation of Her Majesty's tits". As each attempt to clean up the statue failed, the suggestions became more and more outrageous. One foolish fellow suggested the use of urine and was rumoured to be a Marxist sympathizer who wanted to piddle on the royal family. Another expert was allowed to try to clean the bust using a toothbrush and toothpaste. Ever afterward he was ragged unmercifully, and it was suggested that he and his toothbrush were a menace to the opposite sex. An inebriated local MO arrived with a hammer and chisel and wanted to carry out a double mastectomy. However, despite all our best efforts, Her Majesty's bust continued to carry pink traces of colonial service up to the time I left Nyasaland.

The theatre section had considerable talent to draw on, including some ex-professionals, and its performances were much enjoyed. However, as is so often the case with amateur productions, the comedies and farces were the most successful and the serious plays were usually disappointing. This may have been a problem of interpretation, but it was also much easier to imagine old so-and-so dallying with someone else's wife, which he might be doing in real life, than to believe in him strangling his best friend.

Frequently, the real-life triangles added an extra spice to the dialogue, and an apparently innocent line would bring the house down, leaving the players shaken that their friends knew so much about their affairs.

Without television, and with only poor quality high frequency

The Theatre Club – our radio engineer Bill on the right.

broadcast reception possible, most people gravitated to the club during the evening. It was almost impossible to visit the bar without seeing a crowd of people gathered there. The bar provided the nineteenth hole for the golf course, the final analysis point for the tennis players and the buffet for the cinema and theatre goers. You could usually guess in advance the particular group likely to be frequenting the bar by the time of day, although sometimes a session would get going and at a late hour you would still find people in tennis shorts mixed in with a theatre crowd in evening dress.

The club bar was as democratic as an English pub and was frequented by all classes, types, persuasions and ages with conversations going on in most known accents of English. While its democratic acceptance of everyone was one of the club's good points, the gossip that took place at the bar, on almost every known subject under the sun, was sometimes unfortunate. It seemed to be a common human trait to want to impress others with one's own knowledge. This frequently led to embarrassment and concern to those of us having to deal with confidential matters. You could usually learn things at the bar long before they were announced officially. Possibly the main cause of the interest in other's affairs, whether of business or the heart, was the smallness of the European community.

One last picture of the bar I recall, which at the time I always viewed with very mixed feelings, was the sight of the painted and rather overdressed, or sometimes under-dressed, teenagers perched on stools drinking their gins and beers. They looked attractive and sophisticated, but it always seemed a pity that European youth in Africa developed so quickly in an artificial and unnatural way of life.

*   *   *

As the king's representative, the governor, in addition to his official duties and ceremonial appearances, had to entertain extensively. There was in effect a social register. To get on this one went to Government House and signed the governor's book. Colonial staff were expected to do this as a matter of course. You were also expected to repeat this signing after each social visit to Government House and after each absence overseas.

The parties given by the governor and his lady fell into the categories of formal cocktail parties, formal dinners and smaller, more intimate, parties for friends. For the formal parties some governors and their wives stood very much on ceremony; others were much more relaxed and easy-going.

Those given by Their Excellencies who stood on their dignity were usually stratified; also you seldom received a formal invitation to dinner unless you were a head of department or prominent in the community. These parties were often both a chore and a bore to those who were ordered to attend. Protocol sometimes became ridiculous. I remember circling Government House, before a cocktail party, with thirty or forty other cars, to arrive at the exact moment set by God (or the governor's lady). The hosts maintained a dignified and detached manner throughout. When the occasion showed any sign of developing into a real party, the hostess would call the ADC, who would then tell the senior lady present it was time to make a move. We would all queue up to express our thanks (God knows why) and leave again *en masse*.

Fortunately, most governors were excellent and relaxed hosts and, while maintaining the dignity proper to their office, put everyone at ease; and, though the party might be formal, a good time was had by all. Governors and their wives were generally very human people, and those we knew as friends were entertaining and knowledgeable hosts who could be the life and soul of their smaller and more intimate parties.

*   *   *

We lived very simply and modestly and had to follow a number of precautions. All our water had to be boiled and filtered, and we had to take our daily prophylaxis against malaria.

Food supplies were limited. There was some beef and mutton available at the local market, but you were never quite sure whether the animal had died from old age or disease or had been slaughtered. The meat, if you were brave enough to eat it, was usually tough and stringy. Chicken, at least, arrived at your house alive and, as far as you could tell, carried no mortal or communicable diseases. As far as meat was concerned, chicken became our staple diet. We also could get a few tinned meats such as Spam, corned beef and meat pies. Fortunately, our local fish was plentiful and the tilapia from Lake Nyasa a delicacy.

Vegetables and fruit were very mixed in quality unless you were friendly with one of the planters who was growing them. The alternative we followed was to grow what we could in our garden.

Local flour, tea and coffee were good. Rather impure sugar came from Portuguese East Africa. Everything else was imported from

Britain and the Commonwealth, usually tinned or bottled; but this did not guarantee receipt in satisfactory condition owing to the high temperatures in transit. The best grade of tinned Australian butter usually arrived smelling and tasting like ghee, and South African wines would not stand up to the 120° F temperatures on the trains through Portuguese East Africa.

The near addiction of Bantu domestic staff to tea and sugar was a problem we all had. I remember that in our first month we "used" over thirty pounds of sugar. This had to be cut back, under threat of death, but we always had to accept a measure of pinchy-pinchy.

Local facilities for the purchase of food were very limited and the cost of importation prohibitive in relation to the salaries we were paid. We had our local African Lakes Coy store (Mandala), a few Indian stores catering mainly for Bantu customers, and the local market. Without sufficient competition, prices at Mandala and the Indian stores were high and contrasted sharply with the ridiculously low prices at the African market, where two grapefruit could cost you one penny and a chicken (Mkuku) ten pence.

It took a strong stomach to go to the meat section of the market, and most purchases were made by the cooks who took a small "commission" to supplement their incomes. Those of us with private incomes imported delicacies from Fortnum and Mason and other British stores, but you still faced the problem of spoilage due to the lack of refrigeration from the port of Beira.

In an endeavour to reduce living costs and improve supplies, we set up a cooperative with the director of medical services as its chairman. When he wanted to be relieved of these duties I very foolishly allowed myself to be elected in his place. Despite having permanent employees, I then began to realize the problems of running a food store in Central Africa. Because of the transport problem, lead times were completely unpredictable, and you were frequently overstocked or out of stock. You could not afford to have too high an inventory, as refrigerated space and cash resources were limited. Supplies were often damaged or lost in transit. African staff had a habit of "borrowing" things they liked.

All in all, the Co Op was a great success in reducing our domestic costs and expanding our diets. We were pressed to extend our operations to other centres in the country but refused. Although we were prepared to give advice, we already had more to do than we could cope with.

* * *

As far as I know, there were no brothels in Nyasaland. There were, however, several enthusiastic amateurs. The nearest approach to professional operations was that of a local barber. He imported his "sister", a well-dressed but unattractive lady, as his assistant. While cutting your hair he would outline her beauty, talents and prowess, also telling you that she was short of money and would you like to take her to the local hotel? While all this was going on he would be holding a *sotto voce* conversation with his "sister", presumably equating your potential as her customer. This was too much for me, and, although he was a good barber, I transferred my custom to the Bantu barber at the club, who was more proficient in clipping African heads than cutting European hair and had rather low standards of hygiene. At least, he had no "sister" in his shop.

There were very few sexual liaisons between the races, partly due to the different cultures, life styles and educational standards. In the few cases where associations developed between European men and Bantu women, the man was usually ostracized. The term "going native" had real meaning and implications in the Central Africa of those days.

* * *

We had no air conditioning, but the climate, at Zomba's altitude, was generally pleasant except during the very humid rainy season.

Our garden, although rocky and completely informal, was a delight. We had many flowering shrubs and a prolific avocado pear tree. We

Our house, Zomba.

also developed a small vegetable garden where Dixon would build little roofs over the more tender plants, to protect them from the tropical sun, and where our dog stole the kohlrabi and onions. We were also well located, with nearby pine woods above us and the golf course below, so our walks were a joy for both ourselves and our canine friend Nickie. While our "estate" did not compare with the luxurious residences of the CDC, and those of most of the business men and planters, we were very happy and contented in our life there.

*   *   *

Most Europeans had at least one hobby with which to occupy their minds and leisure hours. The interests of many in anthropology, archaeology and the flora and fauna have been mentioned. Other recreational activities were quite diverse. Even in the more usual pursuits of drinking and illicit affairs, striking originality was some-times shown. The latter is not a subject I like to dwell on, and I had no first-hand experience. However, as an example of drinking idiosyn-crasies, a friend of mine evolved the theory that sticking to one type of drink was all wrong and the correct way to remain sober and avoid a hangover was never to take two drinks of the same kind in succes-sion. He called it diversity drinking, and his theory was that the stomach got confused between drinks and could never settle down to absorbing the alcohol. I never had the courage to try it myself, but I have seen him work his way down to, and through, all the liquors in a well-stocked bar without appearing any the worse for wear. Another individualist, having made the mistake of diluting his whisky with gin instead of water, liked it so much that he always asked for this mixture. The effects were more noticeable than with my friend the diversity drinker.

The astonishing hobby of one senior official's wife was inspecting African lavatories, which she felt, probably rightly, were a threat to the health of the community. As far as I know she never discovered the "three old ladies locked in a lavatory" so often serenaded in the club, but she found plenty else and frequently used to regale us with the horrid details at the dinner table. The director of medical services, who had a professional rather than an olfactory interest in the matter, avoided her company in the same way as she seemed to think he avoided the *chimbuzies*. As she was a lady of character, this stirred her to even greater efforts, and there was hardly a convenience, male or female, which was not regularly inspected by her. The surprising thing about the whole business was that, although the sanitary inspector and health department thought her crazy and were exhausted with trying to deal with her complaints, the Africans seemed to regard her activities as quite normal.

I have already described my friend Doc, his interests and the con-tribution he made to development through his road building activities. Nonetheless I should mention the part he played in our lives through his wisdom and knowledge of Africa . He undoubtedly made a great

contribution to the education of his friends about the history, problems, and possibly the future, of Africa and its people.

We had our share of "Houdini Handshakers", possibly related to a
desire to obtain preferment in a small and closed community. I believe
that their influence was extremely limited. The Bantu seemed well
informed about their activities, as I once heard my boys referring to
the lodge as *Mfiti niumba* (the witchcraft house).

We also had our quota of writers in Geraldine Elliot and Denys
Roberts, who were both, in their distinct and separate ways, extremely
entertaining people whose conversation was on as high a level as their
writing.

The hobby which helped me to preserve what I hope is sanity was
amateur radio. When we were boys, my brother and I got to know Mr
Kemp, who had been Marconi's chief collaborator in the early trans-
atlantic radio experiments. Mr Kemp had retired and was quite old,
but through him we met Eric Payne, the radio operator on Marconi's
yacht, the *Elettra*. Eric and my brother had many interests in common,
so we used to get together at our home and on the *Elettra*. We even
saw the great man himself, when he visited the radio room to talk to
Eric. This started both of us on a career in communications. It also led
us to adopt amateur radio as a hobby.

Amateur radio in the early days was technically a far more demanding hobby than it is today, as you had to build your equipment from
components. After the second world war the position became much
easier. It was possible to buy war surplus equipment and modify it to
work in the amateur frequency bands. Later, as the number of amateurs increased, it became profitable for manufacturers to produce
amateur equipment, mainly to meet the demand in the USA. By the
late 1950s the more money you had, the better the station you could
set up.

There were two approaches to operating an amateur station. The
highly competitive one, mainly developed in the USA, was to try to
work a maximum number of countries, zones or stations. The other
way was to make friends all over the world and extend your knowledge

of countries and people. My interest fell in the latter category, although I tried to accommodate the competitive group, who were always anxious to work a rare country.

Through my radio contacts, I got to know Prince Talal of Saudi Arabia, Tondup Namgyal Maharaj Kumar of Sikkim and Father Moran of Nepal. *The latter became a good friend many years later when I repeatedly visited his adopted country.* In addition, I made friends with hundreds of delightful people in all parts of the world. I was also able to keep in touch with the "person on the spot" for information and opinion on events in their countries. This type of contact had to be guarded due to political and security considerations. But, as an example, I had weekly contacts with a fellow amateur in the Kenya Highlands and learned more of the Mau Mau beastliness than I ever could have done through the press or through radio news broadcasts.

It was also extremely helpful to have an advance introduction to people in countries we planned to visit. The world becomes a smaller place to the radio amateur, and I only wish the hobby, as I knew it in the early days, could have been open to everyone.

* * *

One important individual who, through his companionship, contributed a great deal to the happiness of Frankie and me and who showed love, understanding and dignity throughout his all too short life, was Nicholas Dickenson D. O. G. Nickie came to us when he was about eight weeks old as a small, black, cuddly cocker spaniel puppy with a high-domed forehead and long ears. He was extremely well-bred, a grandson of "Lucky Star of Ware", one of the most famous show dogs of all time. He also had good connections locally, as his mother lived with the commissioner of police and his father was the best friend of the director of education.

Almost immediately after his arrival Nickie contracted distemper, and I very much doubted if he could survive. My great dog chum when I was ten years old had died from this terrible scourge despite the attention given by my parents and me. During Nickie's illness, Frankie gave her whole time, night and day, to nursing him, removing the mucus from his eyes and nose and cleaning up his tiny body. We also force-fed him with raw white of egg. After about ten days, during which he became an absolute skeleton, he started to improve, after which he never looked back until his final illness in Jamaica.

Right from the outset Nickie was a wanderer and a keen swimmer. When he was a small puppy, he dived into a fast-flowing stream crossing our golf course and disappeared into a culvert, to appear some seconds later, still swimming vigorously, lower down the stream where I was waiting. Frankie in the meantime was having hysterics at the entrance to the culvert.

Whenever he could sneak away, Nickie would go off on one of his journeys of exploration. He must have borne a charmed life in not being taken by a leopard. He would normally return home after a few hours, usually muddy and exhausted and smelling of anything from the surrounding pine woods to the African *chimbuzies*. Frankie would send out search parties of the domestic staff and sometimes telephone the office to say Nickie had gone again and could I help? We never discovered exactly where Nickie went, although he once turned up tired, weary and dirty at a house we had occupied some years earlier and a considerable distance from our home. On his returns Nickie had to suffer the ignominy of a thorough bath, to get rid of the mud and smell, but he suffered this without protest as one of the facts of life.

Nickie developed an almost unique character. Although Frankie nursed him during his illness, and fed him, he divided his attention equally between us. When I was down with malaria you could not get him out of the bedroom, He would lie there watching me, with only short excursions to relieve or feed himself and with no thought for his usual expeditions. If Frankie and I were in separate rooms he would visit each of us by turn, dividing his time scrupulously between us.

With Frankie's loving tuition, Nickie also acquired a considerable vocabulary and understanding of the human species. If you wanted to discipline him you only had to say, "You go home", meaning you were disowning him, and you had a very upset dog on your hands. He developed some very strange tastes, such as stealing raw vegetables, particularly onions and kohlrabi, and eating beeswax-covered electronic capacitors. The strangest of all was his liking for felt hats. Having taken a large piece out of the brim of my bush hat, he became addicted to these hats, and whenever a guest arrived wearing a felt hat Nickie would beg for it. He once got hold of the bishop's hat and improved its ventilation. Usually, he was very well-behaved and had an almost superior manner.

Nickie did have one trait that we had to tolerate rather than like, and that was his aptitude for producing the most abominable smells. Even Nickie himself could not stand them, and having produced a silent and deadly one he would move to the other side of the room. If you were wise you did likewise.

He had a great family sense; this is what I think hurt him most about the "You go home" business. He was determined that any problems between Frankie and me should be quickly resolved and there should be no side-stepping. This led sometimes to an amusing and embarrassing situation. If Frankie and I were dancing together this was fine, but if she was dancing closely with someone else he would give her a quick nip in the bottom, as if to say "quit fooling around". I never worked out why he didn't attack her partners.

We had to be careful about letting Nickie join our parties, particularly after he had managed to steal any onions or kohlrabi, as he then had the habit of circulating quietly amongst the guests, laying down a most excruciating gas attack. As he looked so noble and innocent, no one had the slightest suspicion that he was in any way to blame, and we found our guests looking at one another with surprise, suspicion, dismay, disgust and sometimes downright horror. I could never bring myself to reveal the true culprit, partly because farting was not a subject for discussion in polite colonial society and partly in consideration for Nickie, who could not stand the smells himself anyway.

Nickie had the habit, when he was tired, of coming to us both, yawning, and then settling in front of the bedroom door. New Year's

Eves were a purgatory to him, and he would lie around yawning and looking miserable until he could finally get us to bed.

Nickie met few other dogs in Nyasaland. His only near acquaintances were Dasher, a yapping and stupid dachshund, and Pip, a large, yellow-eyed, fighting mongrel who hated Nickie's breeding and all he stood for.

When we left Nyasaland, Nickie flew in advance to England, spending his time in the cockpit with the pilot. They nearly lost him in Nairobi when, released to do his business, he tried to take off on another of his missions of discovery. In England, he had to go into prison for six months rabies quarantine before he could join us in Jamaica.

It was only after we moved to Jamaica that Nickie met the opposite sex and reached the full pride of his dog-hood. Then he let himself go, and we were surrounded by dog families of all breeds and sizes but with the common heritage of black coats and long ears.

There was one shocking incident.

Our neighbour's six-year-old arrived at our door to say, "Nickie and Charlie stick on Princess." Frankie hurried out to find Nickie and his son Charlie making love to the different ends of a very long dachshund. Fortunately, Princess was a docile creature, and Charlie escaped the emasculation he probably deserved. Frankie tried to order her dogs to behave, but the trio remained locked in their amorous activities until our neighbour arrived with a hose-pipe and dampened their ardour. Although nearing old age, Nickie continued his philandering, Princess presented her owners with a litter of black dachshunds, and Charlie remained a sexual pervert.

Nickie had six happy years in Jamaica but after two painful operations we lost him from cancer. His son Charlie, the sexual maniac, moved with us to Washington and did something to replace the void in our hearts, but there could only ever be one Nickie.

Chapter 9

Government without Parties or Politicians

Perhaps because of the absence of political parties or any effective opposition, the various functions of government in Nyasaland operated efficiently and without major contention, through the early 1950s and until federation with Northern and Southern Rhodesia was proposed. To understand the later difficulties and disturbances fully, it is desirable to examine the conditions and form of government which existed in the protectorate before federation.

Government policy at national level was decided by executive and legislative councils. The executive council, or upper governmental body, consisted of the governor, chief secretary, financial secretary, attorney general, two other official members and two nominated Europeans as unofficial members.

The executive council was advised by the legislative council, or parliament, which also had the governor as chairman and consisted of nine official members and nine unofficial but nominated members, two of whom were African and one Asian. There were no elected representatives.

These councils were responsible for all legislative action at protectorate level. They also provided direction in the coordination of provincial and district policies.

Local government was in the hands of the chiefs and native authorities. A native authority might consist of a chief alone or a chief helped by advisers or headmen.

District councils had been created to democratize and coordinate local rule in the districts. There was also a provincial council of chiefs in each of the provinces. This gave a line of contact between the provincial commissioner and native authorities/chiefs.

The day to day contact with the chiefs, native authorities and district councils was at district commissioner level. Contact at district level was extremely good, partly because of the requirement that district commissioners must spend at least one week each month on *ulendo* in the villages.

Although the central government structure was not democratic in form, it was well informed on public opinion, had direct liaison with the traditional tribal authorities through the PCs and DCs and was generally accepted and trusted.

Parallel with the government administrative functions, the health and social services and technical departments operated for the benefit of the population. There was also a close association between the health and education departments and the missions in the operation of mission hospitals and schools.

The agriculture department concerned itself in improving native agriculture, the veterinary department in animal husbandry and the public works department with providing and maintaining roads, bridges and other infrastructure. The costs of administrative, social and technical services and infrastructure were subsidized by the British taxpayer. The post office was in a special category. While it provided postal and communication services as a government department it was also revenue-earning and self-supporting.

The national economy, but not government, had a considerable inflow of funds through remittances from migrant workers. There was virtually no industry in the country, and no mineral resources of any significance had been developed. Agriculture production for export consisted mainly of tea, tobacco and tung oil and was largely produced on the three per cent of land in European ownership. There was some production for export by Bantu tenant farmers and cooperatives. This consisted of tobacco in the central province, coffee in the northern province and cotton in the lower river valley.

In the period immediately before federation the British government was, on average, contributing about a million pounds sterling yearly to meet expenses of government, social and technical services. These services needed expansion and improvement, but only so much could done with the funds which could be allocated. Prospects of local funding were limited in such a poor country with few natural resources, subsistence living standards, overpopulation, bad husbandry, soil impoverishment, isolation and costly transportation problems.

Despite the difficult economic position, the bulk of the villagers led a simple and contented life, had basic health services and at least were spared the problems of famine and possible starvation.

One major factor in African opinion, before federation, was the development of a predominantly African civil service. The ratio of African to European staff in the civil service was about 12 to 1. Every opportunity was taken to train African staff and encourage their advancement through promotion.The progress made in Africanization was far ahead of that in Northern and Southern Rhodesia. This largely resulted from the limited civil service budget and the lower cost of African staff. The difference in the staffing arrangements was undoubtedly a major factor in raising concern amongst Nyasaland's civil servants about their future under federation.

African opinion about federation was influenced by the experience of the migrant workers returning from South Africa and the Rhodesias. About 50,000 migrants returned each year to villages all over the country and told of how they were made to live in compounds, with their liberty restricted and without the understanding shown by the whites in their own country. Added to this was the agitation by the African nationalists, although many of these individuals were mistrusted by the traditionally conservative chiefs and headmen.

I believe that federation might still have been saved had the Colonial Office not decided that the administration, through its district commissioners and European civil servants, was not to offer explanations in its support or take any sides in the matter. In consequence many of the population, who had relied on the district commissioners for advice, turned to the nationalists and gave them the opportunity they had been waiting for. It has always seemed incomprehensible to me that the Colonial Office which fathered federation neglected it at birth.

Chapter 10

Federation or What?

The story in African mythology of how the various races obtained the colour of their skins has always intrigued me. According to Bantu legend, God created man with a black skin. After some time, God decided that it would be nice if the people were white. He therefore sent the animals of the forest to all the tribes telling them to go to a distant lake and bathe in its waters, and they would become white. The swifter animals ran to the more fortunate races, and they came and bathed and were white. Unfortunately, the messenger to the African races was the chameleon, which is a poem in slow motion, taking one step forward, hesitating for perhaps a minute, and then taking another step.

By the time the chameleon reached the Bantu tribes, many months had passed, and, although they hurried to the lake, there was no water left when they arrived. They walked right out into the centre of the lake, and all they could find was some dampness in the ground on which their feet touched and on which they bent down and placed their hands. This is why the African has partly white hands and feet, although the rest of his skin is black. This may seem a most improbable story to have gained any credence, but wherever you went in Central Africa the chameleon, which is a harmless and inoffensive creature, was hated and it was almost impossible to get an African to touch one.

If one accepted the premise that there was so little difference between the races, why should colour prejudice have assumed major proportions?

On the European side there were the divisive factors of the different traditions, types of culture and education. Europeans also feared being swamped politically by the overwhelming masses of the Africans, with a loss of many of their existing advantages and a lowering of living standards. Finally, there was the Freudian fear of the loss of purity of the race.

On the African side were equally strong prejudices. While the tribal African was grateful for the removal of oppression and famine, and the provision of social services, he wanted to be accepted as a human being on a common level and resented conditions met by the migrants in the Rhodesias and South Africa. The superior attitude adopted by many Europeans gave rise to a feeling of humiliation and resentment. Development and improvement of the common lot had not proceeded as rapidly as it should have done, and there was a suspicion that the Europeans might be holding back in order to maintain a dominant economic position.

These prejudices were the major obstacles to be overcome in any government based on partnership of the races, such as federation. To do so it was vital that an adequate information network should exist to answer the prejudices and fears of all people. This did not exist, either before or during the early days of federation.

No matter how good, or trivial, a government measure might be, it was likely to create racial problems. Two examples which come to mind were the riots in the Central Province of Nyasaland which followed the order to bund land and prevent erosion, and the demonstrations and violence which followed the introduction of more highly refined sugar from Southern Rhodesia replacing that previously imported from Portuguese East Africa. The nationalists had been quick to spread the rumour that the refined sugar caused sterility and was intended to decimate the Bantu race.

One of the tragedies of Africa was that the first serious attempt to obtain collaboration between the races, developing into a multi-racial partnership in government, should have run into so many difficulties. An analysis of these problems might answer some criticisms of federation.

The federal electoral system was repeatedly criticized as being non-representative. It was, however, much more democratic than those it was replacing. At the stage of Bantu development reached in the federal countries, one might well question whether principles should be placed before progress or whether universal suffrage was more important than honest and enlightened government. From my experience, at the time, I seriously doubted whether the average Bantu villager was ready to play a full part as a democratic citizen. There was always the danger that he would be manipulated as he undoubtedly was over the change in the source of sugar supplies.

Under these circumstances the application of a system which tied political representation and development to economic advancement and education offered a number of safeguards. This was what the federal electoral arrangements were designed to do. There were to be general and special rolls of voters, and those entitled to vote in either classification were persons having certain defined income and property, with a specified educational standard. These standards were not impossibly high when related to the development and economic advancement possible to the African under federation.

Another issue was the fear of permanent European domination and supremacy. The Southern Rhodesia Europeans on their part had cause for concern about including the Bantu masses of Nyasaland and Northern Rhodesia in an electoral arrangement which would allow more and more Africans to qualify for the vote as the general standard of education improved and economic advancement took place.

If federation was so much to the advantage of the Europeans, one would have expected that the Southern Rhodesian vote in the referendum held before federation would have been overwhelmingly favourable. Actually, only 62 per cent of the votes cast were for federation. Most of the white settlers in Southern Rhodesia who supported federation did so as an alternative to the development of closer ties with the Union of South Africa and the introduction of a system based on white supremacy. A break up of the Federation, which seemed likely at the time of writing of this book, would be a betrayal of all that these people had stood for in the cause of multi-racial development.

The Bantu population in Nyasaland feared that the progress made under colonial government in education, social services and African economic advancement would not be maintained. The limiting factor in the past had been insufficient financial resources and aid. With political stability, the federal economy should have become viable and able to provide improved services without dependence on outside aid.

The operation of administrative, social and technical services for a larger unit should have allowed cost savings and helped the development of services. Given these facts it appeared realistic to argue that under federation Nyasaland would obtain considerable material advantage, with more rapid development of social services and education. The Federation also had a more diversified economic structure and was less likely to suffer problems during times of recession.

Another Bantu argument against federation was that the Southern Rhodesian attitude on native affairs was close to the South African one. The Colonial Office had been their protector for seventy years and took an enlightened view and interest in their well-being. The Bantu concerns were partly related to the fact that about 70,000 of the white Southern Rhodesians had come from South Africa. Most of these people were, however, of British origin and had left the Union because of their dislike of apartheid and Afrikaner racial policies.

The initial political and administrative steps under federation were designed to protect the Bantu position. In addition to centralization of many of the technical functions, with an expected improvement in services and efficiency, there was some democratization of government. Nyasaland's legislative council was extended to consist of eleven official and eleven unofficial elected members. The native authorities and district commissioners were to continue to operate substantially as before.

In the federal assembly there were twelve Africans amongst the forty-four elected representatives. A separate African Affairs Board had also been created to watch Bantu interests, and this had direct access to the Colonial Office.

An issue always present in the Bantu mind was the question of land ownership. Although only three per cent was owned by Europeans in Nyasaland, European settlers owned nearly fifty per cent of Southern Rhodesia. There was a real problem here. The suppression of tribal wars and slaving, and the introduction of health and welfare services had caused a population explosion with major population pressures on the land available for use by the Bantu villagers.

A related problem was the Bantu system of cultivation which had been to burn off the land, impoverish it by repeated planting of maize and then move on to other land, thus converting large areas to near-desert and subject to erosion by wind and water. The increase in population and loss of land fertility was creating a need for an increasingly large area to be provided for subsistence crops. Although the European estates, which had nurtured and preserved their lands through proper husbandry and had used it efficiently, were reluctant to give up their land, some European-owned lands had been taken over for African settlers under the Tengata system. There was certain to be continuing pressure, particularly in Southern Rhodesia, for release of land by the European settlers. This was bound to be resisted, and land ownership was likely to be a continuing problem. *Despite independence, how true this is in present-day Zimbabwe.*

Leaving aside the ownership issue it was urgently necessary that all the land available should be cultivated to best advantage and brought into good bearing condition with improved fertility. It was, however, not easy to convince the tribal African to abandon his traditional methods of cultivation, as instanced by the riots which followed the federal government's decision to require contour bunding, which is hard work and never popular.

In many ways the economies of the three territories were complementary, and an economic association was to mutual advantage. Southern Rhodesia, despite its precious metal production and large coal deposits, was essentially an agricultural country with an economy largely dependent on the European-owned estates. These produced tobacco in the north and cattle in the south. Northern Rhodesia was one of the world's largest copper producers. Although Nyasaland produced little of anything, its labour was important to the mines of Northern Rhodesia and the estates of Southern Rhodesia. The Federation with its diversified economic structure was less likely to suffer problems during times of recession.

Faced with the problems developing in the Federation, and seeing breakup as inevitable, Mr F. M. van Edeen, a member of the federal assembly, proposed that Southern Rhodesia and the copper belt should form a white-controlled state with the rest of Northern Rhodesia and Nyasaland forming a British protectorate. This was rejected by the federal assembly and Mr Van Edeen was forced to resign. Since then, the Federation had gone from crisis to crisis due to the activities of the Bantu nationalists, a lack of understanding of the position in the UK and the embarrassment caused by the racial policies of the Union of South Africa.

The introduction of unified federal government and effective administration was also prejudiced by the continued existence of separate governors and executive and legislative councils in Nyasaland and Northern Rhodesia and a separate parliament in Southern Rhodesia. Colonial Office influence also continued to be a factor in government policy and was substantially related to the parochial interests of its former protectorates rather than the interest of the group of countries. If the Federation was to be made to work, it was necessary that the power of the federal assembly should be extended and that the UK government should give full support to the Federation and cease its tacit acceptance of the aims of the African independence movement.

* * *

This book was however designed to be about Nyasaland and not the ever-multiplying problems of the Federation. That Nyasaland became British was largely due to the efforts of the early missionaries, although a cynic could well argue that it would have been better for the British Empire, and certainly the British taxpayer, if the country had been allowed to fall under Portuguese domination. (Additionally, the rest of the Federation would have been relieved of many of its problems.) However one looked at things, Nyasaland was a poor, backward country in which progress had only been possible through British subsidization and the dedicated activities of the missionaries and colonial servants.

The work of the British in Nyasaland over some seventy years should not be thrown away, however great the temptation to avoid facing the problems. The average Nyasaland African was not yet ready to take his place as an enlightened and enfranchised democratic citizen. The European had a place to fill, for many years, in providing administrative and technical leadership. Nyasaland would also, for the foreseeable future, be an economic liability rather than an asset and could not maintain its existing social and technical services without outside help.

What, therefore, was the future of Nyasaland if it seceded from the Federation?

One possibility was that it might revert to full colonial administration as a protectorate. At the time federation was proposed, many of the Europeans in Nyasaland felt that continuation of colonial rule under protectorate status was the best course to follow and was in the interest of the Nyasaland Africans.

Even assuming that the British government was prepared to accept a permanent liability for subsidizing the country, return to protectorate status would probably not be possible in view of the progress made by the nationalists in developing internal pressures for independence. The most likely possibility seemed to be a separate Bantu state. The country was, however, overpopulated and not economically viable, so it would have to continue to rely on financial aid. If it adopted a communist form of government, could it expect help from the communist block and perhaps India, always anxious to extend its interests in Africa?

Was there an alternative which would retain some of the advantages of a continuing association between the countries forming the Federation? One possibility Doc and I discussed was that Nyasaland should become a United Nations Trust Territory, with the United Kingdom and the remainder of the Federation appointed joint trustees. Nyasaland would keep its legislative council, which would continue to be democratized as political education and development took place. This legislature should be fully independent in internal affairs. Local government through the district councils and native authorities, advised and helped by the provincial and district administration, would continue for the time being. As the native authorities and the population became more politically educated, the British staff would be withdrawn.

Economically, the country would continue to be closely associated with the Federation, which would be responsible for defence, internal security and customs arrangements. The technical services, which had been combined to economic advantage, such as medical, communications and the post office also should be coordinated by the federal government but with the safeguard that the civil service posts in Nyasaland should continue to be Africanized as rapidly as possible

It would not be unreasonable to expect a Federation of Northern and Southern Rhodesia to provide economic aid to Nyasaland, bearing in mind its dependence on the use of Nyasaland's migrant labour.

It was possible that as the native population reached adulthood in political matters the advantages of the federal system would be understood, and Nyasaland itself make the move to become part of a future larger Federation.

The possibility of adopting trust status for Nyasaland might, with advantage, have been considered at the outset instead of including the country in a full federation. This would probably have removed much of the opposition to federation and resulted in an acceptable solution for all parties. It also would have provided a multi-racial and economically viable block capable of countering the principles applied in South Africa and perhaps influencing policies there. In view of the progress made by the nationalists this solution was probably no longer viable.

What would happen therefore if, as appeared likely, Nyasaland became an independent Bantu-ruled state?

The aim of the intelligentsia would probably be to create a Russian- or Indian-supported communist state replacing the existing form of government. While the Russians might be prepared to provide advisers and military assistance, they would be unlikely to provide the economic help needed. In view of the overpopulation and inadequacy of resources, Russia might not wish to get involved unless it saw this as a means of creating further problems for the colonial powers in Southern Africa.

The Indians already had a stake in Nyasaland. Many of the left-wing extremists had been educated in India and an anti-white, left-wing state, having ties with India, might be a real possibility. Indian aid might be tied to acceptance of further Indian immigration. The Indians had already extended their slave system of bonded labour into the protectorate and possibly a caste system could develop. (The Sanskrit word for caste is *varma*, which means colour, and was presumably applied by the early conquerors in India to the conquered people.) The Bantu intelligentsia had little respect for the tribal system, and this was likely to disappear. Communist government would in itself be a disaster. A form of communism organized along Indian lines could be even worse.

Under a communist regime the external problems of independence and interdependence were likely to be considerable. A further problem was how the country would be governed internally in view of the dislike of the intelligentsia for the tribal system.

Despite concerns about Dr Hastings Banda's nationalist leanings and public opposition to federation, there was a glimmer of hope for moderate and pragmatic government in Nyasaland should Dr Banda return and come to power. Dr Banda's background and experience over many years in the United Kingdom should have made him realize the need for a moderate form of government and a continuing contribution by European expertise to the development of his country. Although he had followed the line of African nationalist propaganda, and must remain something of an enigma, I believed that he honestly wished to further the interests of his people and was potentially a better leader and less to be feared than the left-wing extremists.

The need for outside assistance would remain a pressing problem. With the common interests established with the Union of South Africa and the Rhodesias through the dependence of those countries on migrant labour, there might be some rapprochement with those countries, particularly if they were prepared to provide financial help.

Chapter 11

Ulendo

One of my first jobs, after arriving in Nyasaland, was to explore the possibility of establishing multi-channel radio systems linking the main centres in the country and providing an international telephone service via Southern Rhodesia.

Much of my early travelling in the protectorate was of the roughest sort, requiring journeys to isolated locations, frequently over nearly impassable tracks, and involving pitching camp miles from any centre of civilization. I will forbear describing all these journeys, but one case may be of interest as an example of the type of experiences we had and generally enjoyed.

For our proposed international telephone system, we needed to make very high frequency radio tests from high points on the Nyasaland border to high points in Southern Rhodesia. A map study indicated that the most suitable practical location in Nyasaland might be on the Kirk Range. A shorter radio path was, however, available from Tambani Mountain, and we wished to explore its suitability.

One morning in December 1951 we set out from Zomba in convoy to Tambani, the Kirk Range and various points in Southern Rhodesia. Our expedition was full-scale, complete with tents, food supplies, domestic staff, bushing party, equipment etc. For transportation, we had two cars and two lorries. The European members of the party consisted of Bill, who would man the Kirk Range station; Roy, who would try and set up a station on Tambani; and I, who would carry out the tests from Southern Rhodesia.

At the time, Tambani was the least known of the mountains of Nyasaland and, although it is around 4,000 feet in altitude, I could not find it on my map. Later, in 1955, it became better known following the discovery of monzonite deposits, and several geological survey teams visited the area.

Tambani had an almost legendary character owing to its Fujiama-like appearance and its isolated location on the border of Nyasaland and Portuguese East Africa. An approach by motor vehicle, through the bush on the Nyasaland side, was impossible. We therefore planned to approach the mountain from the Portuguese side and initially take the Southern Rhodesia road through Portuguese East Africa. This was a corrugated, winding road which was always in dreadful condition from the large amount of heavy traffic it carried.

About twenty miles from Blantyre, the road began to wind its way down into the Shire Valley, finally crossing the river at a point just above the Mpatamanga Gorge. This gorge was an impressive sight. The river falls some 700 feet through a series of cataracts from the upper Shire Valley to the lower reaches near Chikawa, from which point it is navigable by stern-wheel steamers through to the Zambezi.

From Mpatamanga, we continued over a hot, winding section of the road to Mwanza, where we passed through the British and Portuguese customs posts into Portuguese East Africa. After another ten miles, on the Southern Rhodesia road, we turned back along a narrow track through the bush, where we sometimes had to cut a way for the lorries or clear rocks out of the path. After a few miles, we re-entered Nyasaland, this time without passing through any customs post.

Tambani had been visible to us since long before we reached Mwanza, but our route had of necessity been circuitous, and it seemed we would never get there. Now, however, we were approaching it rapidly. But before we reached the rest house, at the foot of the mountain, we had a further problem when a small bridge over a water course collapsed as our last lorry was passing over it. We managed to get the lorry out of the dry river bed and left a party to cut trees and rebuild the bridge, while we pushed on to the rest house. Here, we pitched camp for the boys, put our own things in the rest house, and while Cookie prepared a meal, questioned the rest house watchman and local villagers about possible routes to the top of the mountain. We hired two guides for our climb of the mountain starting at dawn the next morning.

In our talks with the villagers, we learned that the only climb in recent years had been made by a survey team some months earlier. We had heard of this climb just before leaving Zomba, when we were told, to our discomfiture, that the European surveyor was still dangerously and painfully ill in South Africa from blood poisoning caused by insect bites. While the villagers knew nothing of these circumstances, they insisted that this was a very bad mountain with many spirits living on it. It was dangerous to go to the top, as those who did so and disturbed the spirits were likely to come to a quick and painful end. They insisted therefore that, although they would show us the way up the mountain, we would have to climb the last section alone, and they would take no responsibility for our doing so.

By now the sun was setting over the Zambezi, and, after a long day without food, we sat enjoying our meal and watching the glorious sunset. Then, after checking all was well with the boys, who had fed well and were enjoying a sing-song, we prepared for bed.

Presumably to ensure that we had a good night, the rest house watchman told us that a few days earlier he had opened the rest house bedroom door to surprise a leopard, which had then taken off through the window. The window was, we discovered, a hole in the wall without glass, bars or any other restriction. As we made our final preparations for bed, I quietly took my automatic pistol out of my case and put it under my pillow. Bill noticed this and purposefully collected his revolver, a fearsome weapon that looked as if it could kill an elephant. Roy, who had nothing, wandered out into the night to return with a spear and an old muzzle loader which he had managed to borrow. We then settled down to rest.

It was an uneasy and restless night for all of us, partly due to the threat from outside and partly the heat at a lower altitude than we were used to. The leopard did not return, and this was indeed fortunate, as our three beds formed a triangle and we were in greater danger from our own weapons than from any animal misguided enough to enter the room.

Despite our poor night, hot tea and breakfast revived us, and as dawn was breaking we were in reasonably good shape to start the climb. We commenced the long traverse up the side of the mountain following a defined path through thick bush and forest and accompanied by four of our boys and the two guides. We followed the path along the west face of the mountain, coming at last to a ridge where the path began to descend towards Mwanza, on the other side of the mountain. Here, we left the path and turned toward the summit. The trees had now thinned out and, although it was a steep climb, we were walking over open grass that was relatively easy going. We now had an excellent view over the Zambezi Valley and the Kirk Range. We were confident that, based on our experience this far, it would not be too difficult to transport our test equipment or build a road later.

About mid-morning, and after four hours' climb, we came to a rock face, two or three hundred feet from the summit. We traversed this around the summit, but the approach from all sides was precipitous. Without rock climbing expertise and equipment there appeared to be only one approach. This was through a fissure formed by a crack in the rock that offered a sixty degree angle of ascent. This did not look very promising and might prove to be a lion's or leopard's lair. Our guides told us that this was the only way to the summit and was that taken by the survey team. They would not accompany us any farther, as the *mfiti* lived on the other side of the fissure. They would, however, wait for us if we were lucky enough to return, not that they had much hope of this.

Bill and I decided that a reluctant Roy, with his muzzle loader, was less dangerous ahead of us, and was probably best fitted to meet any *mfiti*. We therefore gave him the honour of leading the second team to climb Tambani in living memory. The climb through the cleft in the cliff was not quite as difficult as we had expected, and we ascended the seventy feet or so without much trouble. However, it had become obvious that it would be impossible to transport equipment this way. From the top of the cliff, we found we were only about two hundred feet from the summit, which was covered with large rocks.

From the summit we looked into the chance of bringing up our heavy equipment by an alternative route but finally wrote Tambani off as a possible site for our immediate tests. Having come so far, we decided to rest and enjoy the scenery, and sat in the sun by the survey beacon to do so. To the west, we had a beautiful view over the Zambezi to the hills near Tete in Portuguese East Africa. To the north, we looked over Mwanza to the Kirk Range and to the east we could see Cholo Mountain with Mlanje rising behind it

Bill and I were preoccupied with the beauty of the scenery when Roy suddenly shouted that we were being attacked. He had presumably been watching for the *mfiti* when he noticed a swarm of flies gathering about us, apparently appearing from thin air. Afterward, we realized that they were coming out of crevices in the rocks. Although we were curious about these flies, we decided that discretion was the better part of valour. Taking up our weapons, which were useless against a fly attack, we made a hasty and precipitous evacuation of the summit through the cleft. Our waiting guides and boys, who formed an anxious little party, were glad to see us return alive.

The remaining descent was easy, and we arrived at the rest house in time for a late lunch. Unfortunately, owing to our forced evacuation of Tambani's summit we did not take any photographs of what must be some of the loveliest views in Nyasaland. Nor did I manage to get a specimen of one of the flies. (I learned later that these were not unique to Tambani but lived on at least one other mountain. One of my staff and I were bitten, although not seriously, while carrying out subsequent tests from Cholo Mountain. The effects of the bites were interesting. Although not painful at the time, they developed into circular spots with a central septic area which took months to disappear.)

After lunch, we considered how we should revise our plans and decided that, as Tambani was out of consideration for the present operation, we would concentrate on the Kirk Range for the Nyasaland terminal.

The previous night in the Tambani rest house had been too much for us, and rather than lie there waiting for the leopard or the blast from Roy's muzzle loader, we decided to break camp, with Bill and half our party returning to the fleshpots of Mwanza Border Inn on his way to the Kirk Range, and Roy and I taking the long and difficult road to Southern Rhodesia.

Roy and I finally pitched camp in the bush some fifteen miles short of the Zambezi. We spent the night in tents disturbed by the drums from a village nearby, which continued into the small hours. We were also bitten half to death by mosquitoes.

We were up again at dawn the next morning and reached the Zambezi by 6.00 a.m., making the ferry crossing and finally pitching camp in Southern Rhodesia that evening.

Rhodesia was civilization with its hotels and rest houses, and I will not enlarge on our experiences there. Our tests with Bill on the Kirk Range were not very successful, and we returned finally to Zomba disappointed at the failure of our mission.

Later we achieved successful results in tests between Cholo Mountain and Castle Beacon in Southern Rhodesia and established what was at the time the longest multi-circuit, very-high-frequency communication link in the world, working over a distance of about 350 miles.

*   *   *

Wherever one went in the Shire Highlands one saw the massif of Mlanje Mountain rising at some point on the skyline. It bears some similarity to Mont Blanc in its size and extent and the way it rises almost sheer from the unbroken plain. Only seldom is there snow on its summit, although a layer of cloud is not infrequent. Normally, its colour is grey, tending to mauve in the distance.

In 1951, I first flew over Mlanje following the almost unbroken cliff face on the north side, with its sheer drops of nearly 8,000 feet, and circling over the two main plateaus on the mountain of Chambe and Lucheyna with their green slopes and pockets of Mlanje cedar. In the same year, I also climbed the lower slopes on the south of the range to the hydro-electric plant of the Lujeri tea estate.

This newly completed plant had made possible a new method of processing tea. The normal process was to pick the young, newly formed shoots by hand and then wither them under conditions of high temperature and humidity. The withering broke down the cell structure of the leaf, thus allowing the extraction of the juices and flavour during infusion. The withered leaf was dried, crushed into fragments, graded and packed.

Under the experimental process, the tea shoots were rapidly frozen, causing an even more complete breakdown of the cell structure. The tea quality was excellent but lacked the brown-orange colour favoured by most tea drinkers and was a dirty green/grey. The product was largely used in blended varieties.

* * *

My daughter Rosemary, then sixteen years of age, was visiting us during 1952 and had read Laurens van der Post's *Venture to the Interior*. We accordingly planned an expedition to the summit of Mlanje Mountain. To accompany us on this trip were David, a colleague, and his daughters Jaynor and Anita. We planned to start the climb on a Saturday afternoon, spend two days on the plateau, taking in the climb to the summit, and then return home. Supplies of everything except water, and including an adequate supply of blankets, had to be taken with us.

Arrangements were made in advance for the use of the forestry cottage on the plateau. This had not been permanently occupied since the tragic incident described in *Venture to the Interior*. We also arranged for bearers to help with our supplies.

Unfortunately, David was not ready to start on time and we were further delayed by punctures. When we arrived at the starting point

Mlanje climb: Anita, Rosemary, Jaynor, Bicycle.

for the climb, our bearers had disappeared. It took us nearly an hour
to find three bearers and a small boy called Bicycle.

We finally, somewhat irresponsibly, started the climb about 2½
hours before sunset carrying a fair part of the *katundu* ourselves. We
knew that when we reached the Chambe Plateau, at an altitude of
nearly 8,000 feet, the going should be straightforward. We had first to
climb nearly 6,000 feet over sections which, although not particularly
difficult, were at least arduous and could in mist, or after dark, become
distinctly dangerous.

We had received reports from friends of taking up to four hours
over this section. The forestry people had, however, assured us that if
you hurried it could be done in two hours. It was on this we based
our decision to go ahead, but perhaps without adequate consideration
of the girls' stamina and the loads we would have to carry.

The first two miles were not difficult, involving a steady climb along
the banks of the Likabula stream and passing a beautiful natural pool

which was popular amongst the tea planters of Mlanje as a swimming pool. We had no time for a swim and just had to keep on moving. Soon the slope increased and the path became more difficult. Up and up: sometimes over rock faces and sometimes on slopes of up to 45 degrees. Our lungs almost reached bursting point and our hearts pounded. After a time Rosemary could no longer keep up with us, and we had to stop. "Daddy, I can't go on; it's too steep."

The only alternative would be to give the whole thing up and go back. Unless we went on, and went on quickly, it would be unsafe. We must be over the edge of the plateau in one hour. The bearers and little Bicycle took over the girls' loads, and on we went. Sometimes there were tears amongst the girls, but now they were keeping up better, and we were making good progress. Perhaps, in a way, the extreme exertion was good, as it took our minds off the dangers of the more difficult sections. The bearers, including small Bicycle, who were carrying heavier loads, kept up with us easily. Finally, after the last steep section and just before sunset, we threw ourselves over the top edge on to the Chambe Plateau and lay panting on the grass to recover.

The whole world lay below us, a fanciful and roseate world reflecting the last light from the sun in the western sky. Rising above Cholo was Cholo Mountain with its tea plantations some thirty miles away. In the south, at about the same distance, were the Chiperoni mountains in Portuguese East Africa with their peaks in cloud, a threat of one of the dangers we might meet. Quite close to us was the terminal for the cable hoist used for the extraction of timber.

We had looked longingly at the lower cable terminal before we started our climb, but the forestry people had earlier told us of the dangers of riding the open platform and of an accident when the attendant forgot to stop the winding motor and the lifting cable was broken, allowing the platform to fall freely and smash itself to pieces some four miles away and 6,000 feet below.

After a rest and refreshments, we were on our way again. It was now easy going over level grassland, although dark was closing in rapidly and we had to follow in the tracks of the bearers. Finally, about

Mlanje climb: the plateau.

7.00 p.m., we reached the forestry cottage. Soon, we had a good fire going using the adequate stocks of Mlanje cedar, which burns easily owing to its high oil content and produces a wonderful aroma. By this time, it was becoming distinctly chilly, and the fire was appreciated by all. After a good meal and all the effort of climbing, we were ready for bed. The cottage had two rooms; in the larger of these the girls slept. David and I curled up in front of the fire.

After the others were asleep I watched the cedar fire flicker and thought how much this simple cottage in its isolated location, but with all the beauty and majesty of its surroundings, must have meant to the Frances family before he was washed away and drowned during that unhappy expedition described in Laurens van der Post's book. At last sleep came, followed by the chill inevitable at this high altitude.

Even with four blankets I was cold and very ready to turn out at dawn. It was a horrid morning, with a heavy mist and drizzle; visibility was only a few yards. I felt colder than I had felt for years, as I

The forestry cottage, Chambe Plateau.

walked down to the stream for a wash in nearly freezing water before returning to the cottage to make tea and get breakfast. Calling the girls, we suggested a good wash in the stream before breakfast, to be greeted with "Ugh! It's far too cold." The threat of no wash, no breakfast, brought them to order, and we finally had a good breakfast in front of the fire and discussed our prospects of completing the climb to the summit.

Mlanje is the highest mountain within a range of about a thousand miles. The nearest mountains which even approach it in height are the Nyanja Range nearly four hundred miles to the west, the Nyika Plateau four hundred miles to the north and the Chiperoni Mountains about forty miles to the south. Mlanje, because of its altitude and isolation, attracts extreme weather conditions and is ill-famed for the heavy mist which comes down, almost without warning, and may last for several days. These mists are known locally as "Chiperoni" from the Chiperoni Mountains, where similar conditions apply. We had now fairly obviously been caught in a Chiperoni.

The weather after breakfast had improved slightly. The rain had stopped, and we could see a few yards. By about 10 a.m. we could see across the plateau, although there was still cloud covering the peaks of the mountain. We decided somewhat dubiously to start for the Lucheyna Plateau, from which the main peak rises.

We had a map of the paths on the mountain, and we found that the track to Lucheyna was a well-worn one, which gave us some confidence. We first crossed the river and then climbed to the higher part of the Chambe Plateau from which the Chambe peak rose some 800 feet above us. We were walking across a grass-covered area with delphinium and freesia growing amongst the grass, and a few scattered protea bushes.

Some two miles from the cottage we reached the saddle, an open spur ridge crossing to the main range of the group. We found this less frightening than Laurens van der Post had done, possibly because there was no wind. We were exhilarated by the height and the views to the valley north of us and of the mountain range around us. These were breathtaking. The spur is about ten feet wide, and the slopes on either side, though dangerous, are not precipitous. The worst part was getting down onto the spur from the Chambe Plateau. Here, we had to descend over a rock face with an increasing slope so you could not see what lay ahead. David and I led the way, and the girls followed without too much difficulty.

By this time, the mist had further cleared, and only Mlanje peak was still in cloud, so our hopes for a successful climb were high. We crossed the saddle, which is about 50 yards long, climbed the other side and entered a pocket of montane forest with magnificent Mlanje cedar trees rising some 80 to 100 feet above our heads. Examining one of these trees, David discovered what he insisted were recent marks left by a leopard sharpening its claws. This caused us to proceed rapidly through the forest and view with concern any noises we heard in the undergrowth. Toward the end of the forest area, the path divided, and because of the mist on the peak we decided first to take the track along the north face of the peak, where we should have a good view to the north.

The summit – so near and yet so far.

We came out of the forest onto grassland and climbed over this to an altitude of about 9,000 feet, where we were on a narrow plateau with the peak's rock face behind us and an almost sheer drop in front of us to the valley below. This was one of the most exciting moments of the climb and gave us a superb view over the Palombi Plain in beautifully clear conditions. With our binoculars, we could pick out the buildings in Zomba nearly fifty miles away. We also could see below us Chiradzulu, the changing mountain, which although a mile or so long is extremely narrow and seems wholly different when seen end on.

We were unable to climb the sheer rock face behind us to the top of Mlanje, which was now completely clear. So after a quick lunch we climbed down to the forest and the branch in the paths and followed the other track out of the forest to the Luchenya Plateau, where we started to climb again. Making good progress, we rapidly crossed the grassland to the broken rock face which we had to negotiate on our way to the summit. This was now only a few hundred yards away and about 400 feet above us. Unfortunately, a change was again coming in the weather, and pockets of cloud and mist were forming around us and on the summit. This was a danger sign, and we knew too much of the mountain's history to take any further chances. Reluctantly, we turned and made our way back, looking often to note the cloud rapidly building up on the summit and the mist descending towards us.

By this time Chambe peak was also covered in cloud, and we made top speed to the saddle, which was the danger point. We breathed a sigh of relief as we crossed it and climbed over the difficult face to the easy going of the Chambe Plateau. However, we were now completely in cloud, and, but for the path being well defined, we might have been forced to spend the night in the open. By the time we reached the cottage it was again drizzling with an almost impenetrable mist, and the only thing to do was make a good fire and sit round it telling stories of Africa and thinking of our day's endeavours and impressions.

To most Europeans who have climbed Mlanje, the sense of solitude on a grass-covered and isolated plateau some mile and a half above sea level has a peculiar charm, and the Chiperone mists add rather than detract from this impression. There is a fascination and sense of mystery in the quickness with which the environment can change from a clear, almost alpine, atmosphere, with a landscape giving a distinct impression of Switzerland with its meadows and wild flowers, to darkest Africa, with a heavy blanket of freezing fog.

To most of the Bantu, Mlanje was still feared as a place of spirits and the reputed home of the Nlukuwewe. Our bearers, although we offered them supplies, decided to return to the plain, preferring the risks of the return journey in the dark rather than the certain horror of remaining on the plateau. Some forestry assistants had overcome their fears and now remained on the mountain, but they still did not like it there. It seems possible that a group of Bushmen may, some centuries ago, have taken refuge on Mlanje, perhaps to die out naturally over the years, or to be killed or absorbed by the surrounding tribes.

One can imagine these earlier people of Nyasaland living on the isolated mountain plateau in the fogs and mists, with little in the way of game to support them and driven to descend periodically to hunt on the plain. The effect of these little creatures moving and killing almost silently could well have created superstition and dread amongst the Bantu tribes. As far as I know there had been no anthropological research carried out on Mlanje, but the mountain should offer some scope for such investigations and might confirm what is only a guess on my part.

As evening wore on we prepared our evening meal, and the girls amused themselves singing and reciting to one another. David and I talked quietly about Africa's problems and waded into our one bottle of whisky. This must have triggered his daughters into reciting a poem written by David's father about the evils of strong drink, called "The Hell Bound Train". I remember one couplet: "The boy was full of the best strong beer and the devil himself was the engineer." We were far from any railway, but with the cold around us we were lost to the evils of strong drink. Despite the fire, the singing, the poems and the weighty discussions, we were tired from our climbing, and it was not long before we all wanted to turn in.

Dawn brought a grey, cold day with visibility of only a yard or so. Expectantly, we waited, hoping it might clear and give us a final chance to make the summit climb, but this time it was noon before the sun again started to break through the mist. Any attempt on the peak was out of the question. We therefore spent the afternoon and evening exploring the Chambe Plateau, taking specimens of its wild flowers and looking with envy at the fat trout in the mountain stream. Although I had a licence, fishing had been suspended to conserve the stocks.

During the afternoon, we walked to the gorge between Chambe and Mlanje and looked down to the south and east. It was a lazy, happy afternoon partly spent just lying in the grass and sun-bathing. Tomorrow we had to return to civilization and had to face the long descent to the houses in the valley we could see nearly a mile below us. Again, we were early to bed. This night it was clear but cold, and we had little fear about the weather for the morning.

Dawn broke, we had another cold wash in the stream and an early

Mlanje climb: tea plantations below and Chiperoni above.

breakfast, but it was 9.30 a.m. before we heard the noise of our bearers and could get on our way. The morning was still clear, but as we came to the edge of the plateau the mist came down again and followed us for the first thousand feet almost as if it were providing cover for one of the mountain spirits, or the Nlukuwewe, to track us. Our climb down was not as tiring as our ascent but was more painful in throwing different strains on our tired muscles. By lunchtime we reached Likabula, took a refreshing swim, splashed under the waterfall and had a picnic lunch, using the last of our supplies. Behind us, looking up through the valley, we could see Mlanje peak clear in the sunshine.

I never returned to Mlanje on foot, although David and one of his daughters managed to reach the peak some three years later.

A year after our expedition I was in the air over the mountain with a friend from the Civil Aviation Department, who drove his car as if flying an aeroplane and flew as if he were driving a car. In consequence, we flew over the peak at an altitude of about 50 feet. This gave me a wonderful view and excellent photographs without a telephoto lens but was, to say the least, a very risky undertaking in view of the down-draughts. The director of civil aviation nearly had hysterics when I showed him the photographs.

* * *

Every spring, when the rains were over, the Public Works Department concentrated most of its resources on putting the roads in as good a condition as possible. It was following this annual reconditioning that His Excellency made his annual *ulendo* trip to the provinces. Most other senior officials, if they valued their cars and sometimes their lives, also tried to make their *ulendo* visits then. In my early days, I sometimes had to travel under all conditions but when I headed the department, I wisely fell into the usual pattern.

These visits were a valuable means of keeping in touch with the problems and realities of Africa and meeting one's European and African staff and the population as a whole. *Ulendo* visits usually lasted two to three weeks and might extend to all parts of the country. In addition to the annual *ulendo* trips made by the more senior staff, special visits were necessary by all European staff to deal with specific problems. As we had only one government plane in the country and limited landing facilities, these were normally made by road.

I always enjoyed my earlier journeys and later my annual *ulendo* trips and found a sense of pioneering and romance in setting out on a journey involving long distances where road conditions might be extremely difficult and where perhaps only one car might pass in weeks. In extreme cases, such as the Chendo track from the Great North Road to Karonga, there might only be one vehicle going through each year. Breakdowns were to be feared and every sensible precaution taken. Before starting, you not only loaded the car with supplies of food and drink but saw that the vehicle was in good condition and adequate supplies of spares, tyres, and emergency gasoline were carried. Even so, the inevitable breakdowns occurred.

Once in my early days in the country, and as the rains were starting, I had to visit Karonga with one of my staff to deal with a breakdown in radio communications. On our return journey, we hit a pothole and broke a spring. The car, in collapsing on the axle, cut the brake line.

We were fortunate in finding a native store some few miles away. Here, we obtained some rawhide strips; and, by taking out both springs, selecting leaves from each, and lashing them together with rawhide, we managed to build two fairly serviceable springs. We could do nothing about the brakes and we faced with a journey of some sixty miles to the nearest point at which we could hope for repairs to be made, with only an ineffective hand-brake. This would not have been so bad except that we had shortly to climb 3,000 feet up the Livingstonia escarpment over an extremely dangerous mountain road with an earth surface and twenty-three hairpin bends, some of which were so sharp that it was necessary to reverse back to the edge of a precipice to get around them. (Some years later, when we started a postal Land Rover service to Karonga, we lost two vehicles over the edge of this escarpment.)

Before climbing the escarpment I obtained a heavy block of timber, and on each bend, where I had to reverse, my companion would jump out and hold this under the rear wheels as I slipped the clutch and gently ran back to the edge of the precipice. By this means, we came safely to the top. After that the next forty miles, even without brakes, was child's play.

We had our lighter moments, too, such as the case of a senior official who was a very good friend of mine and was on a visit to the north of the country.

Nyasaland had a common border with Mozambique, which ran through the bush and was in no way clearly defined. A joint Portuguese-British commission was working to define the boundary. The Bantus used to cross the boundary freely as they saw fit, hence the major migration of the Nguru into Nyasaland with all its attendant problems. Many of the roads, including the Great North Road, passed through Portuguese territory, and this gave British bureaucracy its chance to assert itself, although a little more illogically than usual. If you were travelling northward you passed through a Nyasaland customs post when entering Mozambique, but there was no such post when you re-entered Nyasaland. Travelling in this direction, you could collect as much contraband as you saw fit, with little fear of any consequences.

However, government obviously expected those with smuggling tendencies to be government servants, travelling southward to the capital, and you were supposed, when travelling in that direction, to clear customs when you re-entered Nyasaland. The Bantu African customs clerks obviously thought this to be an illogical business, particularly as it would involve them in work that would otherwise be avoided. In consequence, the barrier was normally left up and only lowered when the Bwana collector of customs was expected.

One day, however, a mad Bwana with a conscience arrived and stopped his car, even though the barrier was up. The customs clerk roused himself, fearing at first that it might be the collector and that his friends at headquarters had not advised him of the collector's movements. He was reassured to see this was a stranger and politely advised him that he might proceed on his way. The stranger insisted, nevertheless, that he had a bottle of wine to declare and could he pay the duty.

The clerk remembered that he had learnt something about duties years before, but all he had been called on to do since was to raise and lower the barrier. He felt that the stranger was trying to take advantage of him and told him curtly, but firmly, that customs clerks had far more to worry about than collecting duty and if he would go on his way he would be much obliged. The stranger was a young, recently arrived and enthusiastic member of the secretariat who had travelled north with the senior official but did not know the ropes. His civil service blood was now thoroughly roused. On his return to Zomba, he wrote to the collector of customs in the strongest possible terms pointing out a grave dereliction of duty.

A few days later, his senior officer, having completed his business in the north of the country was on his way home. Following the usual practice of most government servants, he stopped at a Portuguese store near the border to stock up with wine. When he arrived at the frontier he found to his surprise that the barrier was down but assumed that old Joe the collector was expected and appearances must be maintained. He called cheerily to the customs clerk to open the barrier. The latter, licking his wounds from what he had suffered that very morning at the hands of an angry collector of customs, asked if there was anything to declare. The senior official replied that of course there was nothing to declare and the clerk was not there to ask silly questions but to open the barrier.

Although the clerk agreed, he had received his recent instructions in most unequivocal terms and insisted on searching the car. It was only some hours later that the matter was finally sorted out and a very ruffled senior official was allowed to go on his way.

This incident increased the cost of most people's wine by 25 per cent and endeared our new colleague to us all.

*   *   *

In 1955 Frankie, who for the previous five years had been debating going on *ulendo* with me, decided to join me on a twelve-day tour of the central and northern provinces. I was at once faced with the problem of persuading her that she would not require the usual dozen or so suitcases and that priority must be given to carrying adequate spare parts, extra tyres, spare petrol and supplies of food and drink. After these were stowed, there might be room for one small suitcase for the two of us.

At dawn one morning in early July, we started on our long, dusty way to Lilongwe, capital of the central province, some two hundred miles to the north. The road first skirted around Zomba Mountain and then dropped down to the Shire River crossing at Liwonde. We were pulled across the river on a man-powered ferry by some six or so Africans who sang insulting songs about their passengers and seemed

Ferry over the Shire River at Liwonde.

to enjoy their work. After leaving the river the road branched, the right fork going to Fort Johnstone and the lake. The left fork, which we were taking, was the Great North Road. This title was a little misleading, as the road was a corrugated earth track just wide enough for two vehicles to pass and so dusty that you could see the dust cloud of an oncoming car several miles away.

From the river junction, the Great North Road rose up an escarpment to Ncheu, a pleasant hill station on the borders of Portuguese East Africa. Ncheu was the scene of my friend's encounter with the customs clerk. It also achieved some international attention in 1953 when the paramount chief Gomani, advised by one of our militant churchmen, started an insurrection against federation. The churchman had every Marxist/Christian excuse for his part in this matter except knowledge of the people he was advising and experience of conditions in the country. He had some media support for his actions in this unfortunate incident which might, but for enlightened and restrained action by the authorities, have resulted in considerable bloodshed. What hope had Christian civilization in Africa when some of our visitors, however well-intentioned, kept rushing in where angels feared to tread? Fortunately, the angels were still there in the person of people like my friend the bishop.

To the south of Ncheu extending through to Mwanza is the Kirk Range of mountains, which I have described in an earlier chapter. I once spent a most uncomfortable night on the highest part of the Kirk Range during a freezing period in July in an open-neck shirt and shorts.

From Ncheu, which incidentally is pronounced N-cheyu (BBC announcers, at the time of the disturbances, made it sound like someone sneezing), we continued northward. First, along the lake view road which followed the edge of the escarpment and gave a series of vistas of the lake some 2,500 feet below. Here again Africa showed its incongruity. At the highest point, with a view which was out of this world and might elsewhere have accommodated a luxury hotel, was a grass-roofed mud hut, about twelve feet square, with probably one room. Outside was a sign marked "Hoteli".

From here we descended to Dedza, a hill station at the foot of Dedza Mountain. We stopped at the Dedza hotel for a pleasant lunch improved by a dessert of tree tomatoes picked in the garden.

At one time, we had a considerable amount of work in the Dedza area in connection with our radio project. This involved the civil engineering works, including building a road to the top of the mountain. At the time, I spent several days in the Dedza hotel. With little to do in the evenings I would interest myself watching our local engineer's wife flirting with, but resisting the advances of, the local bachelors. I wonder if the struggle finally became too much for her. The marriage broke up, as so many did under the difficult conditions in which the wives had to live.

Alternatively, I would go to the Boma and talk to the local district commissioner who was our leading ornithologist. He was always worth a visit, but I went once too often and got involved in seeing an outdoor film show he had arranged for a mixed audience of Africans and Europeans. This featured a very early silent film, which from its quality looked as if it dated back to the days of Freese Green. The film portrayed Stanley's search for Livingstone. It must have been a serial epic and lasted almost as long as the actual search. After ten reels and

The Great North Road.

A main road bridge. They don't build them like this any more.

about five hours I worked my way to the side of the Boma and sneaked through the shrubbery back to the hotel. I noticed that the European audience had thinned, but the Africans were still sitting on the grass entranced.

After lunch, we were on our way to Lilongwe over a flat plateau, mainly scrub-covered, with massive hemispherical stone mountains standing out from it. Finally, in the late afternoon, we arrived at Lilongwe, the provincial capital.

Lilongwe was the centre of the tobacco-growing industry. Besides the European estates, there were many thriving small African farms. These had brought considerable prosperity to the area. The town itself was wild west looking but had a good hotel, and after a day on Nyasaland roads we appreciated the comforts.

We had a large postal and engineering centre in the town, and I spent the next day visiting it. In the evening, we visited our friends Marjory and her husband Frank, who owned and ran one of the larger estates. Marjory was a member of the legislative council.

Lilongwe was the scene of one of the few cases of irresponsibility we had involving a member of our European staff. Our Lilongwe mail was transported to Chipoka by rail and then taken by contractor's open lorry to Lilongwe. On arrival of one of these lorries at Lilongwe the European postmaster signed for eleven bags of mail instead of the ten actually delivered. When the shortage was discovered, the postmaster insisted that eleven bags had been received.

In the meantime, we had found out that the missing bag contained a bank remittance of forty thousand pounds sent to provide cash for purchases of tobacco from the African farmers. Theft was suspected, and it looked like an inside job. You can imagine the consequent excitement and police enquiries. MI4½ immediately suspected a communist plot to finance seditious activities and started investigating African National Congress activities. The CID were questioning all staff and said they were on the point of making an arrest.

While everyone was having great fun, and the police department was busier than it had been for years, an African villager walked into one of our small offices on the road to Lilongwe with a bag across his shoulder. He said he had found it at the roadside and could he have a tickey (three pence) as a reward. The bag had been carelessly stowed by the contractor and fallen off his lorry. The villager got considerably more than the tickey he had asked for.

The next morning we were on our way shortly after dawn. The countryside was much the same, although broken at one point by the Bua River, one of the few perennial rivers feeding Lake Nyasa. Toward mid-day we reached Kasungu, and after a lunch at the rest house we called on Morris, the DC of this lonely station, for all the news about his district, how our installations and offices were operating and what the immediate and future needs were. I had worked with Morris when he had been a very efficient member of the secretariat staff in Zomba. He later proved to be an excellent DC, well-liked by the local Africans. It was good to see him again and exchange ideas on federation

We were on our way again later in the afternoon, finally rising up from the plain to Mzimba where, after a brief stop at our office, we climbed even farther on to the Vipya Mountains. I have already mentioned this range of grass and bush-covered hills broken by eroded rock eminences, some of which rise 1,000 feet above their grassy bases. The higher points of the range are generally open grassland with many wild flowers and sometimes a few protea bushes. From the higher points there are some lovely views over Lake Nyasa to the east and westward to the valleys of the Kasitu and Rukuru rivers, with Mount Hora, the sight of the slaughter of the Timbuku by the Agoni, in the foreground. Due north, purpling in the evening light, was the majestic plateau of the Nyika some fifty miles away.

Finally, after following the ridge of the Vipya for about twenty miles, we dropped down through the rain forest of Kaningina into Mzuzu, the provincial headquarters and our home for the next two days. Again, we had the prospect of a bath, a meal and a quiet night at the rest house after some 250 difficult miles on earth roads.

For the morning, we had arranged for a Land Rover to take us down the Timberi track to Nkata Bay. This track, which followed the route of an old timber extraction path trodden by many weary African feet, cut the distance between Mzuzu and Nkata Bay from sixty miles to sixteen miles by the simple expedient of going straight down the escarpment and through the foothills to the valley 2,500 feet below. In dry weather the track, although rough going, was relatively safe for a four-wheel-drive vehicle, but with even a small amount of rain many parts of the track became river beds and were impassable. As this is one of the wettest areas of the country, the Timberi track was not likely to become a major highway.

Our Land Rover arrived at dawn, and shortly after we were on our way. We were bumped about a lot by the roughness of the going, but we found the track less frightening than, for example, the Livingstonia escarpment in that it did not follow the edge of any precipices. In some sections, it passed through heavily wooded country; in others, one had an open view of the lake with the blue mountains of Tanganyika in the distance and the low outline of Likoma Island on the horizon.

Despite stops to examine the practicability of running a telephone route up the track, and to look at the views, we arrived at Nkata Bay in time for a late breakfast at the rest house.

Nkata Bay is a lovely spot with a superb situation on the lake. The rest house was located on a peninsula which runs out into the lake and provides the shelter for the harbour, which is one of the safest on Lake Nyasa.

Before starting work, we dropped Frankie off at one of the beaches, a delightful and secluded spot with lovely clear water. The lake was very calm, blue and clear, ideal conditions for the Nkungu fly, and we could count no fewer than eight columns masquerading as water-spouts. Frankie spent her day swimming and sunbathing. We returned to our work at the Nkata Bay office.

There must have been a recent return of migrant workers from the Rhodesias and South Africa, as I had never seen so many African gentlemen with their walking sticks and brief-cases. The effect was rather spoilt by their wives staggering behind them with burdens on their heads and children on their backs. Such was civilization, or the effects of civilization. In the afternoon, we returned to the rest house in Mzuzu.

The following day, after a morning in the Mzuzu office and discussions with the administration in the afternoon, we did the short section to Rumpi, stopping to shop for local supplies at the picturesque market at Ekwendi and visit our office at Njakwa. We were now passing through lower and less interesting country until we approached the Rukuru River Gorge at Njakwa. At this point the Rukuru, which we were next to see almost a mile above our heads, is a clear, rapidly flowing river tumbling over and sweeping around the large rocks and boulders lying in its bed as it finds its way through the narrow gorge.

Having organized food and accommodation at the rest house, we contacted Zomba using the mobile radio equipment I had in my car. But for the telegraph facilities in the offices I had visited, I had been out of touch with base for two days and would be unable to contact them again, through public facilities, until we reached Karonga in three days' time. It was not long before we were talking to Paddy, our postal controller, some five hundred miles away using a length of wire thrown into the nearest tree as an antenna.

Shortly afterward Bill, one of my engineering colleagues, who had been on a separate schedule, arrived. Bill was to spend the weekend with us on the Nyika and had very bravely volunteered to drive us over the Chendo track to Karonga.

We started early the following morning. Our destination for the day was only ten miles away but nearly a mile above our heads. To get there we had to travel about ninety miles, first on the sandy Great North Road and then doubling back and climbing through the broken river valleys, the Brachystegia uplands and finally onto the rolling grass-covered heights of the Nyika. Toward mid-day we reached the Northern Rhodesia guest house on the plateau, and after a wash in the cool mountain water we were more than ready for lunch.

After lunch, we drove across to the Nyasaland forestry project headquarters and had a talk with the forestry assistant. He lived there with his wife and small child. His cottage and the guest house were the only buildings on the Nyika. As was to be expected, he badly wanted us to provide him with some communications.

We learned from our discussions there were tremendous bush fires on the plateau and these were driving large numbers of game before them in a northerly direction. We would probably find our own way to the north blocked on certain of the tracks, owing to the intense heat generated by the fires. We stayed with the forestry assistant and his wife for tea. We also met one of the first Bantu African district assistants appointed by the administration.

On our way back to the guest house we had planned to spend the period through dusk watching the animals watering at Kaulima's Pond, which is the source of the North Rukuru River and the watering place for large numbers of the game on the plateau. I had on a previous visit been enthralled watching the game watering there and seeing almost every type except elephants. This time there was ample evidence, both in the droppings and in the spoor marks in the boggy ground, of the recent presence of large numbers of animals. But although we waited through dusk until after dark, we did not see a single creature. Frankie and Bill were most disappointed and, but for the evidence on the ground, might have suggested that all my stories of lion, wart hog, zebra, eland and roan were straight from Baron von Munchhausen.

I think, despite their disappointment, that Bill and Frankie had begun to appreciate the charm of these rolling grass-covered mountains with their wild flowers, butterflies, birds and (if you were lucky) game. This gigantic high plateau, its bracing air and the tremendous views over Lake Nyasa from the eastern and southern edges, is the finest country I know anywhere in Africa. Not the least factor in its charm is its changeability. When the mist descends, it becomes a dank cold, lost world where one is completely isolated and immobilized.

The fascination of the Nyika had brought me back this time on my fourth visit. On each occasion, the plateau had shown a different character. During my first visit it had been dull and cloudy but with fair visibility and very large numbers of game. The second time it was lush and fresh from recent rains, with an unbelievably clear atmosphere and wild flowers of all types. On my third visit, we barely made it to the guest house through the cloud, and the visibility was as poor as in the London fogs of my youth. We saw nothing and nearly died of cold at night despite our blankets. This time the land was dry and parched under a clear blue sky but with the smell of burning grass in the air.

After our long wait at Kaulima's Pond, we returned to the guest house, our head-lamps outlining the track under the dark moonless sky but with an ominous red glow to the north. We were glad of all the available blankets during the night with temperatures not much above freezing point.

We had intended to make a pre-dawn visit to Kaulima but slept too long. Because of the fires, we probably missed nothing. After a leisurely breakfast, we decided, for the sake of Bill and Frankie, to visit the more spectacular southern part of the plateau. A reasonable track had been cut all the way to the edge of the escarpment above Nchenachena. However, you had to be completely sure of your car's performance at high altitude, as certain of the slopes you had to climb on the return journey were very steep indeed. I discovered this to my cost on a previous visit, when two of us had to help push a friend's car up one of these slopes, knowing that if we failed in our efforts we had a twenty-mile walk in the dark to the guest house. As we had just been watching two lions stalking zebra in the direction we had to take, this was not an inviting prospect.

On our drive to the point above Nchenachena, we saw many francolin, one bustard, the ubiquitous widow birds, with their long trailing black tails, and a few brightly coloured sunbirds. At one point, we saw a small herd of six zebra, but they were nearly a mile away. The view from the track on the final spur above Nchenachena is glorious. You look out over the Henga Valley through to Livingstonia, which stands out on a ridge from the lower plateau. In the background is the shoreline and expanse of the lake. This is not as spectacular as the view looking almost sheer downward from the eastern edge of the escarpment, but this involves a long walk over the Nyika grasslands.

This southern part of the plateau is most attractive in its flora and offers a wonderful, and almost patriotic, display of wild flowers growing in profusion with its red aloes, white geranium and blue delphinium. There is another English impression in the red admiral and painted lady butterflies we know so well in England, besides a profusion of other species which would need an experienced entomologist to classify.

We had a picnic lunch amongst the flowers and butterflies on the southern part of the plateau and then returned along the way we had come to the forestry encampment near Kaulima. Fortunately, Bill's confidence in his car's climbing ability was justified, and I did not have again to test my stamina at high altitude.

From the encampment we took the track to the north and the area of bush fires. Shortly, we saw our first roan antelope and eland standing disconsolately at the track side. From here on, as we approached the grass fires, we saw increasing numbers of game of all types. At one time looking down into a valley from a small ridge, we counted more than a hundred eland, roan and zebra apparently forming one large but straggling herd, the animals pointing unhappily northwards toward the smoke and flames. We left the main track and skirted this burning area, which we estimated was some two miles in depth and ten miles wide.

We managed on our secondary track to find a way through the burning area to a ridge from where we could look over to Msawa, the Nyika's highest point, from which you had the finest view of the rolling countryside the plateau provides. It was impossible to go any further owing to the fires. Depressed by the results of this possibly man-made devastation, we returned to the guest house in the early afternoon and settled down by the fire for a quiet evening and early night. Tomorrow we had to face what we understood was the most difficult car track in Africa. It was seldom undertaken by car and was even difficult in a four-wheel-drive vehicle. I kicked myself for not bringing my radio equipment in case we needed to call for help.

Leaving very early the following morning, we reached the plain before the heat of the day and travelled northward through Northern Rhodesia to Fort Hill, the most northerly village in Nyasaland. After a short visit to the post office, we travelled back a few miles along the Great North Road to Chisenga and then turned eastward on the road to Misuku, which also led to the Chendo track. We had studied our route and knew that the Chendo track was virtually a mountain path which ran first through the Misuku hills and then down the escarpment to the lakeshore plain, joining the Stevenson track which had been the old bearer route connecting Karonga with Northern Rhodesia.

The first ten miles was reasonable, as it carried traffic to Misuku, a coffee-growing area. It was at Misuku where our postal agent "borrowed" £300 to pay the bride price for the local chief's daughter. This fairly good road was almost our undoing. We overlooked the turning to the Chendo track proper, not that there was much to miss other than a rock-strewn path.

When we returned and entered the track, it was a constant nightmare. No section remained straight for more than a few yards, the surface was frightful, consisting largely of boulders, and the track went up and down monotonously, with some sections having a gradient of at least one in three. Fortunately these were all short, and we could get over the top by rushing them, to the detriment of the springs and with me pushing from behind. In other places, the track was made up of loose stones; you could not get a grip, and the car lost way rapidly. Again, I had to supply part of the motive power. In places, we followed natural stream beds which were fortunately dry at this time of the year, but the rocks and sand did not make for any better going. Frankie had collapsed into an uncharacteristic silence, and a grim-faced Bill sat at the wheel listening to the bottom of his car hitting the rocks.

As we progressed, we kept thinking optimistically that it must get better. It could not get any worse, as another car had done it a few years earlier and a jeep had been through last year. If they could do it, we would. This buoyed us up to continue, and finally we reached the edge of the escarpment and started the long run down onto the lakeshore plain.

The track was still frightful, with gullies crossing it, but at least we did not have to rush the hard sections, and I no longer had to push. We even began to take an interest in the countryside and found that this section was really lovely. The whole of the side of the escarpment was heavily treed, and the autumnal shadings were marvellous. Also we had frequent glimpses of the blue lake below vignetted by the colourful trees.

Finally, we reached the lake shore and our last twelve miles into Karonga. This was easy going along the old Stevenson track, the route taken by the old-time bearers carrying heavy loads to Northern Rhodesia. We arrived at the rest house in Karonga as the sun set and could at last take stock of the position. We could hardly prevent laughing at one another. We were red with dust, with just the lids of our eyes showing white. An examination of the car showed a few dents underneath but no major damage.

From the Great North Road to Karonga over the track was fifty-six miles, of which, I estimate, I helped push the car five miles. We started our journey at 11 a.m. and arrived at Karonga at 7 p.m., an average speed of 7 m.p.h. If the sections over the Misuku and Stevenson roads, where we were able to travel at about 20 m.p.h, were excluded, our average over the Chendo track proper was under 5 m.p.h.

I will not describe our journey back to Rumpi, which was the section I had undertaken earlier in the car without brakes. When we arrived, I again got out the mobile radio equipment and established contact with Paddy, to learn all was well at headquarters.

We left Rumpi in our own car the following morning, journeying southward. After spending the rest of the week working in Lilongwe, we ran down to the Grand Beach Hotel at Salima for the weekend. The hotel was managed by an old friend I had first met when he was running the hotel at Cape Maclear. The Grand Beach was opened when the Maclear hotel closed down.

The Grand Beach Hotel had excellent facilities, was extremely well-run and located on one of the best beaches in the world. In 1955 the cost with full board was 25s. per person, per day. It was a shock two years later to find myself paying twenty times as much in Jamaica for a poorer hotel in a less attractive location. Such are the effects of tourism and proximity to a large, wealthy country.

Early on the Monday morning we left for Zomba. We made stops for lunch at Dedza and to pick up Portuguese red wine. After crossing the Shire River at Liwonde, we made one final stop to refresh ourselves in a warm mineral pool which is close to the river and about one mile from the ferry. This pool was fed by a stream which rises out of the ground and gives the impression that it might at one time have been a geyser. The water rises from the rocks only a few yards from, but above the level of, the Shire River and is at near-boiling point.

Late in the evening we arrived in Zomba to be welcomed by our boys and Nickie and to settle down to our normal day-to-day existence. Frankie's first and only *ulendo* was at an end.

*   *   *

Just before leaving Nyasaland, I decided to make my last *ulendo* to say goodbye to my staff and visit most of our main offices. As I had never travelled by lake steamer, I decided to use this type of transportation for at least part of the journey.

My route was from Zomba to Monkey Bay by car, then by lake steamer through Chipoka, Kota Kota and Likoma Island to Nkata Bay, where a member of our staff would meet me and take me to Mzuzu. From Mzuzu, I planned day journeys to Livingstonia and Njakwa, then to return by air via Mzimba and Lilongwe to Zomba.

Leaving early on the first morning by car, we skirted around Zomba Mountain and made a short visit to our training school. We were very proud of this school, which was originally located at one of the bishop's missions. It had since been expanded and removed to our own accommodation with its own hostel. The fact that we had managed to reduce the ratio of European to African staff while carrying out major expansion and development was almost wholly the result of the facilities provided by the school and the dedication of its staff.

In the early years of federation, many visitors came to see what we were doing at the school. These included the Governor General of the Rhodesias and Nyasaland, and Sir Roy Welensky. I took them round and discussed our educational programmes and courses, and I think that they were impressed by what we had achieved.

The chief postal instructor was the wee Aberdonian who once tried the Indian rope trick. Although he never managed to teach this to his students, a number subsequently did a good disappearing act, taking some of our cash with them. Perhaps not surprisingly, many of our postal staff also acquired a broad Scottish accent.

The chief engineering instructor was Len Laycock. Len was what is usually termed a fine figure of a man. Tall and broad-shouldered, with the stance of an army sergeant major and a voice to go with it, he had a commanding personality. The African students were not only impressed by his teaching but also admired him greatly, as the following story shows.

Some year or so before my farewell visit, we were going through some applications for employment. Most of these listed the usual occupations of postal clerk, telegraphist, engineer etc. Len's fame had spread, however, and amongst the applications was one addressed to The Chief Laycock, Laycock's Dept, Zomba. This simply said, "I should like to be a Laycock."

After the visit to our training school, we descended into the Shire Valley and the Liwonde ferry. Before crossing on the ferry, we paused to look at the Liwonde bund, which had been constructed at a cost of some hundred thousand pounds as an advance measure to control the level of Lake Nyasa and secure an adequate flow of water in the Shire River when a permanent dam and hydro-electric station were built.

The hydrological consultants had studied the available records, flow figures and evaporation and had calculated that the level of the lake would fall seriously over the next few years if the bund was not constructed. Africa has, however, an almost unique capacity for confounding experts. After the bund was completed, the level of the lake started to rise alarmingly, and shortly after I left Nyasaland it was necessary to breach the bund to avoid widespread flooding of the lake-shore areas. This was in the future, however.

On the day I was there, the river valley below the bund was empty of water and full of bright yellow flowers. The absence of water below the bund also allowed me to examine the piers of the old bridge across the river, which had been washed away during flood conditions in 1924 and never replaced. We used to watch the crocodiles sunning themselves on these piers before the bund was constructed. Presumably they had moved downstream.

Returning to the ferry, we took our car onto it and were pulled across the river by the team of ferry men. Today there was no water flow, owing to the bund. My thoughts went back to the many times I had crossed with a full river flow, when you always stood a chance of the cable breaking and the ferry going downstream out of control. The ferry men seemed to have lost interest, possibly because of the depressing effects of federation, and the crossing was silent but for the orders of the leader. I felt sad in missing the rhythmic stamping of feet as the cable was pulled along and the songs, even though they were usually so uncomplimentary about the passengers and their ancestors.

On many of my previous trips it had been moving and fascinating to cross the river, frequently on my own, usually in the late evening and after a drive of hundreds of miles, with the last traces of sunset in the sky, the noises of the frogs and insects and with the ferrymen stamping and singing as they pulled you across. Crossing now had none of the old romance.

Once we had crossed the river, we drove rapidly on our way. It was now very hot and sticky at this lower altitude as we drove over the undulating sandy road to Fort Johnstone. This was a densely populated area, and we passed many villages and villagers, who would disappear into the cloud of dust as our car went by. We passed several lorries carrying fresh and dried fish from the lake. There was an extremely heavy (and smelly) traffic in fish over this road, as most fishing activities were concentrated in the southern arms of the lake from which distribution took place to the whole of the southern province.

Vegetation through this area was interesting. The Walt Disney-ish baobab trees look as if they have been planted upside down and have their roots in the air, and the sausage trees have long appendages resembling sausages some two feet long and three inches in diameter. There were also various types of tropical cactus, some of which were twenty to thirty feet high.

Soon we passed Lake Malombe on our right, then rapidly came into Fort Johnstone, an early European settlement. After a short stay there, we followed the lake shore toward Monkey Bay, passing the famous but outdated sign "Beware of elephants on this road". No one had seen an elephant on that road in the last ten years, but it seemed a pity to take the sign down.

Some way up the lake we stopped to say farewell to my old friend Doc, who had left Zomba and built a house on the lake shore. It was very apparent that the lake was not behaving as predicted, and the rise in its level was becoming serious. The beach no longer existed, and the bank, on which his house stood, was being undermined.

After tea we went on to the hotel at Monkey Bay, and I had my first swim in the lake for many months. The beach and water were not as good as farther up the lake, but we had spent many pleasant weekends here. It was near this hotel that we were once chased by a hippo. I had an early dinner and then to bed. I was due to board the lake steamer *Ilala* at 5.30 a.m. next morning.

I was out in good time to a morning prescient with the coming light of day, although the sun had not risen. The lake was like a mirror without a ripple on its surface. Walking a few hundred yards to the steamer jetty, I made my way through a large crowd of Africans who had already gathered to board the ship, see someone off or just to see

Lake Nyasa, the Ilala.

what was going on. To go on board I had to squeeze my way through the talking, laughing Bantus with their bundles, babies and bicycles.

Although it was an hour before sailing time, the lower deck was already solidly packed with humanity and their possessions. Some of these people would be spending one or more nights on the ship. There was hardly enough room for them to stand, let alone lie down. I was fortunate not only in travelling on the upper deck but in having the owner's cabin for my use.

While we were waiting to sail, I watched a continuous procession of more people coming on board, their friends talking and laughing with them. Presently the softness of the pre-dawn light was replaced by the harsher rays of the rising African sun, and the scene then stood out in all its colour accompanied by the humour, and joy, of the passengers and those seeing them off. This despite all the crowding and discomfort.

About 6.30 a.m., we sailed, setting course northward along the coast of Cape Maclear. Here, we passed the ruins of the hotel in which I stayed on my first arrival in the country when it was also the Sunderland flying boat terminal. This was also the site of the first Church of Scotland mission and was one of the loveliest points on the lake with its hilly peninsula standing out between the two lower arms of the lake and its wonderful beaches and clear water. It was also famed for its sunsets. It was not, therefore, surprising that it was first selected by the missionaries as the site for their mission and many years later became the site for the most attractive hotel in the country.

Unfortunately, without modern tropical medicine the location proved to be unhealthy. It was also difficult of access except from the sea, owing to the mountainous nature of the district and the number of streams flowing into the lake. After the flying boat service ceased, the hotel lost its main *raison d'être*. It continued to operate for a few years, but its owners then decided to abandon the skeleton of the building and move the bulk of the facilities to Salima, where they opened the Grand Beach Hotel.

Besides being beautiful, Cape Maclear was a wild and isolated spot. Once, while staying there, I had a rather alarming experience with a pack of baboons. I had taken Nickie with me to a radio station we had set up at the extreme point of the peninsula. On my return, and seeing I was unarmed, the baboons closed in on me in a menacing manner, barking all the time and trying to separate me from the dog. I managed to hold them off with a few well-directed stones and reach the hotel safely. The next day I again went to the station but this time carrying a gun. As I expected, the baboons, although still abusing and jeering me, stayed out of range, posting scouts in the trees to watch closely and moving back as I approached.

Cape Maclear was also famous for the size of its crocodiles. But owing to the clearness of the water, the only recorded case of an attack on a guest from the hotel was when the latter was foolish enough to take a midnight swim.

Once we had rounded the cape, we sailed across the western arm of the lake and docked at Chipoka, the northern rail terminal for the rail line from the port of Beira in Portuguese East Africa. Here was further evidence of the effects of the high water level. An engine pulling four coaches and weighing about 100 tons had tried to approach the dock over a line which had been undermined by the flood water. This was unable to support it, and the train had turned over on its side, where it was being contemplated by a crowd of several hundred Africans, including the railway staff. Fortunately, no one was injured in the accident.

I visited the Chipoka office, wandered about the village and then returned on board for dinner, a talk with the captain about sailing conditions on the lake, and then bed.

I returned to the shore in the morning to see if any progress had been made with the derailed train but found it still lying on its side, surrounded by a large group, with the railway staff preferring contemplation to action. Knowing Africa, I wonder if they ever righted it; or, alternatively, built a new track around this point. In the meantime the overnight train from the south had come in, and several first-class passengers were embarking.

We sailed quite early in the morning. Looking back, I saw Dedza mountain, where we had done so much work, standing out against the morning sky. We were now sailing northward at a distance of about one mile from the west shore of the lake. Soon, we passed Salima with its two tourist hotels of Senga Bay and Grand Beach.

There was now a fresh breeze. Several sailing boats were out from the Grand Beach Hotel. When I was last there, I had watched two Southern Rhodesians taking out one of these boats. Southern Rhodesia is land-locked, and these lads had probably never seen a sailing boat before. Fortunately, they had a native boatman with them, but they gave him a very hard time. Every few seconds they jibed the boat, usually with the boatman's head in the way of the boom. He may have had a thick skull, but finally this was too much for him. Reeling from the repeated blows, he staggered to the bow and lowered the sail, refusing despite entreaties, arguments, curses and bribes to raise it again and forcing his crew to ignominiously paddle the boat to the shore. Seriously, the lake is no place for beginners owing to the speed with which conditions can change and very rough seas develop.

In the late afternoon, we docked at Kota Kota, once one of the main slave trading centres and now a prosperous rice-growing area. I had last been in Kota Kota at the time of the bunding riots, when I had flown in with the commissioner of police, and we had anxiously circled the landing strip looking for obstructions and possible attackers before landing. This evening I was met by the manager of the rice growers' co-operative, who was in no small part responsible for the prosperity of the area and who took an interest in all activities, including our post office. He was a German, with many years experience in Central Africa, and was doing a first-class job not only in developing and extending rice production, thus improving the economic position of the people, but also in organizing trading activities.

After we had inspected the post office and visited his trading store – a model for the country with prices well below the ruling Indian store prices – he took me, at my request, to see the old African ivory carver and his sons who were the last survivors of a trade, probably brought in by the Arabs. The carvings they produced ranged from decorated ivory buttons to tusks carved in their entirety. There was considerable artistry in the design of these items and the standard of workmanship was excellent. The carvers told me that they were facing difficulty in obtaining supplies of ivory, and it seemed likely that the old carver's craft was a dying one. Many of Ali Baba's better carvings had come from this source.

Before leaving, I ordered an ivory chess set. Because of the work involved, the first eight pieces arrived only shortly before I left Nyasaland. I never expected to receive the remainder, but they followed me to Jamaica many months later.

After a drink at my friend's pleasant house, I re-embarked for the night crossing to Likoma Island.

The Mwera was now blowing strongly, and the *Ilala* pitched and rolled as we left Kota Kota, sailing on a north east course directly across the lake. The Mwera is the most dangerous of the Lake Nyasa winds. It caused the capsizing of Bishop Chauncy Maples' sailing boat in September 1885, with the loss of the bishop and most of his crew. The bishop was buried in the chancel of the Kota Kota Church. When the first mission steamer was launched in 1901, it was named after the bishop. Unfortunately, it was very unreliable and had a habit of breaking down, so it became known as the *Chancy Maples*. The *Chancy Maples* continued to operate as a mission steamer until 1953, when it was sold to one of the fishing concerns who still used it in their operations.

During the Mwera season in July 1946, a major lake disaster took place, north of Nkata Bay, when the new 200-ton steamer *Vypia* capsized as reported earlier. Tonight, although uncomfortable, was not dangerous as we ploughed our way across the lake.

At dinner, I met two lady missionaries who had embarked at Chipoka. One, a nursing sister, soon felt the effect of the rough seas and had to leave us. The other, a lady doctor, had recently worked in a leprosarium, if I remember rightly, in Tanganyika. She was an interesting if somewhat horrifying companion as she recounted her experiences and the clinical effects of this terrible disease. As a result of this conversation I itched all over as I returned to my cabin, and made very complete ablutions before going to bed. The fact that such self-sacrificing services were being provided by some missions left me with a sense of humility at the smallness of my own efforts and of pride in these dedicated Christians.

We were up to a golden dawn as the ship anchored some fifty yards off the shore of Likoma Island. The wind had gone down, as it usually does during the early hours of the morning. Sheltered between the island and the Portuguese coast line the sea was dead calm. As soon as the motor tender could be launched, we started for the shore. Likoma Island had an idyllic coast line with its white sand beaches, rocky promontories and green hills rising up to the higher parts of the island. Almost everywhere there were baobab trees, which stood like bewitched people in a fairy story, bare branches held out like arms in supplication.

The arrival of the steamer was an event, and the shore was lined by hundreds of people dressed in all the colours of the rainbow. The bare piccaninnies were in the water splashing themselves and their parents and creating movement to add to the colour of the scene. Drawn up on the beach were several dugouts. A dhow leaving the bay looked as if it dated back to the times of the slave traders.

The lady missionaries, one still looking as if she had made an ocean crossing in a storm, left us here to take up work on the island. I went to have a look at the post office and meet my staff.

Then I made my way to the cathedral, a very large brick building about 300 feet long and 80 feet wide. I had first flown over it when I arrived by flying boat in 1950 and wondered what such an enormous building, set in the wilds of Africa, could possibly be. While impressed by its size, I had also been struck by the incongruity of its galvanized sheet roof. The cathedral was fittingly constructed on the site of a *cipyela*, or witchcraft burning place. The size was needed as the large population of the island was almost wholly Christian and much given to church-going. Our Wilson came from Likoma and, if allowed to do so, would happily attend every church service in Zomba on a Sunday, working his way down, or up, from Catholic to Seventh-Day Adventist.

The increasing population of Likoma Island was a problem despite many of the men being absent on the mainland, or working as migrant labour outside Nyasaland. It was becoming impossible to keep the rest of the population occupied. With the island's limited area and resources, the problem was likely to become more difficult in the future. The island nevertheless gave an impression of well-being and a sign of the order and peace the Universities Mission had helped bring to Africa.

After leaving the cathedral, and with some difficulty, I made my way to the highest point on the island to gain an overall impression of the topography. Seeing the island spread out below provided an aspect of the beauty of the place with its peaceful villages, mission centre and cathedral forming a quiet, if rather isolated, community for Christian teaching.

My friend the bishop, although of another persuasion, had suggested I should call on Archdeacon Cox, who had served at the mission for more than forty years. The morning service had just ended, however, and the road was crowded with thousands of members of the congregation, making access to the mission difficult. Added to this, I could hear the *Ilala* blowing her siren with some urgency. Rather than meet the venerable gentleman, I had to run the remaining quarter of a mile to the beach. I had no wish, however pleasant the community, to remain on Likoma Island until the next steamer arrived in a month's time, or to cross in a dhow to the mainland and make my way home through Portuguese territory. Nonetheless, I left the island with a very real appreciation of how much the mission had achieved since it was first established by Bishop Smythies in 1884.

The usual colourful crowd of Africans thronged the shore and waved goodbye to their friends who were going over to the mainland. We first sailed along the baobab-lined shore to the northern tip of the island, then turned across the lake toward Nkata Bay. As we came out from the sheltered water between Likoma and the Portuguese coast, we again met the Mwera, although the sea was not as rough as it had been the previous night.

During the crossing to the mainland, we ran quite close to two columns of Nkungu flies but they had been partially dispersed, and only a few were blown onto the ship. As the hours passed, the main shore line became closer, and the Vipya Mountains were clearer and loomed higher. Finally, we could pick out the houses on the peninsula guarding the entrance to Nkata Bay harbour. This, which we entered shortly, was almost land-locked. On one of the peninsulas forming the bay, the Boma and rest house stood. As was the case with many lake shore buildings, both were bat-infested and I remembered the times I had stayed in the rest house and these creatures had zoomed past my head while I undressed. Fortunately, as rabies was prevalent, they had no vampire tendencies.

I was to disembark from the *Ilala* at Nkata Bay and was met by John, the senior member of our staff in the northern province. He had driven down that morning from Mzuzu and at times had found the roads so bad that he doubted if he could get through to meet me. It was only then that I learned that on the previous day more than 21 inches of rain had fallen in a few hours. We had lunch on board and afterward called on the district commissioner and visited our office.

I had last been in Nkata Bay in 1956, when we had arranged publicity on the introduction of a Land Rover service replacing what we believed was the last inter-office mail carrier service in Africa. This had operated for many years between Nkata Bay and Chinteche. The Atonga have firm ideas on the woman's place in society, which is wherever and whenever there is hard work to be done; and this service was unique in that the mail carriers were female carriers. The ladies earned about 1s. 6d. for a walk of about nineteen miles through the bush, crossing two rivers, one of which was a favourite haunt of crocodiles, and taking two days on the journey. Each carried about 20 lbs of mail on her head. The mail used to go through twice a week on this basis and with much greater reliability and regularity than it did after introduction of the Land Rover service.

We issued a press release, and the reference to a female mail carrier service attracted worldwide attention. *I recently supplied the Malawi Archives Dept with copies of photographs I had taken at the time.*

Also during my last visit to Nkata Bay there had been considerable excitement resulting from the discovery of the Lake Nyasa eel by the fisheries unit located there. I inspected this monster, which was about three feet long and as thick as my wrist.

After completing our work in Nkata Bay, we left for Mzuzu. I had hoped, for the last time, to go straight up into the Vipya range over the Timberi track, with its wooded slopes and views over the lake. This was, at its best, a difficult road for cars and under present conditions impossible. After a trying but uneventful journey, we arrived at Mzuzu, the provincial headquarters.

Mzuzu had been developed as the centre of a previous Colonial Development Corporation tung-growing project, and tung was still produced in the area. Mzuzu was a pleasant station, but, due to its altitude and located as it was on the windward side of the Vipya range, it was subject to heavy rainfall and frequent clouds and mist. There

Female mail carriers, Nkata Bay–Chinteche.

was a considerable amount of rain forest in the vicinity, and the area had many wild orchids.

I stayed with John and his family. After an early night, we left at dawn to visit Njakwa, Rumpi and Livingstonia, my furthest point north on this trip. The visits to Njakwa and Rumpi, although sad occasions for me in saying farewell to many of my old friends, were not of general interest.

Livingstonia occupied one of the loveliest and healthiest situations in the protectorate. It was located on the edge of a mountain ridge standing out from the Nyika Plateau, with a narrow coastal belt between the foot of the mountain and Lake Nyasa. This ridge was called Mount Laws after the mission's founder. As you stood on the edge of Mount Laws and looked out over the lake, the view was breathtaking. The lake was virtually at your feet, but 3,000 feet below. From this altitude, you could see right across the lake to the mountain

ranges above Songea in Tanganyika. Looking northward you followed
the coastline along Florence and Deep Bays, with their glistening white
sands, to the plains of Karonga. Not only did the lake have its highest
mountains rising on either side at this point but off Deep Bay was the
greatest depth of water – more than 2,700 feet.

The mission at Livingstonia was a township in itself, with a tradition
of Christian service and education. I felt, however, that – given the
superb location with its views over the lake and surrounding mountains – the layout, architecture and standard of the mission buildings
was disappointing and not nearly as fitting as those on Likoma Island
(despite the cathedral's tin roof). I was also a little concerned to note
some lack of maintenance of the premises and a general impression of
untidiness. As I was going down with a bout of malaria, my impressions were probably biased and over-negative. This mission and its
sister establishment in Blantyre had longer records of achievement and Christian progress than any of the other missions in the
country. We had ample evidence of its educational and character
achievements, as we had recruited some excellent staff who had been
trained at these establishments. Our office at Livingstonia was a small
one, and I did not stay long after my tour of the mission, talks with
the missionaries and farewells to the staff.

Mandewe Falls.

Although the road to Kar-
onga passed close to the mission I did not go any farther
northward on this trip. The
road from near the mission to

Florence Bay, which was constructed in the days of the great Dr Laws, runs quite close to a precipice before it starts winding backward and forward down the mountainside. This was the infamous road I had once to climb without proper brakes on my car. From the precipice at the top, a stream rising in the Nyika plunges more than 1,100 feet, mainly in one fall. This fall, known as Mandewe, is one of the most impressive sights in the country. I once climbed down the river when the water flow was low and looked over the edge but found it rather terrifying. There were interesting caves at the foot of the fall, but access was difficult and I never got to see them.

It appeared there might be some prospects of mining activities in the area near the mission, as coal deposits had recently been found and, although broken and difficult of access, seemed to be extensive.

After some fourteen hours on the road and visits to a number of offices, where I had to listen and reply to speeches of farewell, I returned to Mzuzu feeling tired and dispirited and shivering from the effects of malaria.

I spent the next day on local business. In the evening, I had to attend a cocktail party in my honour, where, amongst other old friends and colleagues, I had the pleasure of getting together with the local monsignor who, like his bishop, was doing much for the advancement of his mission and the education of his students, not only in Christian principles but also in the sanctity of work and responsibility to one's fellow men. A French Canadian, he was another of the men who really mattered in the country.

In the morning, the mist was down, and I began to wonder if the plane could get in and I would be able to leave Mzuzu that day. I remembered how I had once flown to the northern province in the government aircraft piloted by the director of civil aviation, who had been a World War II flying ace. The first part of the flight had been clear, but suddenly we found the ground over most of the province covered by low cloud. We flew round for about an hour with our fuel supplies dwindling and little prospect of getting back to Lilongwe in the central province. Finally, we found a small clearing in the clouds and managed to land at Mzimba.

The mist cleared, after an hour or so, and the Beaver in which I was to fly to Lilongwe came roaring in to the short runway. We took off after a short stop and flew across the Vipya, passing Mount Hora on the right and then landing at Mzimba. On the way, the pilot, who was new to the run, told me of the many game he had seen on his flight from Karonga across the Nyika.

Although, due to time pressures and the flight schedules, I had been unable to allow for a stay-over at Mzimba, I was delighted, on getting out of the plane to stretch my legs, to find the whole office staff, including the office messenger, drawn up on the airfield to greet me. The postmaster advanced to the front and proceeded to read a long speech of fulsome praise. He rather spoilt the effect of his long per-oration and rather shook me by ending, "and finally, we are very happy to say goodbye to you, sir." The pilot waited while I expressed my appreciation for their good work and loyal service, and then we roared down the runway and were on our way to Lilongwe.

Flying southward we followed the edge of the Vipya range and flew over the plain broken by Kasungu mountain with its pleasant Boma on the lower slopes. Then we passed the Bua River, and the land started to rise to the central plateau, with Dowa mountain as its highest point. Dowa was a delightful hill station with the mountain rising up to about 5,000 feet. As we flew over I could see our radio masts on the top. Shortly afterward we started to lose altitude before landing at Lilongwe. I had now a raging fever but almost immediately after arrival managed to get the Camaquin I needed to treat my malaria.

I spent two days in Lilongwe, mainly on business but also meeting old friends. I stayed with Ian, the deputy provincial commissioner and his wife Joan, who had lived for some years in the house adjoining ours in Zomba. I also again visited Marjory and her husband Frank, who lived a little outside of Lilongwe and had one of the most attractive houses and delightful estates in the country. Frank was interested in viticulture and was an expert on South African wines, which he maintained, I believe rightly, were amongst the best in the world. Had the climate allowed, he would have dearly loved to produce wines in Nyasaland.

After a final farewell party in Lilongwe, I left by air flying south-ward over Dedza mountain, where I had so many times toiled to the top before we built the road, then over the edge of the plateau crossing the Shire west of the usual route and close to the almost dry Murchison Falls with Zomba mountain looming up ahead of us. Finally, leaving the mountain on our port side, we flew over Zomba township, which I saw for the last time from the air before landing. This was, I may add, not a characteristic *ulendo*, as it was done in comparative comfort.

Chapter 12

To Travel rather than to Arrive

In addition to *ulendo* journeys within Nyasaland, we had some real adventures travelling to and from the country. Travel became an essential part of our lives and indeed was one of the rewards we had from working in the Colonial Service. This chapter describes a few of our leaves and journeys.

I had the interesting experience of flying from England to Nyasaland on a Sunderland flying boat making one of the last flights of the Empire Flying Boat Service. This service operated to India and Africa and was a magnificent conception which, perhaps fittingly, died with the British Empire. It was originally planned to extend the service to Australia, and for many years you could see the larger, nearly completed but abandoned, Princess-type flying boats on the banks of Southampton Water. The then head of British Airways decided that the future of commercial flying lay with the more accessible, higher-capacity, land-based airports. He was probably right, but I have always felt that something special died with the flying boat services which had been used in both the USA and Europe to open up long-distance air travel.

I well remember saying goodbye to my tearful parents, who doubted if they would ever see me again, in the First Class lounge at Southampton. The aircraft took off mid-morning and, at a speed of 200 knots, reached Augusta on Sicily in the afternoon. We flew in over an erupting Etna to land in the sheltered straits near this small town.

The hotel was adequate, and after dinner I went for a walk. I was horrified by the poverty, with communist slogans everywhere. During my walk, I was pestered by small boys who wanted to sell their sisters. The town had little architectural interest and lacked the beauty of nearby Catania. I was glad to escape back to my hotel for an early night. Before turning in, I tried to telephone friends in Vittoria, only fifty miles away, but found the telephone lines were, like everything else, run down and out of service.

We were up at 5 a.m. for a 6 a.m. take off. We flew across the Mediterranean at about 4,000 feet, landing outside Alexandria in time for early lunch and a brief walk. I was intrigued by a lame beggar who kept saying, "Poor man, broke his leg skiing." I wonder what alpinist taught him this.

After lunch, we took off for Luxor, on the Nile, in upper Egypt, where we landed in the early afternoon. After checking in at the Luxor Palace hotel, we had time to visit the Luxor Temple and see the grandeur of Karnak. Although we could look across at the Valley of Kings, outlined by the beauty of the setting sun over the Nile, we had no time for a visit before dark. *One of my regrets in a lifetime of travelling, with several visits to Egypt, is that I never returned to Luxor.*

We left at 5.30 the next morning for our most strenuous day's flying. First, up the Nile Valley, noting how narrow the fertile basin was; then over the Aswan Dam, one of the very few aid projects in Africa partly financed by the Russians. We tried to pick out Abu Simmel and the ongoing work to remove the artifacts, but I am afraid we missed it. After leaving Aswan, we flew out over the Nubian Desert.

The captain had joined us, and I asked him what we did if an emergency forced us to land. He assured me that a flying boat emergency landing, on land, was much safer than that of a conventional aircraft owing to the strength of the hull. There had been one such landing in the Sahara, and no one had even been injured.

Again, we rejoined the Nile and at mid-day landed at Khartoum at the confluence of the White and Blue Niles. We had not much time to see Khartoum, Gordon and El Mahdi's city, rebuilt after the rebellion with a street pattern based on that of the Union Jack. After a short lunch and brief walk through the inner city, we rejoined the flying boat and took off for Entebbe in Uganda. As we left Khartoum, we had a good view of the junction of the two rivers, the Blue Nile clear and swift-flowing from the mountains of Ethiopia and Lake Tana *which I was to visit many years later* and the White Nile brown and muddy from its flow through the desert and the sudd of the Sudan.

Gradually, we left the infertile desert area, flying first over the green banks and sudd filled tributaries of the upper Nile and then over the plateau of Uganda with its cultivated areas and small African villages. We landed at Entebbe, on Lake Victoria, almost exactly on the equator, just before sunset. This was my first experience of one of the African lakes, the African food and African servants. There was little to do in the evening except listen to the frogs and cicadas and talk to the other passengers and crew.

We were up early in the morning for what was, for me, to be the last section. Our flight path was over Lake Victoria and then down over central Tanganyika to the northern tip of Lake Nyasa. This left the mountains of Kenya and Tanganyika well to the east and the Ruwenzori range to the west. My main impression, as we flew over the endless vista of Africa, was of its enormous size and sparse population.

Finally, we came to Lake Nyasa, so clear and blue in the mid-day sun and framed by its surrounding mountains and plateau. This must, I felt, be the most beautiful lake in Africa and probably in the world. I only began to realize its size as we flew almost its entire length, seeing the cathedral and settlement on Likoma Island and later landing at Cape Maclear on the peninsula splitting the two lower branches of the lake.

After lunch, I watched the flying boat take off on its final section to Northern Rhodesia (it flew alternate flights to Northern Rhodesia and South Africa) and spent the afternoon swimming and lazing in the sun. In the morning a short trip by bus to Monkey Bay, and then a one-hour flight by Beaver to Zomba and my new life and job.

*   *   *

Every two and a half to three years the colonial staff in Nyasaland went on home leave. The periods of leave allowed were extremely generous, based as they were on the early conditions in the country, poor medical services and lack of most amenities. As a result, and depending on the method of travel selected, colonial officers were absent from their posts for from six to nine months every three years.

With improved amenities and services, it was questionable whether such lengthy periods of leave were necessary for the health and well-being of the individual. I always felt that it would have been better to shorten the leave periods and use the funds saved to increase the staff's low salaries. This also would have increased working efficiency. The prolonged break in duty was disruptive, and officers lost touch with conditions which might change rapidly during their absences. People acting in their place would seldom be prepared to make policy decisions during their absence. For all the disadvantages to the service, however, these periods of leave could be very pleasant for the individuals and their families.

The Colonial Office was very accommodating in accepting officers' leave plans if they wished to vary the normal straightforward return trip to the United Kingdom. Providing you met excess costs, you could follow any route and use any form of transport you wished. There was, however, a requirement that you should spend the major part of the leave in a temperate climate.

Travelling by land, sea and air became almost second nature to most colonial staff, and it was not surprising that the more individualistic people followed routes which spread out all over Africa, the Middle East, Europe and sometimes the world itself.

One indomitable woman decided to go home overland. She followed a route via Tanzania, Kenya, Ethiopia, Sudan, Egypt, the Arab countries, Turkey and Greece, travelling largely by bus. It always intrigued me how, located as she was in Nyasaland, she managed to get all the necessary visas. Our chief storekeeper bought a caravan and, with his wife and family, crossed from Nigeria through the Gold Coast, Belgian Congo and Northern Rhodesia on his way back to

Nyasaland. Some of these trips were difficult, and they usually involved some discomfort.

Our leaves were not all holiday. I spent one leave writing a thesis.
Another time I spent a month visiting the British Post Office, research
establishments and various manufacturers and bringing myself up to
date on the latest developments in postal and communication facilities.

While at the beginning Frankie and I took the normal direct routes
to and from Europe, we had some adventures, such as being declared
mutineers by the captain of one of the liners, who, owing to a change
in schedule, wanted to disembark all his Beira passengers at Cape
Town a thousand miles from their destination. On another occasion, I
had to repair the engine of our train in the wilds of Portuguese East
Africa. I was, however, intrigued by the exotic journeys made by our
friends. Finally, our opportunity came when we learned of the Shaw
Saville liner, the *Southern Cross*, making round-the-world trips and
calling at Durban.

*   *   *

In June 1956, having managed with some difficulty to get a cabin on
the *Southern Cross* sailing out of Durban for Liverpool the long way
round, we set out on our most ambitious leave journey. This involved
four days travelling by train and nine weeks by ship. Frankie, who
believed the amount of luggage one needed increased directly in
proportion to the length of the journey, out-did herself; and, despite
my protests, the minimum I could get our luggage down to was two
cabin trunks and five suitcases.

A few days before we were due to leave, misfortune struck. Frankie
went down with flu and was not really fit to undertake the four-day
train journey to Durban. However, we had paid our passages, including the excess we had had to meet, there were only two trains a week,
and it would have been impossible to take our mountain of luggage
by air, so we had to stick to our schedule.

The night before our departure, we stayed with our friends Hilda

and Hans in Limbe. A Swiss couple with a young family, they somewhat understandably went in for cuckoo clocks. These apparently
presented problems in the synchronization of the hands with the
cuckoo. For the sake of the children, the clocks were set on the basis
of sound rather than sight. When therefore I set my watch before going
to bed at 9.00 p.m. it was actually 9.45 p.m. Additionally, the wretched
clocks were not synchronized with one another, and all night long a
cuckoo sounded off every few minutes.

When our friends called us at apparently 4.30 a.m., I did not realize
the true time, and thought they were rather overdoing things. I therefore had a leisurely shave, shower and dressed while a heavy-headed
Frankie remained in bed. I left her to get ready and went into the
dining room, only to return a few seconds later to tell her we had
twelve minutes to reach the station, which was more than a mile away.

Hilda and I went ahead in one car to stow the baggage and try to
delay the train. At 6.05 a.m., five minutes behind the scheduled time
of departure, Hans and Frankie arrived just as they blew the whistle.
I just managed to push Frankie on board and jump in as the train
gathered speed. We came that close to missing our round-the-world
trip, and I have hated cuckoo clocks ever since.

To reach Durban by train from Nyasaland involves a journey of over
2,000 miles, first travelling south to Dondo, in Portuguese East Africa,
then west to Umtali in Southern Rhodesia, north east to Salisbury,
south west to Bulawayo, south through Bechuanaland to Ladysmith,
then east to Johannesburg and Durban.

Besides nearly boxing the compass, the rail line has to fall from 3,000
feet to sea level, rise again to 6,000 feet and then return to sea level as
it twists, turns and snakes its way over the difficult African terrain.

As we were travelling by diesel coach over the first section to
Dondo, we had sent our two trunks ahead by steam train with the
promise of our railway friends that they would be on the night train
from Dondo to Salisbury.

Slowly, as the morning passed, we wound our way across the
southern part of the Shire highlands to Luchenza, then down the

escarpment toward Chiromo following the valleys of the Tuchila and
Rua rivers, which turned and twisted in all directions with Mlanje
sometimes to our side, sometimes in front of us and sometimes behind
us. As we descended, the country flattened, and the heat increased. In
mid-morning we reached Chiromo at the confluence of the Shire and
Rua rivers. Here, we crossed the Shire over a new bridge constructed
in 1950 and replacing a previous bridge washed away during severe
flooding. This was a picturesque point, and we could see two old stern
wheelers anchored by the shore with a third vessel coming downstream.

Shortly afterward we crossed a temporary section of line where the
embankment had been washed away during a cyclone earlier that
year.

The lower river valley was cotton country, hot, humid and climati-
cally horrid, although the river was rather beautiful and many of the
old-timers talked with nostalgia of the good old days they spent there.
Personally, I was always glad to get away from it and back to the high
plateau.

Although there were some heavily treed areas, and timber extraction was one of the local industries, the countryside was flat and open.
It was, in many places, swampy, with large areas of elephant marsh.
Mosquitoes in their thousands destroyed even the peace that the
coolness of evening might otherwise bring and with the other insects
and frogs created an absolute cacophony through the night.

Gradually, we made our way southward, crossing, in the early
afternoon, the bridge over the Zambezi at Santa Ana. This was more
than two miles long and was, at the time, the longest railway bridge
in the world. The bridge and this part of the line were built by the
British to provide Nyasaland with an outlet to the sea. When the
concession expired, ownership would pass to the Portuguese. The
bridge, which was low and on a series of piers, was impressive as an
engineering achievement but had little architectural merit.

The lower Zambezi Valley through which we were now passing was
flat, hot, dry and scenically uninteresting. However, not far away was

Mount Gorongoza, which had been declared a nature reserve and had some of the largest herds of elephant and other game existing in Africa.

Slowly, the long day came to an end, and, as the sun sank over the Zambesi Plain, we arrived at Dondo Junction, some twenty miles from Beira, with a wait of nearly two hours before the night train to Umtali was due. We spent this time on the platform, travel-tired, hungry and tormented by mosquitoes. At last the steam train, on which we were to travel to Rhodesia, pulled in.

Things seldom go right on the African railways. Our first problem was that two scented Portuguese gentlemen were fast asleep in the beds of our reserved compartment. They had obviously had a farewell party, as there were several empty bottles on the floor. Although the compartment was clearly numbered with the number shown on our tickets, the African guard was reluctant to move these members of the ruling race; I had to take the initiative. After a lot of argument, the Portuguese gentlemen finally let us into the compartment but sat staring at us with dislike until I told them that Frankie, who was obviously ill, was suffering from a mysterious and infectious African disease which was probably fatal.

Having lost our friends, our next shock was to find that, although we had had no breakfast or lunch, we would have to stay hungry, as there was no restaurant compartment on the train. There was not even water to drink or wash ourselves in. Worse was to follow; a visit to the guards' cabin led to the discovery that our trunks were not travelling with us as promised.

Dirty, hungry, tired and dispirited, we turned into the previously occupied bunks, which smelled as if drunken pox doctors' clerks had been sleeping in them, and tried to sleep as the train lurched through the heavy African night. As dawn arrived we were climbing through the hills to Umtali and at least some amenities normal to a civilized existence.

A rapid wash in the station waiting room, and breakfast in the restaurant, made us feel much better. I sent a telegram about the missing trunks, requesting a reply to Salisbury. Shortly afterward our friends Jed and Betty arrived and cheered us up even more. Jed, who had previously been the director of geological survey in Nyasaland, had, on retirement, settled in Umtali, one of the loveliest parts of Southern Rhodesia. Umtali is located in a high, delightful valley, at the foot of the Vumba mountains. An attractive town, its surroundings were outstanding with easy access to the massive grandeur of the nearby Nyanga downs.

We had last visited Umtali by car in 1953 and had stopped at a place called Hot Springs some forty miles to the south. Although the springs were public property, a character in a kilt appeared to have established squatter's rights over the area and was offering a popular, and apparently profitable, "cure all" service. If one could believe him, the allegedly radioactive waters would cure anything from asthma to Zollinger-Ellison syndrome. Fortunately, the Southern Rhodesians were a healthy people, and probably no one came to any harm. I personally found the water very hot and the smell of sulphuretted hydrogen terrible.

After our talk with Jed and Betty and a wait of about an hour, we boarded the Southern Rhodesia train for Salisbury and puffed our way up the valley and through the pass to the high plateau. This was pleasant and not very heavily populated country leading into the tobacco growing areas around Marandellas and Salisbury.

Looking out of the train window at Marandellas, I was surprised to see my sister-in-law, who had motored over from Salisbury to meet us. We rapidly disembarked, leaving our bags in the train, and were on our way by car with the pleasant prospect of being in Salisbury for lunch and not having to rejoin the train until evening.

Salisbury and the full comforts of civilization in my brother's house were much appreciated. So was the news that the Trans Zambezi Railway had sent our trunks through on the previous train, two days earlier, and that they should be lying at Salisbury, or Bulawayo. However, the Salisbury station master knew nothing of them, and we began to wonder if we were being passed down the line.

In the evening, on our return to the train, we were pleased to find ex-Nyasaland Post Office colleagues Brian, Malki, Jimmy and their wives, who had transferred to Federal Headquarters in Salisbury, waiting to see us off. It was nice to talk of old times in Nyasaland and about Federation.

Again in the early evening we were on our way across the plains of Southern Rhodesia but this time in comfort, as there was a good dining car, and our coach had washing facilities. In the early morning, we reached Bulawayo, the second city of Southern Rhodesia and an industrial centre of some importance. Although I had not been there before and would have liked to see the city, it was a dank, cold, cloudy day with a strong wind. We decided to stay on the train. I did, however, go in search of our trunks and finally found them amongst a pile of other baggage for the Union of South Africa. Once these were on the train, I felt I had seen enough of Bulawayo.

Toward mid-day the train pulled out, and we spent the rest of the day and night crossing the Bechuanaland Protectorate with its grassy plateau and cattle ranches. In the middle of the following morning, we reached Mafeking, a wild-west-looking town.

Late in the evening, after hours spent crossing the seemingly endless veldt, we drew into Johannesburg, where we had arranged to break our journey and stay with friends. Johannesburg that evening was freezing, and we were glad to gather round a good fire and exchange reminiscences. It was, however, only a short break and early the following morning we left the skyscrapers and broad streets of Johannesburg for Durban.

Most of the day we continued across the veldt, passing the yellow cyanide hills and mountains of mining slack extracted from the gold mines around Jo'burg followed by the waste from the coal mines near Newcastle.

During the night, we descended to the Natal Plain through one of the most beautiful escarpments in southern Africa. We had already motored through this area, however, and were happy to catch up on our sleep. At dawn, five days out of Nyasaland, we arrived in Durban.

After putting Frankie to bed in our hotel, I went to check our passages, make sure the errant trunks had arrived safely and take some of our suitcases to the docks. Again, the trunks were missing. After several hours search I found them at a completely wrong berth and now in bond and seemingly immovable. A little bribery, a lot of persuasion and the help of a friendly taxi driver enabled me to transport them to the correct berth, and I felt I could at last relax for the next nine weeks. With nothing better to do, and exhausted and hungry from my struggles with our baggage, I went to a waterfront restaurant and had a light meal of wonderful Indian Ocean prawns.

I then decided to do something I had never done before and take a rickshaw back to the hotel. I had always hesitated about doing this on previous visits, as I disliked allowing another human being to pull me, when I had legs of my own. However, I had been intrigued by the Durban rickshaws, which were colourfully decorated and bore slogans of their owners' prowess. They were in no way comparable to the sad vehicles and people one sees in the Far East. The rickshaw boys were dressed almost as if for carnival and often wore the massive horned Zulu head-dress. Best of all, they were a cheerful bunch, who obviously enjoyed what they were doing. This was what finally persuaded me to take a ride.

The real thrill of a Durban rickshaw was its method of motivation at speed. As it started, it was a simple two-wheeled vehicle pulled by a human beast of burden. When it picked up speed it became a complicated problem in dynamics, with the rickshaw boy a skilled athlete who delighted in showing his ability.

The rickshaw travelled at an estimated speed of 10 to 15 m.p.h. Balanced precariously on its two wheels, the rickshaw boy was lifted high in the air on the shafts for most of the time, with his swinging legs touching the ground for a brief period only during each stride. This looked and felt a most hazardous business, but there were few accidents, and any sudden stop threw the weight forward and gave immediate increased stability. In a Durban rickshaw, any loss of dignity was on the part of the passengers, who were just stage props

Rickshaw, Durban.

for an artistic performance. The rickshaw boys thoroughly enjoyed themselves and were proud of their skill, as well they might be. Durban would be the poorer when it lost these happy balancing artists, but I believed it would only be a matter of time before progress and convention would cause them to disappear.

On return to the hotel, I found Frankie had recovered somewhat, so we contacted our friends Jim and Flora, who normally lived at their sugar plantation on the Natal coast, some eighty miles to the north, but who were staying in Durban for their son's wedding. Jim was a member of the South African Parliament and appeared to know everyone in Durban. From that time on, our life was one continuous round of parties and social activities, culminating with Richard's wedding to the charming daughter of the Norwegian owner of a whaling fleet.

The wedding took place on the day before we were due to sail. At

the wedding, we met Lois, Jim's cousin, who was also sailing on the
Southern Cross as far as Australia. The next afternoon tired, but no
longer travel-weary, we boarded the *Southern Cross*.

*   *   *

The *Southern Cross* was a remarkable ship, and opinions on her facilities
and services are likely to be almost as varied as the 1,160 passengers
she carried. The concept of a wholly passenger vessel making four
complete round-the-world trips each year was magnificent. That
the ship managed to maintain its schedules and dock and sail
almost to the minute of her published arrival and departure times
was a sure endorsement of her capabilities and the skill and sea-
manship of her officers and crew. For a ship with a large superstructure and without the steadying effects of carrying cargo she was
generally a good sea craft. She was one of the first ships to be fitted
with stabilizers. Unfortunately, in bad weather these had to be
withdrawn to avoid damage, and the ship could then become very
uncomfortable indeed.

For a one-class ship, the *Southern Cross* was well appointed, and the
cabins were reasonably roomy. The use of air-conditioning throughout
the ship made cabins without portholes or outside access both practical and comfortable. There were two deficiencies which could be
criticized. There were washing and ironing rooms but no laundry-
service. More than 1,100 people had to wash their own laundry and
then iron it. Additionally, the builders seemed to have overlooked the
need for sound insulation between the cabins. Despite the annoyance
of noise and a possible cause for embarrassment, this created some
human interest, as domestic quarrels and the usual domestic triangles
were the subject of rather better informed comment than usual at the
breakfast table.

The *Southern Cross* had been designed to meet the needs of two groups
of people. The first were the round-the-world tourists. The second group
consisted of people requiring passages to and from Australia and New

Zealand. This latter group was subdivided between the new immigrants and the colonials travelling to and from Europe.

The groups were dissimilar in character. Round-the-world passengers were mainly well-to-do, middle-aged people who could afford to make use of all the amenities and take trips on shore as they felt inclined. The immigrants were uncertain of themselves, often full of concern about the decision they had taken and what might await them in their new country and usually having to watch their expenses carefully and take no shore trips. The colonials were divided between the young, likeable and extrovert Australians who had saved up to see something of the world and a retired group of well-to-do people similar to the round-the-world travellers.

These are, of course, generalizations. People of all incomes, social backgrounds, educational and cultural levels were on board. The cross section of humanity added to the interest of the voyage, although sometimes the exuberance of some younger passengers tended to conflict with the quieter life favoured by the older people.

The general impression we gained was of a happier ship from Australia onwards than existed on the first section from Durban to Fremantle. This probably resulted from the progressive replacement of the infestive immigrants and the young colonials who had spent all their money by a fresh, green batch of exuberant youth from the southern continent setting out on a great adventure.

The design of the ship and its schedule were, of necessity, a compromise. We considered the accommodation in the public rooms and the facilities provided were rather overcrowded. We felt that she would be a happier and more comfortable ship if she carried a hundred or so fewer passengers.

As tourists – though we understood that the length of time spent in port must be limited to meet a tight schedule – we would have appreciated longer stops in certain of the more interesting ports. It is a very long way to New Zealand to spend only three days there and see only part of the North Island.

Even the crew, from what we saw of them enjoying themselves in

Quinn's Bar in Papeete, would have liked to stay longer than the twenty-four hours allowed. Not surprisingly a number deserted ship there. Probably, but for Frankie, I would have done so myself.

Our impressions of the places we visited were kaleidoscopic, because our stay in each country was seldom longer than the average politician allows himself on a fact-finding tour.

*   *   *

What of the people we got to know on the ship? First was Lois, who left her heart in Natal and who deprived us of a very good friend and comrade when she left the ship in Sydney to visit the outback and the Great Barrier Reef before returning to her job as almoner in a London hospital. Rita and Klaus, with their artistic temperaments, were the good friends who later nobly helped us to dispose of the Australian wine but not the bottles, who helped us deal with Madam Fare Iti and who accompanied us on most of our sightseeing trips. It was only at the end of the voyage that we learned that they were on their honeymoon, with the prospect of separating immediately after arrival in England – Rita to rejoin the Düsseldorf Ballet and Klaus the Hamburg Symphony Orchestra, then performing in Edinburgh.

At 7 a.m. each morning I would join an old retired American railway engineer as he took his constitutional. After fifty years of driving a train, he was now spending his retirement from travelling travelling. He was a remarkable man with his wealth of experience and stories of his early days in the wild west. Bearded, with an extremely fine face, he might have been someone out of a Conrad novel, and I believe he had now found his true vocation at sea. The previous year he had been around the Horn and Tierra del Fuego. He insisted that the natives were still as wild as those who boarded the *Firefly* and were so discomforted by the tacks Joshua Slocum had scattered on the deck. Not the least interesting thing about this old gentleman was that his luggage consisted of a small cardboard box tied up with string. One's needs when nearly eighty are very small indeed.

In contrast was Wilma, the German beauty queen, with a different dress for each appearance. She looked her best, however, in a bikini. Although most of her own sex were jealous of Wilma, and she was much in demand by the younger men, we saw a lot of her and found her to be an intelligent, charming and friendly person.

We were extremely sorry for the old couple at our table, both over seventy years of age, who had never been outside the Union of South Africa. They had saved up for the trip and were looking forward, with ever increasing anticipation, to seeing Tahiti. When they arrived there, the husband was too ill to go ashore and his wife too devoted to leave him.

On the journey from Papeete, Janine was with us. A successful businesswoman, half French and half Tahitian, she was taking her sister to finishing school in France and then spending six months in her apartment in Paris. She partnered me at deck tennis, and we had common interests in painting and photography. Unfortunately, Frankie lost her address and telephone number.

We had to suffer the old sheep farmer who sat at our table and worried about his considerable wealth and how he might lose it in an uncertain world. This was his one and only subject of conversation.

From Fiji came the socialist police officer who knew everything except how to treat his inferiors. He thought tipping was demeaning and after four weeks of excellent table service shook hands with the table steward instead of tipping him.

One character who intrigued us was the little man who wore a cloth cap at every meal. The cabin steward said he also wore it in bed. Then there was Norman the retired schoolmaster, with his goatee beard, who almost created a riot at the ship's concert. Lastly there was the immaculate, supercilious, bald-headed man who would never go ashore without his bowler hat. We called him BBB (the bald headed blighter in a bowler). We thought he must be something in the city until we arrived in England and saw him try and take two of our suitcases.

*   *   *

After we left Durban late in the afternoon we passed close to two whalers, each with a dead whale in tow, and had time to marvel at the size of these leviathans and regret their passing.

As we followed our course eastward, with our next port Fremantle 4,300 miles away, it was interesting to look back at Africa with the setting sun creating a golden glory behind us and outlining the hills of the Natal coast and the skyscrapers of Durban. This was the last we were to see of land and of ships too, as the route from Durban to South West Australia was not very usual.

Every day the promise of Australia came closer, raising excitement amongst the returning colonials and increasing the depression and pessimism of the immigrants.

Although the Australians were largely of British descent, an underlying bar to understanding stemmed from the country having been colonized by Britain as a penal settlement. You had to remember that everything depended on the point of view and try to see this from the Australian side. The Australians were fine and intelligent people in an attractive and potentially wealthy country and had loyally supported Britain in two world wars. Nonetheless, the people of both countries saw things very differently. A nice example of this was a story of an Australian soldier who wished to marry a British girl and take her home after the latest war. Her parents would not agree and said, "You can't possibly go to Australia; that is where we sent all the criminals." The boy went home on his own but was so depressed that his parents asked him what was wrong. When he told them they said, "You can't possibly want to marry an English girl; that is where all the criminals came from."

If Australia was known as the thirsty land, the Australians could deservedly be called the thirsty people. Statistically, the Australians drank more beer per head than any other people on earth. In case the beer ran short, they managed to eke out supplies with some excellent, locally produced wines and the usual local and imported spirits. What was surprising to most foreigners was that the Australians had been able to set records in liquor consumption while hindered by some of the most restrictive licensing laws existing anywhere. To get a drink in a Sydney pub during the 5 p.m. swill hour when the procedure was to line them up by the half dozen or so per person, was a considerable achievement.

The Australian loves freedom, and I believed the excessive drinking habits were a direct result of the ridiculous restrictions. When, however, I suggested this to the wife of an Australian friend, she said, "They are bad enough as it is; can you imagine what they would be like if they could drink all day?" It would be wrong to comment on the drinking habits of the men without stressing the temperance and restraint of the Australian women, many of whom were teetotallers and did not smoke.

Australia was until relatively recently a lonely and isolated continent, with the outback an unexplored hinterland to the pockets of coastal settlement. It was only in 1813 that Lawson and Wentworth managed to find a way from the Sydney Plain through the precipitous Blue Mountain range to the fertile plateau beyond, and wider settlement of Eastern Australia became possible. Always in Australia there was a feeling that – leaving aside New Zealand, another equally lonely land – the nearest areas of European kinship were the USA 6,000 miles to the north east and South Africa 4,000 miles to the west. With the countless Asian hordes and overpopulation to the north and north west, this was a disquieting thought.

Australia had become an area of European settlement due almost wholly to the harshness of the British courts and legal system in the eighteenth and nineteenth centuries. If you stole a sheep, or poached a few hares because your family was hungry, or if you did anything to seriously annoy the establishment, you were likely to be sentenced to transportation for life. From 1787 until the middle of the nineteenth century, about 150,000 convicts were transported to penal settlements in Australia. Tolpuddle, near my birthplace in Dorsetshire, had, in its memorial cottages, a monument to the first trade unionists who were so transported. Australia had hers in the self-reliant, independent,

extrovert, progressive and sport-loving descendants of the early settlers, with their innate kindness and hospitality.

I had always liked the Australians, both those I met and worked
with during the war and the friends and colleagues I knew in England.
The men were usually lithe and healthy-looking – not all sunburnt
gladiators from Bondi Beach, but good-featured and more athletic in
build than the average European or American. They were seldom
given to the niceties of society and were direct and down to earth. They
hated prevarication and quickly got to the point. They were hard
working, competitive and able. They always showed their respect for
their women, possibly owing to the shortage of women during the
early settlement days, but loved to pull their legs unmercifully. A thing
I liked about both sexes were the wrinkles of sun and laughter in their
faces.

I had only met a few Australian women before going to Australia,
but as a result of my radio contacts Frankie and I met several families
while we were there. My salient impression was how different the
women were from their more emancipated sisters in Europe and
America. An Australian woman's home was largely her world, but it
was a world of which she was the centre. Australian women were
tremendously proud of their husbands, their children and their homes.
They were happy in their domestic surroundings and, although they
might appear to be in the background, were generally better informed
than an English wife about their husband's job and their country's
problems. They appeared anxious to play a supporting role rather than
assert their own personalities. There were few career women in Australia, nor were there the equivalents of the dominant, culture-hungry
American matriarchs.

One thing that jarred me in Australia was the ugly and unmusical
intonation and accent prevalent in colloquial talk. Perhaps worst of all
was the ubiquitous use, and monotonous repetition, of the great Australian adjectives "bloody" and "lousy". However, Australian slang
and idiom were rich and colorful and were making a valuable contribution in the development of a living language. The paradox was that

a nation that had produced vocalists of the calibre of Melba, Austral, Dawson and Sutherland, and literary giants such as Henry Lawson, J. G. Robertson, Eleanor Dark, W. G. Hay and Judith Wright should be so unmusical in their day-to-day speech and sometimes show an absence of discrimination, variety and capacity in its vocabulary.

* * *

In first visiting Western Australia, the last of the states to be colonized, Frankie and I were really starting the wrong way round, although perhaps fittingly in that upside-down country.

The gentle privateer William Dampier was commissioned by the Admiralty, in 1699, to make the first accurate survey of the west coast of Australia. He formed a poor opinion of the land, calling it the barrenest spot on the globe. He thought the aboriginals were miserable, filthy, nasty and unpleasant.

A convict settlement had been established in New South Wales in 1788 following the charting of the east coast by Captain Cook. Despite Dutch and French interest in the west coast, it was not until 1826 that the first British settlement was made on King George's Sound. This was followed a few years later by the settlement on the Swan River under Captain James Sterling, which had today grown into the capital city Perth and the adjoining deep-water port Fremantle.

Western Australia had been one of the most rapidly growing areas of Australia with a population of 5,000 in 1850 increasing to 500,000 in 1950. Nevertheless, with an area of 976,000 square miles, it had a population density of only one person for every two square miles. More than half the population lived in Perth/Fremantle, so the rest of the state was very sparsely populated indeed.

Based on what we knew of its history and surroundings, we expected Perth to be an overcrowded, ugly frontier town and Fremantle even more unpleasant due to the squalor which usually seems to exist at sea ports. We also expected to see a sandy, inhospitable and infertile coast. Even the prospect of seeing the black swans in their natural habitat held little attraction. Those brought to England had always seemed sombre and funereal compared with our native white variety.

Actually, we found Fremantle a clean and well-laid-out city with excellent amenities. We were more than charmed and delighted by the situation of Perth on the fertile northern bank of the Swan River. The view over the city from Mount Eliza in King's Park was magnificent. The wide estuary with its many inlets provided a foreground to the fine buildings of the city, and on the skyline, some twenty miles away, was the blue haze of the Darling Mountains.

We spent some time at the University of Crawley, a fine series of buildings of which Western Australians were justly proud. Crawley gave not only an impression of dignity and learning but also the sense of tradition one finds at Oxford and Cambridge. In the gardens of the university, we found many plants and flowers new to us, such as the waratahs, honey and crane flowers.

We spent some time in the center of Perth mingling with the shoppers. It was a Saturday afternoon; and, as we learned from conversations in the shops, a restaurant and bar, many people were in town from the surrounding cattle and sheep ranches, the fruit farms and vineries, in addition to the half of the state's population which lives in the twin cities.

As the discovery of gold did much to populate and develop Western Australia, I suspected there were also diggers, although we did not meet any. There were probably also a few lumberjacks from the nearby karri and jarrah forests.

Incidentally, we saw the black swans in their hundreds, preening themselves in the sunshine, on the blue waters of the Swan River and looking completely in place with their surroundings. We left Perth with an impression of a lovely city, a friendly people, a dislike of the harsh unmusical speech and twenty bottles of assorted Australian wines.

What with sampling the Australian wines, we saw little on our way to Melbourne except a whale on our port side which "blew" about half a mile from the ship and then sounded. How fascinating to see the spout of air and water rising so high above the sea from the lungs of this giant mammal. It was our first live whale and vividly brought to mind many sea stories but most of all Herman Melville's classic *Moby Dick*. The empty bottles were by now becoming a problem, as we had no porthole and the steward only came round once each day.

*   *   *

Melbourne was preoccupied with its preparations for the Olympic Games. This, the second city of Australia, had a population of one and a quarter million, had spacious public gardens and many fine buildings. However, it was obviously far more interested in the forthcoming Olympics than in a few tourists. Organized tours of the city seemed to have been suspended. We did manage to find one tour through the orchards of Victoria and the Dandinong Mountains, with their views over the range and southward over the city. Otherwise we were left to make our own enquiries and find our way around using taxis.

We visited Sherbrook Forest with its eucalyptus trees. But the much touted lyre birds were unncooperative and were obviously saving their displays for the Olympic Games. As cricket aficionados, we visited the Melbourne Cricket Ground, scene of Don Bradman's greatest triumphs; the Games committee had had the effrontery to rename it the Olympic Stadium.

We also visited the Shrine of Remembrance, which from the outside looked like a Berlin air raid bunker. It was, nevertheless, impressive in its interior and showed an imaginative conception – possibly based on the solstice stone at Stonehenge – in that a slot in the roof was so placed that at 11 a.m. on 11 November the sun shone directly on the Cross of Remembrance. The views over the city from the top of the shrine, standing as it does on the major eminence of Domain Hill, were impressive. We went to inspect the Yarrah, the upside-down river, which certainly lives up to its name in muddiness but provides an attractive foreground to Government House.

Captain Cook's cottage in the Fitzroy Gardens had me puzzled for

Captain Cook's cottage, Melbourne.

more than a year. I had read of Cook's voyages and could not understand how, when travelling along the south coast in 1770, and without the aid of an Olympic Games Committee, he had managed to build an English cottage in so unlikely a place. It was only much later that I learned that the cottage had been given to the Australian nation and moved, stone by stone, from Cook's birthplace in Marston, Yorkshire.

From Melbourne, we went quietly on our way, leaving it still busily preparing for the Olympic invasion. Fortunately, stocks of wine were not reserved for the Olympics, and we managed to take further supplies with us.

*   *   *

Have you ever been on a liner when someone goes overboard? This happened to us in the Bass Strait one day out from Melbourne. We had just gone to the bar for our pre-lunch drink when the ship started to keel over alarmingly. The sea almost came up to the superstructure windows on one side, while we pivoted about a point in the sky on the other side. The bar steward answered an unspoken question by saying it was unusual to turn at full speed and possibly someone had gone overboard.

It is only in such circumstances that one realizes the immensity of the ocean and the smallness of a human being. For nearly an hour we cruised slowly around. The captain, crew and many passengers scanned the waves through binoculars. We learned that the person facing eternity in that wilderness of water was an under-cook who had decided to end his troubles by jumping out through a waste hatch. Although he then changed his mind and started swimming, he owed his life to a lonely albatross with sight much keener than any human eyes. The circling bird in an empty sky above an apparently empty ocean led the captain to take the ship in that direction, and we finally saw a head rising occasionally above the waves. This was more than a mile from the marker buoy dropped when the alarm first sounded.

A near-tragedy turned into comedy when the lifeboat was launched to pick up the swimmer. Most of the oarsmen seemed to have had no boat drill experience, and the boat careered all over the place. The boatswain finally sorted them out and managed to get some directional control. The under-cook was blue with cold but otherwise none the worse for his experience. However, I believe he had to walk home from Sydney, as no ship would take him.

*   *   *

Sydney must have the loveliest harbour in the world, surrounded by its green hills and sandy bays, with its fantastic bridge and hundreds of miles of coastline. Even the haze and drizzle of the June morning on which we arrived could not spoil our sense of anticipation and enhanced the effect of the bridge looming through the mist. This bridge is nearly two miles long and its arch rises 500 feet into the sky.

A colleague of mine, an ex Fleet Air Arm pilot, was court-martialled during the war for flying under this bridge. He maintained that, with a clearance of 180 feet above the water, this was much easier than landing on an aircraft carrier and was neither difficult nor foolhardy.

Despite advance contacts made by radio we found it difficult to learn much about a city of two million inhabitants in a few days. We remember the contrasts in the transport system: the terrible and frequently overcrowded trams and the expensive taxis with their not very helpful drivers. However, the ferries were similar to the vaporettos in Venice and took one comfortably and romantically across the bays to the suburbs.

We remember the Heads of Port Jackson with their bare cliffs and rocks washed and battered by the spray of the Pacific waves; the sparkling waters and calm beaches of the harbour with its hundred thousand small boats and the houses lining its tree-clad shores; the orange crush bars, used mainly by females and foreigners, with their wonderful fresh juice; the all-male crush in the pubs at swill time when it was a fight to even get near the bar; the cars in their thousands and the traffic jams in the city streets.

We were not impressed by Bondi and the other Pacific beaches which are so often portrayed in tour posters. These were generally small (the tour brochure photographs foreshorten them and give a completely false idea of distance). The sand was reasonably fine but was disturbed by the Pacific rollers, so the water was seldom clear. Durban beach was far more impressive and attractive, had the rollers necessary for surfing and even had the tiger and white sharks if you enjoyed swimming in such unpleasant company. Give me the beaches of Lake Nyasa, or the Caribbean, any time.

We visited Vaucluse House and saw the exhibition of stage coaches which had operated in many parts of the country. We thought at once of Wells Fargo and the American west. We spent an interesting half day at Taronga Park and were thrilled by the birds and animals, including the crazy kookaburras and, finally, some lyre birds not preparing for the Olympic Games. The platypus, so long regarded by naturalists in Europe as a practical joke in bad taste, unfortunately refused to show himself. The stars of the zoo were unquestionably the koala bears who subsist on an all-dry diet of blue gum leaves and who unlike so many Australians have no need for liquid refreshments. What charming, woolly, toy-like creatures these are, with their wide, appealing, yet sleepy eyes.

We went one day from Sydney to Katoomba in the Blue Mountains. Climbing from the plain and following the cliff drive, we caught just a glimpse of the Three Sisters, then the mist came in and obscured the whole escarpment. We stopped at Echo Point and peered down into the abyss but could see nothing. We were, in fact, to see nothing further of interest that day, although we later allowed ourselves to be lowered down the cliff side near Katoomba Falls in a most dangerous-looking contrivance which was used originally in the extraction of coal from the cliff face.

Before leaving Australia, we went in search of the few souvenirs we could afford to buy. For Frankie, this was a black opal. This is probably the best investment we have ever made, as it has appreciated at least 1,000 per cent. I contented myself with a boomerang, costing a few dollars. It seems strange that, although we did not know this device in the Western world and thought the aborigines had invented it, the ancient Egyptions were using similar throwing sticks more than two thousand years ago, as shown by those discovered in the pharaohs' tombs.

Our last experience in Sydney, the night before we left, was a farewell bottle party held on deck by the Australians sailing with us and attended by all their friends and relations. This was certainly some party, and I am surprised that the right ones were left on board and the friends and relations were finally persuaded to go ashore, as dawn crept in and the ship cleared the quay side. One belated passenger had to chase the ship down the harbour by speedboat to avoid being left behind, and several non-intending passengers had to leave with the pilot in his launch.

* * *

We sailed from the calm of the harbour through the Heads into the rising sun, over the Pacific, on a swell which lightly rocked us. Our crossing of twelve hundred miles to Wellington was comfortable and uneventful.

Wellington was like an aging queen of the theatre. Seen from the auditorium heights of Mount Victoria looking northward the city, the harbour and the Hutt Valley were a magnificent sight, with the green of the hills, the blue of the harbour and the multi-hued buildings. When we descended into the city, we saw the untidy drabness of the streets and the garish colour of many buildings, often with the paint peeling off. There were some fine new buildings but these were frequently hedged in and crowded by the painted and often dilapidated wooden buildings. It was understandable that in an area prone to earthquake shocks there was a very good reason during the nineteenth and early twentieth centuries, and before the development of modern reinforced concrete structures, to use wooden buildings.

After Australia, with its happy, extrovert population, the white people of New Zealand seemed desperately, dourly dull. The early settlers did not have the advantage of a prison education and came in the main from Scottish Presbyterian homes, where life was hard, ruled by the scriptures and with little light-hearted joy or amusement. They were earnest, good, honest and religious people much given to hymn-singing. Although there certainly were many cultured, talented and brilliant New Zealanders of Scottish ancestry, who had a great sense of humour, the white population on the whole contrasted greatly with the happy-go-lucky and sometimes irresponsible Maoris.

We were not sorry to leave Wellington on our tour of the North Island. The first part of the journey was pleasant, the route passing first along the coastal road and then turning inland through a green, sheep-dotted countryside. It was a greener and more fertile land than any we had ever seen. After lunch at Taihapi, a trading store centre, we were on our way again and the country changed completely as we crossed a grey, lava-strewn desert with isolated tussocks of coarse grass. We followed the desert road almost to the foot of Mounts

Ruapehu and Ngurahoe. These are almost perfect volcanic cones and are the source of the desert lava. There is a hot water lake in the crater of Ruapehu.

After Nguarahoe, the desert road descended to the fertile plains around Lake Taupo, with the first signs of thermal activity now appearing ahead in the form of white clouds of steam, almost as if from a stationary railway engine. Taupo is a lovely lake with its clear water, its islands – one of them an ancient Maori burial ground – and the snow-clad mountains in the Tongariro Park rising to the south. The lake and the Waikato River which it feeds offered some of the finest trout fishing in the world. In the small town of Taupo, we crossed the Waikato River and turned away from the lake towards Wairakei some six miles away. There was now a tremor in the air, with clouds of white steam, and we could hardly wait to arrive in the thermal area.

The environment had, unfortunately, suffered great changes, and we found on arrival at the Wairakei Hotel that the noise of two geothermal bore holes was almost unbearable. The bore holes had been sunk for a government project to tap the steam power potential and later extract heavy water for atomic development. These man-made bore holes were emitting enormous jets of steam with pressures of about 400 lbs per square inch. The generating plants had not yet been installed, and not-very-effective silencers had been fitted in an attempt to reduce the noise.

The concept of usefully exploiting this thermal energy was an exciting one, but some concern was felt about a possible loss in geyser activity as the underground steam concentrations were tapped. We found that this idea was very much in the minds of the guides, who insisted there had already been a reduction in thermal activity since the first bores were made in 1950. One other possible cause for concern may be the pollution of local rivers, including the Waikato, from the chemicals in the condensed effluent.

One of the first things I did after checking in at the hotel was to find my way to the warm mineral water pool. It was dusk, and the pool was crowded with the Maori drivers of the tour cars, who were

New Zealand: where you can catch a trout and cook it on the hook.

relaxing and thoroughly enjoying themselves. On my arrival, they seemed amused by my appearance. Owing to the steam rising off the water into the cold air, it was only when I entered the pool that I discovered that I was the only one wearing a bathing costume. Frankie and I returned to the pool at about 11 p.m., when we had it completely to ourselves. By this time there was a heavy frost on the ground. It was a relief to get into the water and required considerable will power to come out into the freezing air.

We spent the next day in the Wairakei thermal area, with an afternoon visit to the Huka Falls. Wairakei takes its name from the Wairakei stream that flows through the geyser valley. Throughout its length, this valley billows with steam, and the smell of sulphur catches in one's throat. The waters of the stream were augmented by the outflow from the hot pools and geysers, and the green of the vegetation was contrasted by the silica and sulphur deposits on the rocks.

The Wairakei geyser was the one we were told played less frequently than formally and we saw it only from a distance. We did, however, have a close view of the beautiful "Prince of Wales Feathers" geyser in operation. The various boiling mud pools also fascinated us.

Some three miles to the south of Wairakei is the Karapiti blow hole, which was believed to be the safety valve of the thermal area. According to Maori records, this blow hole had been discharging a continuous jet of dry, superheated steam for more than five hundred years. The pressure at the orifice was 180 lbs per square inch, and stones thrown into it were hurled high into the air. (We were again to see the power of this blow hole at night, when the guides lighted an old hessian sack and threw it into the vent, producing a pyrotechnic display some hundred or so feet high.)

Escaping from the inferno, we returned to the Waikato River and visited the Huka Falls not far from where the river leaves Lake Taupo. The Waikato, New Zealand's longest river, which finally discharges into the Pacific some two hundred miles away, falls nearly a thousand feet between Taupo and Cambridge and generated about one megawatt of electricity as it passed through nine separate hydro-electric plants. The Huku Falls were the first on the river and, although the drop was only eighty feet, were unusually attractive due to the volume of milky blue-green water channeled over a ledge only about fifty feet wide.

The next day and night we spent at Rotorua. This was a typical spa with its gardens, pavilions and baths, and in many ways was reminiscent of many of the European spas. The diversity of types of mineral water available was probably unique. Rotarua's situation on the banks of Lake Rotorua, looking out over Mokoia Island, is most attractive.

To us Whakarewarewa, which we quickly shortened to Whako, was the high spot of our visit to the Rotorua area. This geyser valley is similar to that at Wairakei, although the boiling kaolin pools were much larger and more tempting to those whose wives have annoyed them. Incidentally, Maori wives were obedient, docile and disinclined to nag their men. Across the bridge over the Kauaka stream were the geyser flats, with pools of near boiling water contained in rocky depressions. This was the point where one could catch a trout in the Kauaka stream and turn around, and cook it in the geyser flats without standing up or taking it off the hook. Also here, facing out on to the geyser flats, was an old Maori township which was still occupied, although the Maoris were tending to migrate to European-style houses in Rotorua.

This settlement had considerable interest and beauty with its carved wooden buildings and its gaily coloured meeting house. The many pools on the flats, some of which had been carved out by hand centuries ago and which were at various temperatures, were still used by the townspeople, on a communal basis, for cooking, bathing and washing. The hot water facilities were obviously the reason a settlement was established at this place. We saw and photographed several delightful Maori children in one of the pools. We also saw their parents in a more relaxed atmosphere and much more natural surroundings than elsewhere.

A short distance from the geyser flats and stream was Pohutu, the most impressive of all the New Zealand geysers. While it was quiescent, we could walk right up to the geyser and look down into a circular, well-like, hole in the rock some twelve feet across with the clear, near boiling water about ten feet below. The rock walls fell sheer from the sulphur-coated, wet and slippery rock flat on which we stood. There was no protection for the careless or suicidally inclined. This was one of the most dangerously fascinating places I have ever seen.

To see Pohutu playing was really something. First the slow surge of the waves of water coming over the lip of the orifice, followed by the scalding jet with its plume of steam rising about two hundred feet into the air, accompanied by the rainbow effects produced by the drops of water falling in the sunlight. Then you thought and wondered how it was possible that a few minutes ago you were standing on the edge and looking down into this frightening wonder. It is as well that geysers keep to a regular time schedule.

Close to Whako was a reconstructed Maori fort which was essentially tourist-orientated. While it had probably been carefully planned to follow the original design of such forts, it looked dead and unlived in and was an anticlimax to the living charm of Whako village. This was also where the tourist people had arranged a show consisting of Maori chants and *poi* dancers. We found this disappointing, as the performers were the older women who, in typical Polynesian fashion, had gained in substance rather than grace over the years.

We had hoped to go to the Bay of Plenty, but time did not allow this and we had to return to the ship and sail the next day.

In contrast with the wild, all-night party in Sydney, the New Zealanders sent us off with the crowd of well-wishers and friends on the quayside singing the hymns "Abide With Me", "Nearer My God to Thee" and "For Those in Peril on the Deep".

* * *

During our visit to Wellington, I picked up a newspaper in which a report about an incident in Fiji, our next stop, caught my attention. It referred to a sea mystery almost as unique as that of the *Marie Celeste* but having a distinctly modern feature.

The *Joyita*, a modern, well-found vessel 75 feet long, with a crew of three, was discovered deserted and drifting some distance off Vita Levu. There was no trace of any struggle on board and nothing to explain the absence of the crew. The ship had been built in the USA and commissioned as a yacht but had later been converted to a refrigerated deep sea fisherman. She was virtually unsinkable, had a cruising range of 3,000 miles and, at the time she was discovered derelict and towed into Suva, had ample supplies of water, food and fuel on board.

The weather between sailing and discovery had been fair and the seas normal, and anything unusual in local conditions would have been reported by one of the other fishermen, several of who were operating in the same area. It was from one of these that a most unlikely story originated. This crew reported that a flying saucer had passed over their boat and appeared to land on the sea in the direction in which they knew the *Joyita* to be. Imagination – perhaps – but the *Joyita* was undoubtedly found derelict, and I had before me as I wrote these comments a cutting of the Suva Bay paper giving notice of the auction of the *Joyita* then lying in Walu Bay, Suva.

We only had time to visit Suva, the capital of Fiji, and its immediate surroundings. It was a familiar feeling, on our arrival at the quay side, to find a police band, in typical colonial style, playing the same old numbers as did their colleagues in Nyasaland on every festive occasion.

Generally speaking, Fiji depressed me, as the whole economy seemed to be in the hands of East Indians. Some Chinese and many East Indian indentured labourers were originally brought in to work on the plantations. The East Indians had prospered, brought in their families, multiplied exceedingly and numbered 150,000, about 20,000 more than the native Fijians. The East Indians had taken over most of the trade and business and some plantations. Little assimilation had taken place and Indian trading practices and treatment of the Fijians appeared little different from those they had employed in Africa. The Chinese, in contrast, had largely been assimilated and had fitted well into the society and economy.

There was, I sensed, a feeling of despondency amongst the native Fijians about the Indian stranglehold on their economy, and they showed little of the Polynesian gaiety of the Maoris or of those Parisiens of the Pacific, the Tahitians. The white and Negro races of Africa might have done well to study the Indian population explosion and the development of Indian economic power in Fiji.

The island of Vita Levu is green and mountainous with some excellent beaches. The economy was still largely based on sugar, with some production of copra, rice and bananas. There was also "gold in them thar hills" and some production of this precious metal. Efforts were being made to develop tourism on the south coast. We found Suva an unattractive town, but the surrounding areas in the hills and looking out over the sea were very pleasant.

We visited an ex-Nyasaland colleague who was the PMG and had an attractive house in this area. The visit also gave us the chance to discuss conditions in the islands. We went out to a sugar plantation in the country. This was smaller and not as well run as those we were to know in Jamaica. On our journey through the countryside we were interested in the Fijian villages. Although conditions of life were primitive, the villages impressed us as cleaner and the houses more spacious and light than the mud huts of Africa. The houses were built with pandanas palm walls and roofs on wooden frames.

On our return to Suva, we had the chance to take a swim at a club on the outskirts but declined. The sea here was full of sea snakes with a venom as deadly as the mamba. One of the strongest arguments against a sea-level canal across Central America is that sea snakes could then cross from the Pacific into the Caribbean and would probably breed freely there.

Our last search before leaving Suva was for the *Joyita* which we found without difficulty but were unable to board.

I have since been back to Fiji on several occasions, once with Frankie who met Raymond Burr who was doing great things for the Fijians on his privately owned island. I would however have little to add to the above comments and believe my first impressions were reasonably accurate.

*   *   *

Perhaps from the earliest dreams of our youth we all carry in us – be we tramp or tycoon – our own picture of an earthly paradise. In many of us, this will be linked with palm trees and pirates, lagoons and lakes, the sea breaking on a coral shore, a life free of all endeavour and worry, long sunlit days, nights under a tropic moon, and beautiful girls and handsome men. Brought up on Robert Louis Stevenson and, when my parents allowed, Somerset Maugham, I had been an island addict since as a small boy I sailed amongst the islands in Poole Harbour. I virtually started life with no resistance to places such as Tahiti.

Following this, a liking for the poems of Rupert Brooke and the paintings of Gauguin began, many years ago, to fix Tahiti in my mind as a mecca for the future.

What was the secret of Tahiti's fascination for all her lovers? One can analyze perhaps the beauty of a woman but not her charm, or her appeal, to her lover. The resolution of Tahiti's charms was equally difficult. Perhaps the most fascinating thing about Tahiti was its eternal capacity to thrill and delight. Every person who knows the island, or for that matter every book one reads about it, looks back with nostalgia and states that Tahiti is not what it was and that soon it will not even be what it is. Nevertheless, the "is" remains an enchantment to every newcomer.

There were other tropical islands of great beauty, but few, if any, had the strangeness of the Tahitian skyline with such a range of mountains compassed in such a small area. There were lovely coral beaches and palm trees elsewhere – some West Indian beaches on the turquoise Caribbean were superb. Handsome men and beautiful girls lived on islands in other parts of the world, but I doubted if there was a gentler, happier people than the Tahitians, or one that had all the virtues except conventional morality.

The physical characteristics of the Tahitians have been shown in the pictures of many artists and in the photographs published in travel magazines. Except perhaps in the pictures of Gauguin, none of these do justice to the Tahitians. In portrayal there is too often a heavy, sleepy expression and a complete failure to catch the ephemeral, indefinable characteristics seen in the living face. These were sometimes as quick and fleeting as the movements of the people themselves. I took many photographs of the Tahitians but all showed a flatness of expression which belied the life and gaiety we saw in their faces.

If your needs were simple there was little the Tahitian countryside, and seas, could not provide. An inexpensive existence was still possible there. For these reasons, Tahiti still substantially offered the same attraction to both the poor and rich. Some day, however, the great American public would discover Tahiti. There was also, disaster of disasters, talk of an international airport. This could result in a welter of tourism and exploitation of the tourist similar to that taking place in the Caribbean. Tahiti would surely then no longer be what it was.

The charm of Tahiti was not only in the beauty and attraction of its people and landscape. History had also contributed to it. Tahiti may well have been originally populated by Thor Heyderdahl's red-bearded white men before the Polynesian conquest. It would provide a fitting background for those legendary people. However, this is all guesswork, and we are not even certain when the Polynesians arrived, although we have a good idea when they made the ocean crossing and settled the Hawaiian islands.

European discovery was by Captain Samuel Wallace, who claimed the island for Great Britain in 1767. The following year, Louis de Bougainville claimed it for France. The ubiquitous Captain Cook arrived in 1769 to reclaim it for Britain and observe the passing of Venus – and I mean the planet. A Spanish expedition arrived in 1772, also with claims to the island. They were followed in 1788 by Captain Bligh of the *Bounty* who called to collect breadfruit plants to be used to feed the slaves on the West Indian plantations. The mutiny on the *Bounty* followed, caused partly by the sanctimonious beastliness of Bligh and partly by the attractiveness of the Tahitian girls.

A subsequent British expedition successfully brought breadfruit to the West Indies. A close friend of mine, and chief of the engineering branch of the company I managed in Jamaica, was a descendant of the botanist on this expedition. In 1840, the French, who had returned to the island, declared a protectorate over Tahiti during the reign of the Tahitian chief Pomaro.

Although its history has been varied and cosmopolitan, the island has today an essentially French character. The French colonials are a part of the island in the same way as the island is a part of France. The French have brought much of their charm and culture to Tahiti, which through the works of Gauguin has given its own characteristic art form to the world.

These attempts to provide a frame for the Tahitian picture do not provide an adequate explanation of the island's enchantment. Perhaps that is what it really is. Certainly, it was impossible to analyze the living spell which might show itself in a glance, an intonation, the slant of the sun on the lagoon, the moon seen through the palm trees, or any of a thousand things.

*   *   *

We approached Papeete at dawn over a calm and oily sea. Behind the shore, the peaks and pinnacles of the mountains with their fantastic shapes reached toward the sky like an unreal theatrical backcloth lacking as yet the detail in depth the sunshine would shortly bring. We still seemed detached from the shore in a completely different world, and yet, as we had so many times read, the land breeze brought us the scented aphrodisiac air, a lure and a promise to all arriving at the island. This, at last, was the paradise we had waited for and hardly dared hope could actually exist.

We watched the ship docking at the quayside, anxious to go ashore as soon as we could. Even the dockside itself could not depress us, for here we were not surrounded by the usual cargo vessels with their utilitarian air of commerce, rust and dirt, but by the romantic inter-island schooners and some of the loveliest yachts I have ever seen, coming from all parts of the world. Admittedly the ugly tin sheds hid Papeete from our view, but seaward we looked out on the opalescent lagoon, with Moorea in the distance purpling in the rising sun.

We had arranged to spend the morning in Papeete, and as soon as the French customs officials had finished with us – and they were particularly tiresome, possibly wishing to keep the joys of Tahiti to themselves – we went ashore and out through the market into the town.

The market in the morning was one of the sights of Papeete, crowded by all races – Polynesians, Asians, Europeans and Americans – either shopping or sightseeing. Amongst the Caucasians, it was interesting to contrast the French residents so correctly dressed in European-style suits with the American visitors often wearing the Tahitian *pareo*. It seemed astonishing that a nation so logical, so fond of comfort and inclined to indulge itself in other respects, should maintain the conventions of European dress in a country where appearances mattered little and the *pareo* was simple, inexpensive, practical and comfortable.

You could buy almost anything in the market – vegetables, fruit, meat, bread, flowers. Whether you wished to buy anything or not, this was the morning meeting place. All the races of Tahiti were equal there and mingled freely with one another. You could hear Tahitian, French, Chinese or English spoken. As you stood at the top of the steps looking down into the market, the whole impression was one of inter-racial understanding, freedom and, above all, colour.

The smell of Papeete in the early morning was intriguing, reminiscent of a small French town yet having a character of its own. We tried to define it, and the nearest we could get was the scent of frangipani flowers we had noticed from the boat adulterated by the dockside smells of copra and vanilla and mixed with the smell of newly baked French bread, coffee, garlic and humanity.

Papeete was just recovering from the first phase of the July 14th celebrations, although the gaiety was far from over and the Tahitians would continue to commemorate their storming the Bastille for several weeks. What might, but for its superb waterfront and colourful people, have appeared an ordinary small French coastal town was enlivened by the fern- and flower-covered dance platforms, stalls, open air restaurants and all the paraphernalia of a fairground. Though it was early morning the streets were crowded with the local citizens and people from the surrounding countryside, with here and there groups of grass-skirted competitors taking part in the Otea dance competitions.

We had not gone far in our walk through the town before the noise of the drums called us to the grounds in front of the Municipal Building. This was wonderful and free entertainment. The drums of Tahiti had a sound of their own: at first a monotonous regular beat, which would suddenly be broken by a change in the rhythm, an interruption in the cadence. We tried to follow the sequence and anticipate the changes, which were supposed to be based on ancient Tahitian poems, but we always failed. Nevertheless, the drums had

Tahiti: dancers.

the metre of poetry with a strangeness perhaps related to the curious vowel enunciation of the Polynesian languages which is fascinating in its complexity. On top of this was the quite astonishing spectacle of the dances themselves. Just how much the drummers were inspired by the dancers or the dancers by the drums I do not know. Never had we seen such perfect synchronism of movement and music.

The Tahitian dances were nothing like the heavy hip-gyrating hula of Hawaii and the American movies. They were light and fluid, the movements astonishing in their quickness and almost as varied as the Americanized version was monotonous. The old-timers would tell you that the modern dances were emasculated compared with the sexual gestures and indecency of the Timorodee, suppressed years ago by the missionaries, which originally were performed by the young unmarried girls to excite the men. What would the tourist not give to see these dances in their original form? Again, it was the old question of

Tahiti not being what it was. Nevertheless, we found the present-day drumming and dancing an exciting, pulse-quickening spectacle.

What of the rest of the island? We had arranged to take a tour, which we found was conducted by an extremely aggressive French woman who was obviously anti-Tahitian, one imagines embittered by years of having to compete with young and more attractive Tahitiennes. Perhaps as a result, her attitude towards the native population, and for that matter towards ourselves, was, to say the least, objectionable. She insisted in calling the native girls *poule* and the men *cochon*. I think the Tahitian drivers had her measure, as, out of her hearing, they called her Madam Fare Iti. Thinking this must be her name, I also called her this, to be first treated to an incredulous stare and on the second occasion by a torrent of invective. It was only later I learned that the translation of what I was saying was "Madam 'Little' House". Fortunately, we had Rita and Hans as kindred spirits in the car. Frankie spoke good French, and the driver was helpful and knew his island well. So it was not difficult to detach ourselves from her odious presence and too-orderly convoy. Thereafter, we used our driver as a guide.

The island presented unrivalled seascapes and mountain views. The countryside was extremely fertile and largely covered by lush tropical bush. Against this green setting, and perhaps seen more vividly as a result, were a profusion of flowering shrubs, including most of those we had known as exotics in Africa. One other characteristic of the vegetation of Tahiti was the presence, in the forest glades and gullies, of many varieties of wild ferns that added to the beauty and seclusion of these cool green wonderlands.

As a result of heavy rainfall, spread over most of the year an abundance of water flowed in the rivers and streams which had their source in the mountains. The interior of the island, with its mountains and precipitous green slopes, was largely uncultivated and not readily accessible to a short-time visitor, as the one main road followed the coastline round the island.

One of the charms of Tahiti was that it was not heavily populated.

The population density was only about a seventh of that of most of the West Indian islands.

During our tour of the island, we visited Point Venus, scene of Captain Cook's observations, where stood the delightful house of James Hall, who worked with Nordhoff in writing *Mutiny on the Bounty*. My wife has, perhaps justifiably, a suspicious mind, and every time I mentioned the significance of the transit of Venus, she treated it as a poor joke and seemed to think Cook's observations were probably anything but scientific.

Beyond Matavai were the black volcanic beaches, a reminder of Tahiti's volcanic origin. We stopped here to allow Frankie to collect coral specimens from the beach and to talk to some small boys fishing from the rocks. One of the places on the north coast we should have liked to explore further, had we had the time, was the valley of Papeeno, Tahiti's longest river, whose source was in Mount Orohena, 7,400 feet above and Tahiti's highest point. Papeeno had a place in the history of Tahiti. In the days of human sacrifice its isolated hidden valleys were a sanctuary for intended sacrificial victims and for offenders against tribal law. Papeeno seen from the entrance to the valley and framed by its fantastically shaped mountains seemed a lush and verdant paradise.

Next to Papeeno, and famous for the beauty of its *vahines*, was Hitiaa, where Gauguin found his first companion on arrival in Tahiti. As I already had a companion, all I was allowed to seek were a few rather indifferent and emotionally dissatisfying photographs.

Tahiti and Tiarapu, or little Tahiti, have an outline similar to the figure 8, Tahiti being the larger part of the figure and Tiarapu the smaller. We crossed the isthmus joining Tahiti with Tiarapu at Taravao. Tiarapu, although hilly, had not the majestic grandeur of Tahiti with its impossibly shaped mountains climbing to the sky. The isthmus joining the two islands was quite narrow and low-lying and led directly on its south side into the coastal plain of Papeerii, where the American Harrison Smith created a botanical wonderland, much of which was now overgrown. A considerable amount of copra was being produced here. With it came a reminder that this Garden of Eden is not perfect. Every bearing palm carried a metal guard to protect the nuts from the rats which plagued the island. With syphilis and tuberculosis, this was another of the benefits civilization brought to the islands.

The next place we looked for, and one I particularly wanted to visit, was Mataie, where Gauguin first settled with his fourteen-year-old *vahine* from Papeeno, and where most of his early Tahitian works were painted. Mataie, with its reef-locked lagoon, the lush surroundings and the stream and track leading up to Lake Vahaira, are of interest in their beauty, history and legend. Lake Vahaira, with its memories of Rupert Brooke, was surrounded by green-clad mountains nearly 5,000 feet above our heads. Brooke visited it, but the climb itself, partly along the bed of a stream and, where this was too steep, through almost impenetrable undergrowth, took a full day and was out of the question as far as we were concerned. One can imagine the sombre mystery of this still, green lake high in the mountains, which had given rise to the legend of the Tahitian princess who was lost in the lake and from whose union with a water spirit the first eel man was born.

These eel men with little ears, part eel, part men, were reputed to live in the stream which flows from the lake to Mataie, where the princess once lived. The legend goes that they may fertilize any *vahine* careless enough to bathe in the stream. We walked some way up the stream and peered eagerly into the water but saw no eel water spirits. They were certainly much less in evidence than the *Wärmflasche mit kleinen Ohren* which we were warned about during the early days of the occupation of Germany. The eel god appears frequently in Polynesian mythology. We had also heard about it in Fiji, where legend has it that the fire walkers of Mbangga obtain their immunity and ability to walk over the heated stones from one of these eel spirits.

Beyond Mataie was the plain of Antimaono, the largest in the island, where the infamous William Stewart lived at Montcalm, his cotton plantation. Stewart imposed a state of slavery on his workers and frequently took the law into his own hands. Possibly due to his lavish

Tahiti: the lagoon.

entertainment of French officials, including the governor, no action was taken against him. Stewart finally died a pauper as the law was about to catch up with him. Montcalm is today a ruin.

* * *

The *mareas* of Tahiti were the places of worship of the old Polynesian gods and the scenes of human sacrifice. Following the conversion of the islanders to Christianity, the *mareas* were destroyed and were now scattered ruins, where it was hard to even guess the original form. The Tahitians were still extremely superstitious about these haunted spots and the Tupapus, or spirits, they said lived in the vicinity.

The *marea* we visited was Arahuraraho. This was the most accessible rather than the most famous, or infamous, of the Tahitian *mareas*. To us the fallen stones conveyed no impression of a malevolent and primeval past. In fact, seen in the sunlight with a crowd of colourfully dressed tourists buying souvenirs and taking photographs, it was just like any other tourist trap.

In an endeavour to increase tourist interest, several excellent wood carvings had been made reproducing, presumably fairly accurately, the frequently obscene carvings of earlier times. The most explicit of these were protected by a grass hut. We found these interesting and an experience which followed amusing.

The most revealing of the statues might have had for its model the man in a well-known Tahitian story who was suffering from elephantiasis and pushed what are to a Tahitian vital organs ahead of him in a wheelbarrow. We noted two middle-aged spinsters from the boat viewing this work of artistic imagination with both fascination and horror. They were so preoccupied that they did not notice us. In consequence, we were enlightened by the following conversation:

"Doris, surely that isn't . . .? I think it's disgraceful; it must be the French influence on the poor natives."

"I agree it's disgusting to show people things like that: I shall complain to the captain and ask him to have it cut off."

*   *   *

Farther along the south coast and shortly before we again reached Papeete was Punaauia, one of the loveliest coastal districts on the island, looking out over Moorea. Here, Gauguin had his last home, from which he was driven as a result of his feud with the Protestant missionaries. Gauguin had little love for missionaries of any denomination. Before his tragic death in the Marquesas, he quarrelled equally with the Catholic Church in those islands.

At Punauia was Chez Rivnac, a centre for artists and famous for its wonderful Tahitian food and Tahitian dancing. However, they did not serve the native dish of *fufufu*, probably for hygienic reasons. This was made in Tahitian households by throwing all the fish one caught, and did not like, into a barrel, where it was left for a month or so. As with Chinese eggs, the bacteria finally die, and the end product is not dangerous to human life. It consists of a fishy-smelling jelly.

We will never forget the evening we spent at Chez Rivnac – the beauty of the sun setting over Moorea, the native Tahitian meal and the *otea* dancing which followed. Our favourite course was the marinated tuna pickled in lime juice, very good indeed. The main course was pork wrapped in leaves and cooked by placing it between hot stones and burying it in the ground. This was excellent. We tried everything, including all the Tahitian vegetables and fruits served with the meal. Afterwards came the dancing, lit only by the moon and the palm frond torches carried by the male dancers. This had the same fascination, but in a much more romantic setting, as that we had seen earlier in Papeete. What a fantastic performance this was, the movements almost unbelievable in their quickness, the changes following exactly the strange cadences of the drums. I have seen many native dances in Africa and the Caribbean, but compared to this the movements were clumsy, formless, prancing postures.

Chez Rivnac was also an hotel, and I was a little shaken by a story the proprietor told me of a young American who complained bitterly that he had not been supplied with a *vahine*. If this idea of Tahitian hotel facilities gets around, you can understand my concern about a possible mass tourist invasion of the island.

Having exhausted the joys of Chez Rivnac, we took a taxi to Hotel les Tropiques, the most sophisticated centre for late revellers. This was on the outskirts of Papeete, and its terrace was built out over the lagoon. Its dance band played excellent American jazz and European dance music. A floor show followed. The performers were Tahitian, with some excellent singers and dancers in the modern idiom. Not the least interesting thing about Les Tropiques was its international character, with people of all races dancing together and enjoying themselves. We liked Les Tropiques, and it was very late, or early, when we returned to Papeete.

We had not explored all the night life of Papeete and had still to visit

Quinn's, the most famous bar in town. We found it bursting at its seams with people of all types and colours, including half the crew of the *Southern Cross*. The dance floor, with its *vahines* struggling to dance with amorous, drunken sailors and tourists, had hardly an inch of spare space on it. We could not find a single seat, let alone a spare table, and after a short time withdrew and took a quiet walk along the front to get the smoke out of our lungs.

Although it was now well after three in the morning, the fair was still going strong, and you could still win a *pareo*, a doll or a bicycle at one of the many games of chance. These were less sophisticated than those in the West and showed considerable ingenuity in using spinning cycle wheels, where you had to guess the position in which they would stop, and live rabbits going through one of a number of trapdoors on which you placed your bet. The Tahitians found it all good fun, and we enjoyed mingling with them and watching them gamble.

We returned to the ship just before sailing time. We sailed again at dawn to the music of drums and guitars from the quayside. The players could have had no hope of any financial reward and must only have been doing this for our enjoyment. We felt that the Tahitians were a materially poor but happy people, with a wonderful capacity for sharing their happiness with others.

As we left Papeete, we threw our leis overboard and looked back at the Diadem catching the first rays of the rising sun. As we looked, it was suddenly hidden in a rain squall. We turned our backs and went below to sleep, leaving Tahiti behind us but carrying its memories with us.

In 1974, we spent a week in Tahiti and visited Moorea. Tahiti was certainly not as it was but still enjoyable. The International Airport was operating; we landed there. The place was so crowded with tourists that the international chain of hotels, which had confirmed our reservations months before, could not accommodate us and had booked us into a Tahitian hotel, where chickens ran around the grounds outside our room and local children played in and out of the sea. This was probably a plus, and we enjoyed it no end.

When we went to an Otea festival the dancing was as good as ever.

Unfortunately, many of the Tahitians had picked up the bad manners and the lack of honesty frequently produced by tourism. For example, I gave a taxi driver, who had agreed to pick us up later in the evening, a sizable note to pay his fare, and he drove off at high speed taking my change with him. He did not return later, and we had some difficulty getting back to the hotel. We had been lucky in seeing Tahiti in better days but it probably still fascinates the newcomer.

* * *

Six days of sunshine, trade winds, porpoise and flying fish. Six days of deck tennis, sun bathing and swimming in the ship's pool. Then the equator, and King Neptune came on board with his retinue. Seldom have I seen an uglier bunch of scalawags, largely made up of the Australians who had partied all night at Sydney. They had the usual diadem, sceptre and fancy dress. In one respect, they made a welcome departure from protocol in substituting Australian beer for the more usual draft of sea water inflicted on initiates.

They would have loved to get their hands on a bikini-clad Wilma, but she, and all the other round the world passengers, had suffered their torture on the way south. The victims were therefore largely made up of the Australians and New Zealanders going north for the first time. They did have one female beauty to initiate in the person of Janine's little sister, but with the innate gallantry of most Australians they were kind to her; and, after she had quaffed the beer and eaten the raw herring, she was allowed to jump rather than be thrown into the pool. Without sufficient interesting female victims, they finished the large supplies of beer themselves and, looking more disreputable than ever, fell into the pool to cool off and sober up.

Another two days of sunshine, sun bathing and swimming, then suddenly the temperature fell by ten degrees and we were sailing over a grey ocean under heavy skies, a sign we were in Humboldt's Current and approaching the coast of South America.

* * *

Panama City, founded in 1519 and sacked by Henry Morgan in 1671. Panama City with its hot, heavy, damp, blotting-paper atmosphere. To do anything in Panama City you must have dollars, and we had very few. The power of the almighty dollar was absolute, and we only had British and German currency. As in most countries, we found there was an unofficial bourse, this time for some strange reason in the YMCA.

Klaus, Rita, Frankie and I shared expenses and took a taxi into this city of contrasts. American skyscrapers and old Spanish buildings dating back to the sixteenth century. Streets thronged by well dressed, obviously well to do people and by beggars. Everywhere, lottery and sweepstake ticket-sellers. One thing which impressed us immediately was the beauty of the young girls and children, with their mixture of Indian and Spanish blood.

We saw some of the city's buildings and monuments and were interested in the statue to De Lesseps at the scene of his failure. This was more impressive than that at Port Said, where he achieved success. We found Panama very expensive, and, as we had been virtuous and not changed currency, the only things we allowed ourselves to buy were Panama hats. These were of much poorer quality than those in Ecuador.

We sailed into the canal the next morning and, as we expected, found it completely different from the Suez Canal. Suez, which has no locks, has long straight sections and easy curves with palm-edged sandy banks and the desert beyond dotted with camels and felaheen. Panama raises ships in transit to 85 feet above sea level and winds about following the line of least resistance, making use of existing river valleys with their banks green and lush with tropical vegetation. Seeing the type of countryside, we appreciated the problems met in construction of this canal and the near impossibility, with the technology available at the time, of De Lessep's original concept of building a sea-level canal.

The problems were not only those of overcoming the engineering

Panama Canal lock.

obstacles but, more seriously, the medical scourges of yellow fever, malaria and dysentery. Construction of the railway which preceded the canal, and the various attempts to build the canal, cost an estimated 40,000 lives. Incidentally, Gauguin and his fellow artist Charles Laval worked as labourers on the canal.

After passing through the Culebra cut and before entering Gatun Lakes, we passed the 1,150 foot prominence known as Mount Balboa from which, in 1513, Balboa first saw the Pacific Ocean. One of the confusing things about the canal, which you discover when looking at the charts, is that, owing to the shape of Panama, it runs from south east to north west in passing from the Pacific to the Caribbean.

To me, the great interest of the canal was the locks which had made the project possible. These were typically American in their efficiency, with a filling time of only fifteen minutes and with the electric mules moving the largest ships as if they were shunting railway rolling stock in a siding. The canal was operated by, and under the control of, the American government.

* * *

We entered Caracas Bay, Curaçao, at 3.30 a.m., with the ship due to sail again at 11 a.m. We had heard so much about Willemstadt and its Dutch colonial buildings that we were walking around the streets before it was light. This was a charming town with superb shops. It was also a free port, and shortly before we sailed we did some shopping. There was a most intriguing pontoon bridge which was driven sideways by propellers on its pontoons to clear the channel for shipping entering the harbour. I went on it to photograph the floating market and was almost shanghaied when it started to move.

The floating market was a particular feature of Curaçao. It consisted of a quayside against which many small sailing vessels, from the South American mainland, were anchored, selling fruit and vegetables off their decks. Curaçao is a small arid island whose economy is largely dependent upon its refineries and the handling of Venezuelan oil. It

Curaçao: floating swing bridge. It no longer exists.

was hard to believe that it had a population of about 100,000, nearly three times that of Tahiti.

Besides looking around Willemstadt, we went to a point near Caracas Bay to see Henry Morgan's house. This was another memory of the famous pirate who ultimately became governor of Jamaica.

*   *   *

Trinidad, and steel bands in the morning. What a place this was! Discovered first by Columbus in 1498 and fought over since by the British, French, Dutch and Spanish, the population was nearly as mixed as the island's history. The miscegenation here, with a mixture of Negroes, Europeans, Arawak Indians and Asians, including both East Indians and Chinese, would have driven Mr Malan and the Afrikaners crazy. Trinidad was a very gay and friendly island, similar in some ways to Jamaica, where I was to take up an appointment in 1957.

It was impossible to go anywhere as a tourist in Trinidad without being greeted by the ubiquitous calypso singer. These were of all ages from six to sixty, and whenever you stopped your car they appeared to serenade you. There were, of course, calypso singers and calypso singers. Some were first-class entertainers and had achieved world fame. Others used it to earn a pittance instead of begging. We were later to know the mighty Sparrow, a Trinidadian and probably the best of them all, and Lord Jellico, a Jamaican who was the most outrageous with his Big Bamboo.

Nonetheless, the street calypsonians had their merit and were usually topical and amusing. This was almost wholly a male occupation, with gallantry to the ladies and a tendency to take the mickey out of the men. The ladies generally would be complimented on their appearance and dress. Their male companions would be subject to outrageous leg-pulling. We laughed with a seventy-year-old cleric who was serenaded with "Don't leave any babies in Trinidad."

Trinidad, which lies close to the estuary of the Orinoco, had few good beaches. The best was Maracas Bay on the extreme north of the

Trinidad: steel band.

island facing Tobago, which has the beaches Trinadad lacks. Strangely, it was at Maracas Bay that I saw my first case in many years of serious snake bite. We swam with Klaus and Rita and I took photographs of the girls modelling the grass skirts they had bought in Tahiti.

What else was there to see in Trinidad? The pitch lake out of which many of the roads in the civilized world had been surfaced without any appreciable fall in lake level was interesting but not exciting. The surface was quite firm and level as we walked out on to it. The villages were squalid, over-populated and not very enthralling.

The night life in Port of Spain was terrific, with the floor shows having their own particular West Indian character and setting a very high standard. They featured steel bands, calypso and limbo dancing. We were unfortunate, or fortunate, in not being in Trinidad at carnival time, when the whole place goes wild. *Although I spent ten years in the Caribbean, I never managed to visit Trinidad at carnival time.*

*   *   *

After leaving Trinidad, we had the ship's concert and captain's dinner. The concert was the usual disaster, as the professionals on board, including Rita, stayed well away from the organizers. Unfortunately, many of our less-talented passengers did not. Three groups labelling themselves "No laundry on board" tried to exploit the comic aspects of this deficiency. Janine and her sister did an *otea* dance which was received enthusiastically by the younger male passengers but did more to show off their figures than any innate dancing ability. This appeared not to have been passed on from the Tahitian side of their ancestry. Wilma showed the extent of her talents by singing very well in both English and German. At the end, she slipped from her evening dress to display her more usual bikini. This brought the house down. I preferred the evening dress and singing.

Following Wilma, and while the young Australians were still glassy-eyed, Norman, our goateed schoolmaster, came on the stage to sing a song he had written called "The Wise Old Owl". Unbeknown to the audience, this had forty-four verses; not only that, Norman was tone-deaf and had no idea of singing. The older passengers were restrained by the presence of the captain, and the young Australians were still dazed by what they had seen of Wilma, so the owl's admirer managed to get to about verse twenty before the audience began to get restive. Having managed to get so far, the singer now felt sure of himself, increased his DB level and persisted with the torture of his unwilling listeners. When he was in his mid-thirties and still aiming at forty-four, it became too much for even the most polite of us and he finally had to leave the stage to a barrage of catcalls. His bird did indeed get the bird in no uncertain terms. This brought the concert to a rather ignominious ending.

There was little of interest at the captain's dinner other than a well-justified speech of thanks for the performance of the ship and its staff. The usual free champagne was appreciated by all, even though it was an Australian brand (and very good). One side issue was of some interest. The bar steward, who ran a daily tote on the ship's run, had been persuaded to take bets on whether the passenger who wore the cloth cap would also wear it at the captain's dinner. Such were the social pressures for full evening dress that the odds were three to one that he would follow the dictates of convention. I had complete confidence in my man, and sure enough, there he was wearing his cloth cap.

So at last we came to the United Kingdom and later to Frankie's home in Germany. England was quiet and orderly, as we expected. However, when we arrived in Germany, where Frankie's parents invited us to stay in a small hotel near Bonn, we were involved in a fantastic Russian spy episode. To our consternation, we learned that this hotel was the centre of a spy ring complete with hidden microphones, tape recorders, German and foreign agents, East European couriers and behind it all the dear old white-haired proprietress with whom we often took an evening glass of wine.

One final comment on ourselves was that one of the cabin trunks containing what Frankie termed were essentials was not opened from the time we left Nyasaland until we returned eight months later.

Chapter 13

White Man's Burden

In the late 1950s, when I was writing this book, Britain and the other colonial powers were willingly, or under local and international pressures, divesting themselves of their colonies. India and Pakistan had been independent for a decade. East Africa and Nigeria were in process of becoming independent, and similar plans were in hand for the Caribbean countries. The Federation of Central Africa was facing almost insurmountable problems, and it seemed that this one experiment in interracial cooperation, with a gradual and orderly extension of the franchise, was certain to fail.

I believed that the process of granting political independence and a universal franchise should have been undertaken only after a study of existing conditions and consideration of the benefits which would have resulted from continued European participation in the government of many of the countries. The most successful approach was that of France, which granted independence to the more politically developed countries in North Africa while incorporating the governments of Algeria and their island empire into the national assembly, as part of the government of France.

In the case of Algeria this subsequently proved to be a disaster and gave rise to a bitter war for independence. The problems extended to France itself with acts of terrorism and attempts to overthrow the national government.

At this time of change, I found it interesting to examine the widely held view that the colonial powers had exploited their colonies to their own advantage. There was considerable evidence that the reverse had been the case, at least over the last decade. In fact, the one-time subject people were exploiting their previous masters, infiltrating their countries, burdening their social systems and influencing their policies in international and home affairs. Frequently this was against the better interests of the indigenous population, as well as European culture and well-being.

The suggestion that upside-down exploitation existed was certain to be challenged by the colonial territories and the migrants who had settled in the UK. However, the facts spoke for themselves.

During the post-war period, every family in Great Britain contributed an average of about £60 each year towards the cost of colonial development and welfare. This direct aid was only part of the picture. Commonwealth preferences and quotas raised the cost of food and other items over the cost of purchases made in world markets. Costs of welfare for the colonial migrants, with their large families and low skills, was another burden on the British taxpayer.

It was suggested that the Commonwealth provided a large market for British goods. This might have been true in the past, but increasingly countries such as India were taking over the bulk of the textile market throughout the Commonwealth. The development of new industries, in many of the developing countries, further complicated matters. These were frequently helped by subsidized financing, which unfairly lowered production costs. They also took full advantage of the Commonwealth preference system.

At the time I left Nyasaland, most textiles, the major item of trade with the local people, were being obtained from India. Imports from Britain consisted almost wholly of equipment and materials for British-financed development projects. Other projects were increasingly being financed through the international development agencies and subject to international procurement.

A frequent criticism of the colonial powers was that of exploitation of natural wealth and materials. As these resources had not been tapped before the Europeans came, the real question was whether development of the resources had benefited everyone who had a stake in them.

Ownership of land and resources was a very open question, particularly in South Africa, where the Europeans and the Bantu arrived at the same time. The development of large-scale agricultural, mining and industrial activities had been possible only as a result of European investment, initiative and expertise. Most of these developments had brought better living standards and social services to local people. Projects developed by the private sector were economic ones and not helped by concessionary aid and subsidies.

The United Kingdom had already a population pressure problem, but every year increasingly large numbers of African, West Indian and Asian migrants arrived and, through their British nationality, claimed full rights of citizenship. Was it reasonable, or logical, to accept these people, of alien race, while denying similar facilities to Europeans with whom we had common cultural interests and a similar racial background extending over many centuries?

I believed that the British Commonwealth had become an anachronism. The ideal of an association of nations made up of all races was a lofty one, but surely its very form was schismatic, and interests must be conflicting owing to the different racial and cultural outlooks and the divergence between the standards of living and stages of economic development reached. Were the members' interests even compatible?

The Malthusian question of pressure of living space and growth of population was a fundamental issue which might, in the not too distant future, become an almost insoluble problem. Within the Commonwealth, you had the case of India, with a population growing by over one hundred million each decade, and Great Britain, with a total population of about fifty million. Were the common interests to be met using the predominately European-inhabited colonies of New Zealand and Australia and the less densely populated parts of Africa to absorb the Asian population explosion? Would the ex-colonies, who were better able to do so, even accept this surplus population? *Tanzania was later to eject most of the Asians it already had.*

British politicians loved to refer to the Commonwealth as a bulwark for peace. This was as much a nonsense as many of their other pronouncements. Could we rely on any real help from the ex-colonies in time of war? Even in the last war, South Africa, a white-governed country, entered the war after a very narrow vote, with the country divided between the pro-British element and the pro-Hitler, Malan/National Party with its associated Ossewa/Brandwag neo-Nazi movement.

With the development of communist and near-communist sympathies in many of the colonies and ex-colonies, were we likely to get any support in the future? Even access to strategic materials was likely to be of little value as we were likely to face another, possibly atomic, blitzkrieg which might last only a few weeks or even days. Remember that Hitler came very close to success in his first assault during the last war. The initial period of any future war was likely to be decisive and would not wait for prolonged debates on possible participation and the importation of strategic materials from places thousands of miles away. The Commonwealth with its divided policies and loyalties was as much a bulwark for peace as Chamberlain's "Peace in Our Time" agreement with Hitler.

What held the Commonwealth together? It was surely not a question of common wealth and common interests. The British, as responsible Europeans, had certainly some interest in preventing the countries they had helped develop from falling under communist domination. They also might wish to protect their investments in these countries and preserve the rights, lives and properties of their citizens who had settled there. These were justifiable aims. What is overlooked is that this might also be in the interests of the countries concerned. However, in the case of the Central African Federation, we were, at best, being half-hearted in protecting British interests. I wondered if we ever again would take a stand in protecting these.

Was our continuing political influence of value? We had tried, in the past, to achieve social and economic improvement and the development of democracy in all the colonies. However, we now faced the situation of a white nationalist apartheid state in South Africa, black dictatorships and oligarchies developing elsewhere and a disintegrating and possibly communist-influenced Central Africa.

Was there any sign of universal friendship within the Commonwealth? Every year the representatives of the African, West Indian and Asian countries, both within and outside the Commonwealth, became more and more angry over Great Britain's policies if these showed any self interest, or Britain tried to take a strong line in maintaining law and order. Many leaders of the ex-colonies conveniently forgot the lack of freedom in their own countries while introducing motions in the UN condemning the racial policies of the white-ruled countries. These policies were, in the South African case, admittedly wrong but were usually less repressive than those in the countries raising the complaints. India, one of the main complainants, was the only country able to claim that it had a system of slavery still in existence.

Although atrocities were common in many ex-colonial countries, every racial disturbance in the UK, however small, was greeted with angry cries and criticism of the finest police force and fairest judicial system in the world. All that Britain had done for its colonial empire, including its willingness to grant self-government, was conveniently forgotten.

Were there any cultural ties? European culture was a direct descendant of the Grecian and Roman cultures and had been carried to the countries where European immigrants had settled in influential numbers. America had inherited a European culture. Its leadership in many sciences and certain of the arts was based on the European heritage.

Culture depends on many things. It is partly related to the history and accumulated knowledge of the people and partly to the genius of individual members of the population. If it is to have favourable conditions for growth, it is also dependent on national or individual wealth.

Europe with its national, papal and individual patrons had been a fertile area for cultural development. America, with its wealth and resources, was continuing this tradition on both a national and an individual basis. India, with the wealth of its maharajas, had developed an alien/different culture. Most parts of Africa had little other than their tribal societies and what the Arabs and Europeans had brought in. Within this context, British cultural interests, for the foreseeable future, would lie with Europe and America.

If the Commonwealth had so little to offer to the indigenous white British subject, what was its value to the ex-colonial subjects? The main advantage was the possibility of exploiting the ex-colonial powers on an international, national and individual basis.

For the ex-colonial nation this involved obtaining aid, frequently without economic justification; provision of subsidized educational facilities; and freedom from the disciplines resulting from misgovernment and mismanagement which often brought deteriorating social conditions and economic collapse. It also provided a means of influencing policies in favor of their own country and the Asian and Negro races as a whole.

For the individual, it gave freedom of movement into the home country to take advantage of the social services, job opportunities and other facilities available there.

Based on these factors, I believed that all countries – including in particular the USA, which had pressed so long and so strongly for freedom and independence for the colonial territories – should accept that the colonial and ex-colonial powers could now advance an even stronger case for freedom from the burdens created by the ex-colonies they had helped to develop and started to bring into a twentieth-century world.

Should we continue to try to make the Commonwealth work? I felt that this was against the best interests of all white British subjects, that charity begins at home, and that we had a debt to pay to our own people before we continued to provide massive aid to our ex-colonies and let their people have free access to all we had built up and had to offer. I also hoped that, with the development of freedom in Europe, a closer association with those having a common culture and interests would follow. With these thoughts in mind, I made some suggestions for our future national policies in my next and final chapter.

Chapter 14

What to do about it all

In order to provide a sound basis for future British policies in Africa and correct world opinion, it was essential that Britain should be far more objective in its publicity on British policies and aims. Our worst failure in explaining the British position had been in the case of our best friend, America. How were we to correct this?

We should try and get our American friends to forget about the American War of Independence, with its aftermath of ill feeling and distrust of colonialism. The British colonial system had achieved a great deal in pacifying and helping the backward races and under-developed countries.

We should publicize the progress and good which had been achieved through enlightened British rule by dedicated persons whose main concern had been the advancement of the country and the people they governed and protected.

We should emphasize that many Bantu political leaders cared little about the interests of their countrymen. Unfortunately, these persons had the advantage of reaching and exploiting public opinion through the most influential and educated Negro racial block in the world. This, through its racial sympathies, was usually biased in their favour.

We should point out that there were many Europeans, even outside South Africa, with no home other than Africa, who, by their own and their ancestors' efforts, had developed estates out of the wilderness and brought industry, gainful employment and ever-increasing prosperity to people of all races in Africa.

The world should be fully informed about the Mau Mau atrocities, committed in the name of independence, how primitive many of the tribal Africans were and how much they needed outside leadership and knowledge in addition to the guidance and leadership of their traditional chiefs.

Totalitarianism and communism were unlikely to make any real progress under British rule, or the gradual development of a local constitution supported by Britain, but many of the Bantu nationalists, through their training and indoctrination in Russia, China and India, favoured such political structures and policies.

We should make it clear that thousands of colonials and ex-colonials wanted to see the Bantu progress in our way of life and take his place in government and at all levels of society. To help achieve this, it was necessary to apply every pressure we could on South Africa to look for an alternative to apartheid. The principles adopted under the Central African Federation of treating the community as one unit and basing the vote on economic and educational standards would provide orderly progress to real democracy.

The least South Africa should be expected to do was to give the blacks and coloureds some right of self-determination. South Africa should also abandon apartheid and provide free association between people of all origins and colours.

We also should try to convince South Africa that, while it might be able to control the position in the Union for the time being, it was unlikely to be able to do so indefinitely. In the meantime, it was prejudicing the position of the white African colonials and destroying the hopes of establishing moderate multi-racial governments in neighbouring countries. By following repressive racial policies the Afrikaners were helping the nationalist extremists by providing a basis for propaganda to influence world opinion. Finally, they were creating doubts in the minds of white people throughout the civilized world about the morality of the European position in Africa. This was likely to result in large areas of the continent falling into the hands of totalitarian or communist regimes.

In the case of the Euro/Asiatics from Russia, we should record our concern about their aims and objectives and our dislike of their methods. Hopefully the deficiencies of their own inefficient and repressive system would ultimately catch up with them.

What to do with India? We should stop all aid and assistance, other than humanitarian aid, until she ended the slavery of the caste and bonded labour systems. We should also tell India that while slavery exists in India, she is not regarded as a civilized country whose council is acceptable in Commonwealth affairs.

We should press India to take action, within the country, to limit the growth in population. Surplus population should be India's problem, not Africa's. We might well let India see if she could get greater help from her Russian friends and burden the Russian economy. Perhaps, the Russians might be persuaded to open the steppes for India's surplus population.

*   *   *

Faced with the developing trends in the Commonwealth, what policies should Britain follow, both in its own interests and those of European culture and order?

In Germany I was involved in the provision of communications for the North-West German Iron and Steel Control, which was the first concerted attempt at European economic cooperation after the war. I became convinced that full membership of a European Community was an alternative to the Commonwealth and offered greater strength and security for the way of life we stood for.

The first-class powers were those which had advanced furthest technologically and developed the greatest economic strength. In a modern world, small units could not operate efficiently without adequate markets and economies of scale. The wealth and leadership of the United States was related to its size and population.

The US economic structure and its sciences were substantially based on work carried out by foreign nationals and the heritage of the smaller

European countries. Undoubtedly the people of Great Britain, France, Germany, Italy and Spain still had the basic ability, but with the advance in scientific and industrial development, and the ever increasing investment involved, the individual units were too small and conditions not conducive to the development of an industrial/technological society comparable with the USA. In consequence there was still a brain drain to the USA.

The idea of a European Federation had been proposed many times before. It would make a larger unit than the USA and could, I believed, achieve more. The cultural ties were there, and, although natural resources were more limited than in the USA and Russia, development of more competitive pricing structures and trading arrangements with countries having these resources could overcome this deficiency.

We had made some progress toward a unified Western Europe through the Iron and Steel Control trade and customs agreements. The need for a much more complete integration was becoming a matter of extreme urgency on both economic and security grounds. This was vital to the defence of Western civilization from communist infiltration or aggression. It was also pivotal to the development of a stronger economic structure with better standards of living and the resources to defend itself against the threat from Russia.

It could be argued that European Federation, although in the interest of the Europeans, would do nothing for the ex-colonies and would have some adverse effects in denying them protected markets. I believe that a united Western Europe could, over a period, attain the economic strength of the USA and would be better equipped than the individual ex-colonial powers in providing both the capital and technical assistance needed for development. Also, a more rational organization of industry would lower production costs, open larger markets and create additional demand for raw materials which were increasingly having to be obtained from the underdeveloped areas. This in itself would provide a spur for economic aid and development.

In the changed circumstances existing in the Commonwealth, I believed that our aid policies needed urgent review. One major change should be the elimination of all aid to those countries with avowed communist sympathies and which were not dedicated to democratic principles. Let them become a burden on the Russian economy. In time it might be an unsupportable one.

Humanitarian aid should continue to be given, but where it was needed because of the failures and weaknesses of the governments concerned, the facts should be well publicized. All other aid should be based on sound economic principles with the elimination of subsidized development which had no economic justification. Uneconomic projects result in the development of agriculture and industry on an unsound footing with unfair competition in world, Commonwealth and local markets. On the other hand, aid directly related to a nation's willingness to develop its resources, whether in materials or manpower, and which would offer an economic return on investment, was a wholly different matter and should be encouraged.

In everyone's interest, and to increase economic development, aid projects should wherever possible be undertaken using equipment and materials supplied from the country providing the aid. Provision of aid is obviously less of a burden if one is able through so doing to increase employment and produce at marginal cost. This would lead to increased wealth, adequate employment and over the longer term increased ability to help the underdeveloped world.

An important corollary to economic development was that it should parallel – or lead – educational advancement. Far too often in the colonies I saw the unfortunate results of education without opportunity. This was one reason for the mass migration to the United Kingdom with its attendant and future colour and employment problems.

I realized that strong moral objections could be raised against holding back extension of educational facilities and the provision of grants for scholarships. I had, however, to weigh my experience of the contented villagers against the detribalized and discontented intellectuals, with no faith in their own or in our society. The happiest Africans I knew were not those who attended secondary school or university, but the uneducated tribal Africans living contentedly in their villages, lying in the sunshine and watching their womenfolk working in their maize patches, while giving their own time to quiet contemplation.

We might well ask whether we should subsidize university attendance for everyone in Britain. This might be socially desirable but is certainly uneconomic. It is hard to justify education of large numbers of the population to school certificate and degree standards in a country which, at its present stage of development, consists of a primitive tribal society based on subsistence-level agriculture. Such education, without economic advancement, leads to dissatisfaction and unhappiness, with an understandable wish to escape from, or exploit, the community. We should therefore look very carefully at educational grants and subsidies and relate them to the needs of the country's economy.

Although I had a great affection for the Bantu race and appreciated its many good characteristics, it was obvious that mass migration to the developed countries must be a matter of concern. I have earlier dealt with some problems, but not that of the mixing and inter-marriage of the Caucasian and Negro races. This has social and ethnic aspects which are bound to be the subject of individual prejudice and often hardship. On the other hand, continued segregation in any country creates problems of interracial feeling and jealousy. The social problems involved in absorption and integration in the community, given the cultural, religious, language and ethnic differences, can only be resolved over time and become more extreme as the number of migrants increases.

One other social problem is the loss, by the more advanced developing countries, of their better-educated nationals and those who show the greatest initiative. This is related to the educational problem. In helping to educate, we are almost certainly increasing the level of migration. Where the development of the countries' economies has created a need for these people, they are creating a shortage of expertise through their migration. I faced this difficulty shortly after arrival in Jamaica, where, having set up advanced overseas technical education facilities, we had to drop the scheme when we found that most of our trainees went to better-paid jobs overseas. We found, incidentally, that any form of indentured system was useless when the people could move freely out of the country.

I believe that British policy on migration should be related to the actual labour needs of the United Kingdom and subject to full recip-rocal facilities being given by the migrant's own country without any restrictions, either way, on rights of property, person or citizenship.

Epilogue

1. Jamaica, 1957–67

In 1957, I left Nyasaland to join the Jamaica Telephone Coy, first as chief engineer, and later as managing director.

Jamaica was another world. For the first time, we were living in a truly interracial society with people of all racial backgrounds and colours fully accepted in the community and having the chance to advance to any position. For example, the minister of trade and industry, responsible for all commercial activities including those of my company, was a mixture of Arawak Indian and Negro. The prime minister, whom I had to meet on a number of issues, claimed to be 60 per cent Irish, 30 per cent Arawak and 30 per cent Negro, the total of 120 per cent being, he maintained, why he was better than other politicians.

My staff were of all races, colours and origins. One senior engineer, the blackest man I ever met, claimed I was his father. This was an unlikely conclusion, as he was about my age. When I asked him about our stated relationship, he said that it was a compliment and showed his great respect and regard for me.

In place of our small army of domestic staff, we had one maid and one gardener. The maid was a character. She had a very poor opinion of Jamaican men and had no intention of supporting one, although she appeared sometimes to find them useful. She had five children but hastened to assure you that they had different fathers. This free and easy life style was common amongst one's domestic staff. A friend's

The author with staff members of the Jamaica Telephone Coy.

Jamaica. Sir Alexander Bustamentamente (Busta) opening subscriber long distance dialling.

maid produced a rather light-coloured baby. The lady of the house questioned her about the father. The clear yet ambiguous reply was, "If you sit on a bag of nails, how you know which one stick you?"

In addition to having a major commitment in running a large company, I became involved in a number of public activities and professional responsibilities. These included setting up and later becoming president of the Jamaican Institute of Engineers, chairman of the technical committee advising on standards for the introduction of TV, chairman of the Post Office advisory committee and member of the Scientific Research Council's technical committee. I was also a member of the advisory committee for the College of Arts, Science and Technology.

My own country asked me to serve as the local chairman for the Western Hemisphere Exports Council and as a member of the Federation of British Industries Scholarship Committee.

If this were not enough, there was a very full social life, with a need to attend parties two or three times a week and a considerable entertainment commitment, both within and outside my company.

*　　*　　*

We had come from a colonial society where all the senior colonial officers were from Britain. My department in Africa had been organized along hierarchical lines, with most of the senior positions held by Europeans. Our domestic arrangements were substantially based on a feudal system, where you were very much the lord and master. Socially, we only had very limited contact with the Bantu and Asian population.

Although we had always tried to avoid racial bias, it was undoubtedly good for us to experience the different conditions in Jamaica where the governor general was a black man, most of the ministers of government black or coloured, and one's colleagues and friends from all backgrounds and races.

Was there colour prejudice? Perhaps in a reverse kind of way. If you wanted to succeed in politics, because of the preponderance of the black electorate, you were preferably coloured or at least had a coloured wife. There was virtually no prejudice in business, which, although often still controlled by British and American interests, was open to all races whether Bantu, Arawak, European, Mid-Eastern or Asian.

Although it lacked racial divisions, the country suffered from a major division between the well-to-do/middle class and the extremely poor. This was accentuated by the very high population density, the high birth rate (predominantly illegitimate), the limited amount of land available for extension of agricultural activities, the lack of industrial development and the migration of large numbers of the unemployed to squatter settlements in Kingston the capital city. There was widespread use of marijuana in all areas. These factors contributed to a high crime rate, with some crimes of violence, most of which were drug-related, although not in the accepted sense of providing money to feed the addiction.

Marijuana/ganja/cannabis was readily available at little or no cost. Marijuana is known as hashish in the East, and the word "assassin" was derived from this. The effect on its users when fully under its influence is to remove inhibitions, compassion and feeling. People in the developed countries who urge legalizing this drug may be unaware of its behavioural effects.

There were several sector movements in Jamaica. The most prominent, the Rastafarians, regarded Haile Selassie as God's representative on Earth and used ganja as an aid to religious experience. The association with Ethiopia was interesting as, to my knowledge, no Ethiopians were ever brought to the West Indies as slaves. The Rastafarians' acceptance of the Lion of Judah as their messiah was largely related to the special significance of having a black person as both the secular and religious head of a feudal but cultured black civilization.

Since I left Jamaica, the whole world has become aware of the Rastafarian movement through the music of Bob Marley. The Rastas have, to some extent, become glamorized, with rock singers copying their long dreadlocks and repulsive appearance. At the time I was in Jamaica, most people, although concerned about the Rasta doctrine of interracial hatred and their extensive use of ganja, regarded them with tolerance. I personally hated their naming an extremist racial sect after Ras Tafari, the civilized, cultured, Christian gentleman I had known in the late 1920s.

We numbered many Jamaican artists and writers amongst our friends. There were also dedicated and efficient Jamaicans of all races, and mixtures of races, in all walks of life. These people could make a useful contribution to society in more advanced civilizations anywhere in the world, and many migrated to better-paid jobs overseas. They were also desperately needed in Jamaica, and this drain was a loss to the economy and society.

My job was always interesting and sometimes stressful. To add to the complications of running a company involved in highly technical operations in a developing country, I had the problems of a highly

Union delegates and self at company party. Terrance ("Blood must flow") is on the right.

vociferous and organized staff and a political structure where the unions were effectively the two political parties.

I spent many hours in union negotiations with Michael Manley, who later became prime minister. We developed a friendly and cooperative relationship, helped by Michael's sense of humour. During a strike at another public utility, the union ordered a "go slow" in my company as a measure of sympathy and solidarity. I immediately countered by discharging three hundred casual staff as, with the permanent staff going slow, casual staff output would be negligible. Michael telephoned, "You can't do this to me, Dick." I replied, "It's done, Michael." Michael came back at once, "If they don't go any slower than usual, is that OK with you?"

We also had our own strikes. During one of these, I had to pass the picket line to get to my office. As I did so, the chief delegate shouted, "Blood must flow." I replied, "Whose blood, Terrance?" to receive the astonishing reply, "Not yours, you're a good bastard."

After I had been ten years in Jamaica, my company was sold to an American company, and, as they wished to introduce policies which concerned me, I resigned.

Such then was the Jamaica in which we spent ten opinion-forming years, a Jamaica in which many senior members of the community, colleagues and friends were coloured or black, a Jamaica in which I got to know most of the politicians, business people and my staff by their Christian names. This helped in maintaining good public and staff relations.

When we left Jamaica, we took with us a sense of the warmth of the country and of its people of all colours. More than anything else, we appreciated the innate kindness and sense of humour of the Jamaicans, which helped to resolve the most difficult situations and make life easier than it might otherwise have been in a poor country with many inequalities, shortages and hardships. But for the violent crime, which has become more severe since we left the island, it would have been our intention to retire to Jamaica and rejoin our many friends there.

2. Washington and other Places, 1968–78

I joined the World Bank in Washington on April Fool's Day 1968. Three days later, Martin Luther King was assassinated. As I was staying in the centre of Washington, I was surrounded by demonstrations, riots and arson. I began to wonder if I was not the proverbial fool for leaving quiet and relatively peaceful Jamaica and coming to this centre of racial feeling and intolerance.

When peace was restored, I settled in on my modest job where, as a senior staff member, I was responsible for leading appraisal and supervision missions of telecommunication and power projects all over the world. I also directed or took part in several seminars.

Providing you were not looking for career advancement, this was one of the most interesting jobs you could have. It was also my licence to travel and to get to know people, in industry and government, in many countries. This was rewarding and satisfying, when related to the contribution one could make to development and the extent to which one's efforts were appreciated. I felt that over thirty years of experience and knowledge in a technical sector, gained in Europe, Africa and Jamaica, were being put to good use. This was also a period of personal study and learning, particularly about economic factors, and the relation and contribution of each sector to the economy as a whole.

One refreshing aspect of work at the Bank was the degree of camaraderie which existed amongst the staff at all levels. This was particularly important during our missions to developing countries when the mission members had not only to work together as a team but virtually to live together. Usually we stayed in the same hotels and most of the coordination of our activities was done at evening sessions. Meals were often taken together, and even our recreational activities and excursions were usually planned as joint rather than individual efforts. Members of the missions were genuinely concerned about the health and wellbeing of their fellow mission members. They even tried to protect them from dangers of all kinds.

Before leaving on a mission to Pakistan one of our secretaries asked me to contact a friend who was living in Pakistan and take her one or two personal things. After arrival in Pakistan, I telephoned the lady and asked if she would like to join us for dinner and pick up her things. When she arrived we found her to be young, attractive and very well dressed.

Initially, our guest seemed restrained and I suggested that she might have preferred younger company but she replied that she found older men more interesting. As she got to know us, she became both entertaining and outgoing.

I mentioned that I had bought my wife a sari. Our guest at once said, "Why don't we go to your room and I can show you how a sari should be worn?" The other mission members immediately expressed an interest in also learning how saris were worn – it was probably important to project evaluation – and joined us for the demonstration. They remained loyally at my side until we had escorted the lady to her car and she was safely on her way home.

While at the Bank, I worked in more than thirty countries on all the continents. These were days of travel, hard work, long hours and, due to the long and frequent absences, a disrupted home life. One needed a very understanding wife and the dedication of a workaholic. Nonetheless, it was a fascinating job.

My interests extended well outside the projects I was working on. I tried to study the culture, history, ethnic background, governmental systems and social structures of the countries I was visiting. I also, at my expense, tried to visit other areas and points of special interest. I met some fascinating people and had several adventures.

*   *   *

In Nepal, I arranged one weekend to make a trek from Pokhara into the foothills of the Annapurna range. With a maximum altitude reached of 4,000 metres, it was not mountain-climbing as such but certainly sorted out the men from the boys. I was in the latter class. The views were

Nepal: Nagar Kop, Himalayas.

Everest from the pilot's cabin.

Nepal: pagoda.

magnificent, and the insight into how the people lived extremely interesting.

Another weekend, we tried to reach the Tibetan border over the road the Chinese had constructed. After a gruelling four hours, our Chinese vehicle had to turn back because of a land slide about five miles from the border.

In Kathmandu, I met Boris, that most unbelievable of all "characters" on the subcontinent. I was intrigued by his stories of life in the Russian ballet, his escape from Russia, his time at the Calcutta Gymkhana Club, where he met his Scandinavian wife, and more recently in Nepal, where he seemed to know everyone from the king to the social outcasts. The Yak and Yeti, the restaurant Boris ran, was the meeting place for the international, social and mountaineering sets. Boris understood and loved good food and wine and frequently used them as an aid to telling his Rabelaisian anecdotes and ribald stories.

I saw the child goddess Kumari whose deity would end with puberty. I was also introduced to several of the large number of hereditary generals who attained their commission at birth.

I made a friend of the Anglo-Indian pilot who flew us all over the country, often inviting me to join him in the cockpit of the DC3s, similar to those in which I had flown in and out of Berlin during the Russian blockade. Between two of my visits my friend crashed into the side of a mountain, when trying to fly into Kathmandu in cloud. There were no survivors.

The closest friend I made in Nepal was Father Marshall Moran. We had a common interest in amateur radio. I made several visits to the father's seminary on the slopes of Pulchowki mountain and got to know him well. He had been in the country for thirty years and was a fascinating raconteur who probably knew, and understood, more about the country and its people than any other Westerner alive.

Nepal was always a joy. The countryside was magnificent and the culture and architecture fascinating. Despite the primitive conditions in many parts of the country, no one appeared hungry. Funds sent home by the soldiers serving in the Gurkha regiments were being supplemented by a rapidly growing tourist industry, and the country could afford to buy most of the essentials not produced locally.

*   *   *

Nearby Bangladash, which I had to visit repeatedly, was another story. I usually saw things at their worst, and even at their best it was hard not to be depressed by the problems of the country and its people. I also felt some sense of national guilt that partition, which caused countless deaths, untold misery and a bitter civil war, had been introduced by the British. Despite the poverty and suffering, some of the river scenery was lovely and the constant boat traffic very interesting.

Some of my visits to Bangladesh were at times of national disaster. Once, before the civil war which led to the separation from Pakistan, it was in the chaos and misery following a typhoon which flooded wide areas and killed thousands. Despite the devastation and loss of life this was in a way an enlightening experience. Working with me on behalf of the Pakistan government was my friend Abdu'l, a descendant of Abdu'l Qadir, one of the founders of the mystic Sufi sect, the brotherhood of poets. Abdu'l was not only capable and hard working but was the personification of a good and dedicated (I almost wrote Christian) human being who showed both understanding and compassion for those who had lost so much in this national disaster.

Abdu'l and I developed considerable mutual respect and regard for

Bangladesh: river scene.

one another and talked of many things including Christianity, Islam and humanitarianism. At these times, I quoted from the Kasidah which had so influenced my thinking. He countered by quoting from the poems of Hafiz which contained so many similarities. Abdu'l could not believe the Kasidah had been written by an Englishman. I told him that Richard Burton had studied Islam and made the Haj. Burton had also been initiated into the mysteries of Sufism and become a Qadiri. I hoped this would lead to a discussion of the mysticism of his sect but Abdu'l avoided further discussion. I had too much respect for him to pursue the matter.

*   *   *

Shortly after the civil war between East and West Pakistan, which resulted in the creation of the separate country of Bangladesh, I was a member of a United Nation's relief mission led by Frau Erna Sailer,

Austrian ambassador to India. This was an interesting, but in some ways a distressing, experience due to the widespread devastation, suffering and famine. The one encouraging fact was that the rest of the world was trying to provide help. During this mission I worked with, and got to know, the UN resident representative Toni Hagen who cared deeply about the position and the problems of Bangladesh. Toni had earlier been in Nepal and had written what was probably the definitive book on Nepal. It also contained many excellent photographs.

The poverty, over-population, shortages and lack of any hope for major improvement in Bangladesh would have touched even the hardest-hearted. Worst of all, the Bengalis appeared incapable of working together for the common good. The UN relief mission had worked closely with President Mujibur Rahman, who was an impressive leader. When it seemed that he might pull the country together, he was assassinated.

* * *

On a later visit to Bangladesh I had an annoying experience. I was sitting quietly reading in the hotel lounge when two men approached and asked if they might join me. I said that I had no objection. They at once started a conversation criticizing government and the political leaders in extreme terms and saying how much better conditions had been under Pakistan government. When they asked my opinion I realized that they might be "agents-provocateurs". I told them I thought we should be like the three monkeys who could see no evil, hear no evil and speak no evil. Disconcerted, and perhaps annoyed at the monkey reference, they left me, probably to seek another victim.

* * *

Some years after this I was leading simultaneous missions to Pakistan and Bangladesh. Whilst working in the latter country, and despite having had all my "shots", I developed all the symptoms of cholera. As a result of the almost continuous vomiting my eyesight was affected and I had some difficulty in reading. A few days later the cholera symptoms had cleared up but, when flying to join the mission in Pakistan, I found that I had lost the sight in one eye.

My colleagues were disconcerted at having to work with a one eyed Jack and seriously concerned about my sight problem. Abdu'l, who was working with the mission, was a great source of strength and help to me at this time. Amongst other things he arranged for me to see the leading Pakistani eye specialist who diagnosed a detached retina in one eye and developing problems in the other. The specialist wanted to operate immediately. Failing this he prescribed complete rest, until an operation could be performed.

The mission members performed nobly, taking over most of my commitments. Those meetings I had to attend were held in my hotel room. Abdu'l spent most of his time with me and, together with the mission members, became my eyes in reading what I had to read and my presence in dealing with his colleagues. As a result of them all working almost night and day and with the cooperation of our Pakistani friends we were able to leave four days later.

Abdu'l came to see us off at midnight, Diffidently he took me to one side and said, "I am praying for you as a brother Qadiri. I hope you will recover your sight and come back soon. For now I shall miss you and our talks on what it is all about. My thoughts go with you."

My colleagues led me back to Washington, a three hour operation, laser treatment of the second eye and weeks of strictly controlled convalescence. When I returned to duty I was promoted to take charge of power and telecommunications projects in Latin America. Sadly I never saw Abdu'l again.

*   *   *

I spent a considerable time in East Africa and was disappointed in much of what I saw. I had known the area well when in Nyasaland and had accepted the case for independence. I hoped the East African community would build on what British colonial rule had started.

Beware of this fellow (blowing dust).

Pussy (lioness).

Buddies (zebra).

"Where did you come from?" (cheetah).

Pygmies, Congo area.

Instead, the incipient tribal and national ambitions came to the surface, and an association important to a balanced economy broke down.

Kenya, with the strongest economy, remained the best-off and most stable of the three countries. Tanzania expelled most of its Asian population who controlled much of the economy. It also took over the land of the large estates for its resettlement projects, which were less productive, and experimented with collectives, using Chinese advisers.

Worst of all, and moving back into the Dark Ages, was Uganda. I went there many times while Idi Amin and Milton Obote were in power. I saw misery which I would have preferred not to see and heard many details of atrocities.

One weekend, a friend offered to take me and two other members of the mission to the Queen Elizabeth game park. We had been assured that Europeans were safe, even outside Kampala, and accepted with enthusiasm. On the way back to Kampala, we were followed by a military jeep, which stopped and looked appraisingly at our car when we filled up with petrol at one of the small towns. It then began to trail us as we left the protection of the town. Fortunately, we had the faster vehicle and outstripped them. We learned later that, during the previous week, two American journalists had been murdered in this area by military personnel and their car stolen.

During my visits to East Africa, I had the pleasure of visiting most of the national game reserves. To me the most impressive was Amboselli. Not only for its wild life but also for the scenery, with the snow-capped peak of Kilimanjaro always looming in the background. I also had the joy of driving down into the Congo Valley, where there was a small pygmy (Bushman) settlement. I took them presents and was invited to one of their feasts and dances. It was hard to imagine these small and gentle people as the dreaded Nlukuwewe of Nyasaland folklore.

*   *   *

Iran was one of my favourite countries, despite the reports of corruption at high level. Incidentally, the Shah was never directly named. I travelled widely in Iran, saw them catching sturgeon from the Caspian, skied on the higher slopes of Mount Demavand and visited Iran's major cities and Persepolis. I went into the desert and saw the *qanats*, the fascinating underground irrigation systems with their blind white fish. I also, as a result of my introduction to Persian poetry through the Rubaiyat and Burton's Kasidah, made pilgrimages to the tombs of Saadi, Hafez and Omar Khayyam.

My final visit to Iran was at the time of the rioting and civil disobedience when the Shah was deposed. I overnighted in London and checked conditions with Iran Air. They assured me all was quiet in Tehran. I arrived at midnight to find all hell had broken loose. A curfew was in force, although most people were ignoring it. I managed to bribe a taxi driver to take me to my hotel, the Hilton, which fortunately was on the outskirts of the city. There, I learned that the Intercontinental, where my colleague Andre was due to stay, was on fire, with shooting in the area. I booked the only remaining accommodation at the Hilton, the honeymoon suite, and left a message at the airport for Andre to come to the Hilton. Fortunately, he received the message and arrived about three in the morning. His complaint, "What am I to do in the honeymoon suite on my own?" was typical.

Omar Khayyam's Tomb, Neshapur.

The following morning, our taxi was shot at as we tried to reach the government offices. The taxi driver wanted nothing more to do with us and bundled us out of his taxi. We had to walk the last hundred yards or so. The officials we were to contact said their staff were on strike and in an ugly mood. They asked us to return to our hotel to avoid provoking the lower-grade staff. Fortunately, they provided a car to get us back to the hotel.

We contacted the government minister, whose department we expected to work with, by telephone, and he advised us to leave the country as soon as possible. This was not easy, as the airline we had booked with, to take us to Pakistan, had cancelled all flights into Iran. With some help from the United Nations, we managed to get out four days later, flying west to Turkey.

Surprisingly, our mission obtained most of the information we wanted, although circumstances overtook its objectives. We worked from the hotel and held discussions with the minister and government officials concerned. I think they were glad to be away from their offices, which were under siege and in a state of chaos.

*   *   *

When visiting microwave radio station sites, I travelled into the back-ward parts of Papua New Guinea, with their hundreds of languages and light-hearted tribal skirmishes where they play "touch" with Stone Age axes.

In South Korea all members of our mission were invited to dinner at a high class Ki Sang house. While the girls were intent on serving, entertaining and making our visit enjoyable they were certainly not prostitutes and followed the best geisha traditions I had earlier seen in Japan.

Visiting India I saw the beauty of the Taj, the bureaucracy of Delhi, the poverty and despair of Calcutta and much more.

Indonesia had the lakes and volcanoes of Sumatra, the ruins of Java and the temples and dances of Bali. The Ketjak ceremony fascinated me with its chanting cadences and the mass hysteria and near ecstasy this created.

In Jordan I visited Jerash and the Dead Sea and saw the isolation and mystery of Petra and the Nabateans.

I visited the Saudi desert with the remains of its petrified forest and its prehistoric underground water supplies. They wanted to take me to the mosque square to see them cut off the hand of a thief. The Koranic code has almost eliminated murder and crime but I refused the opportunity of seeing it in operation.

I saw the sophistication of Beirut before its destruction, the ruins of Ba'albek; the Hebrew, Christian and Moslem heritage of Jerusalem; and the beauty and culture of Taiwan.

These were a few of my travels and adventures when working for the Bank. I enjoyed the travel and was happy with my work. However, over the years a process of disillusionment took place. I had looked for high ideals and principles in the governments of the developing countries. This applied in some countries, but in others there was dishonesty, corruption, tribalism and nepotism. Accountability was often missing and a sense of responsibility lacking.

The Bank was doing a good job in appraising, financing and supervising development and social/economic improvement projects which would reduce the gap between developing and developed countries. This despite the country problems and the international nature of the Bank's management and activities (and the complicating factor of having more economists per square foot than any other entity on Earth). The Bank was a remarkably efficient organization. It was also an excellent employer and fully deserved the loyalty and dedication it received from most of its staff.

I made friends from many countries and disciplines and at all staff levels while I worked in the Bank. I also worked with, often admired and, I hope, helped the government and sector executive staff in the countries in which I was responsible for projects and seminars. Most of the people I worked with had the best interests of their country and organization at heart. Many, of all races, have remained our friends since I retired from the Bank.

*   *   *

What of our private lives in Washington? After my initial baptism of fire, we enjoyed all the cultural and other amenities the city had to offer and the beauty of the surrounding countryside. We made many friends of all nationalities and colours, mainly amongst the better-educated and comfortably off. We also met many good, honest and hard-working black people at all levels of society, including the not-so-fortunate classes. However, we quickly learned that Washington was truly the crime capital of the world.

Reports in the media might lead one to believe that the crime population was largely made up of politicians and TV evangelists. Unfortunately, we had more violent and desperate criminals. It was not possible to walk at night in most parts of central Washington without fear of being molested. Many of the younger blacks still worked on the principle of "Whitey, you owe us something, and we are going to take it." Given the chance, they appeared to enjoy insulting and intimidating you, and, when they could get away with it, beating you up. Friends and colleagues were mugged, many of us were abused, and a number suffered thefts. My wife was threatened, with the police arriving in the nick of time. Our house was once broken into.

While the anger-driven and anti-social behaviour of some of the coloured population was directed against the whites, many of the older, law-abiding blacks, including in particular the taxi drivers, were also attacked and robbed. It was almost impossible to get a cab at night unless you ordered it to come to a specific address. Undoubtedly a lot of this crime was drug-related.

We moved from Washington to our retirement home in Florida in 1978. We left Washington with sadness that the lawless, arrogant and demanding black section of society had so little feeling for their own people and were, through their activities, prejudicing racial under-standing in the community as a whole. This attitude had never been present in either Africa or Jamaica.

After leaving Washington, I intended to divide my time between Florida and Switzerland. Through 1986, however, I continued to be asked to undertake consultancy work for several national and interna-tional organizations and companies. This has taken up a great deal of my time.

My time in Jamaica and the USA provided the framework of expe-rience and increased knowledge, on a world-wide basis, within which I tried to review my comments in the earlier chapters of this book and to write the next two sections of this epilogue.

3. Africa and Colonialism, 1994

A. In Retrospect

Looking back over the years since I wrote my earlier comments, the change in the Africa I loved and worked for has been almost wholly for the worse.

The first movement to grant independence in the central African area, that in the Belgian Congo, resulted in a state of anarchy, with the rape of Belgian women and children, murder of Belgian nationals and a civil war killing thousands of Bantu Africans. I believe that the loss of all order in the Congo resulted directly from the granting of independence under outside pressure before the Congolese were ready for it.

Patrice Lumumba stated he would take help "from the devil". Kruschev may not have appreciated this obvious reference to himself, but he certainly supported Lumumba. While all this was going on, the United Nations, disunited as was so often the case, did not know which side to support in the civil (Katangan) war. When they finally intervened tens of thousands had already died. One fortunate short-term effect of the Belgian Congo debacle was that the adverse publicity on the results of Bantu rule led to some moderation of African Congress activities elsewhere.

The first serious attempt at interracial understanding, and progressively interracial government, in the Federation of the Rhodesias and Nyasaland, collapsed and was replaced by the separate black-ruled states of Zimbabwe, Zambia and Malawi. Malawi, under the enlightened rule of Dr Banda, and with economic help from the UK and South Africa, has done better than most people expected, despite being flooded with refugees from neighbouring Mozambique.

The economies of Zambia and Zimbabwe have gone through a period of great difficulty, with the devaluation of currencies, nationalization of some companies and government seizure, or control, of many financial assets. Intertribal fighting and some terrorism has been reported from Zimbabwe. The need for aid to economies, which under the Federation would have been self-supporting, has increased substantially. A few international companies have invested funds in Zimbabwe. However, the tight exchange controls, and the steady decline in the value of the currency in overseas markets, has discouraged outside investment in Zimbabwe.

The Europeans, who were largely led into supporting the Federation by their own politicians advised by the Colonial Office, have cause for major complaint. Many have been forced to leave all that their ancestors built and have migrated from what were Northern and Southern Rhodesia.

*   *   *

What of the rest of Africa? One vital factor is that populations are growing faster than are locally grown food supplies. The food produced *per capita* has, it has been estimated, fallen by 20 per cent since colonial times. Africa's present population of about 650 million is increasing at nearly 3 per cent *per annum*. In the absence of more effective birth control measures it may exceed one billion by the year 2010.

The major increase in Africa's population has already started to cause serious humanitarian and environmental problems. Shortages of food and famine are becoming extreme in many areas. Forests are being cut down for fuel and burnt off for planting. Desert areas are increasing due to poor husbandry and over-cropping. Less and less space is available for the wildlife. In many areas the wild animal population is being decimated by poachers driven by poverty and the need to obtain food for their hungry families. How are food supplies and even the basic needs of the increased population to be met in the future?

In many countries, dictatorships have been established, with little sense of democracy or regard for basic human rights. Hundreds of thousands have died as a result of intertribal wars, famine and the breakdown of health services. Economies are often in difficulty due to

African Ambit

mismanagement, graft and inefficiency, this despite available man-power and material resources.

There has been a breakdown of law and order in countries such as Uganda under Idi Amin, and Milton Obote, with military despotism and intertribal wars taking an untold toll in human life and suffering. In a 1988 TV interview, the Ugandan ambassador to the USA estimated the number of innocent people massacred in her country as over 300,000. The number has been reported elsewhere as more than 700,000. Little has been said about this by the media or black leaders in the USA. What would have been made of the position if even one tenth of one per cent of this number had earlier been killed in one of the colonies? I was interested to note that the lady ambassador did not follow the usual line of blaming the colonial system for Uganda's misfortunes, but the CIA, UK and Israeli intelligence, who she suggested had brought Amin and Obote to power.

Order has been restored in Uganda, but intertribal wars continue elsewhere with a need for humanitarian aid to alleviate the effects of misgovernment and inter-tribal hatreds. Having said this, one must, in fairness, mention the successes of black African rule in countries such as Malawi, Senegal and Cameroon.

One of my failures in writing the original chapters of this book was that, although I commented on the lack of leadership above the tribal level, I failed fully to appreciate the likelihood of intertribal conflict when colonial rule ended. But the tribal system had worked well in colonial times and had formed an integral part of the governmental system. It had also maintained the traditional cultural background for the society.

The evidence of likely intertribal conflict was there. I had written about the intertribal wars which existed before colonial government was established. The replacement of the central integrated government structure which the colonial system had provided by a vacuum, or by leadership which had limited acceptance, would almost inevitably result in the tribes starting to fight it out amongst themselves.

Tribalism remains a major problem. There have been, or are ongoing, tribal wars in Zaire, Mozambique, Angola, Nigeria, Liberia, Rwanda, Burundi, Uganda, Upper Volta, Chad, Ethiopia, Eritrea and the Sudan.

Sadly, tribalism, and the often related sectarianism, is not unique to Africa. Such conflicts have existed for decades in Northern Ireland, they have caused the division of Cyprus, the destruction and foreign domination of the state of Lebanon and the bitter conflicts in what was Yugoslavia. Even the USA, with its Ku Klux Klan and Nation of Islam, is not free of ethnic and sectarian intolerance .

* * *

I believe that through their opposition to colonialism and their support of the nationalists, America, the USSR and India contributed to the breakdown of law and order in many African countries. These conditions might have been avoided under a gradual process of democratization within the colonial system.

However, the colonial powers, on their part, failed to develop and outline their programmes for democratization of government in their colonies, and explain the dangers of proceeding too far too fast. Adequate publicity, both within the countries themselves and on an international basis, was essential to an orderly transition to democracy. Additionally, the colonial powers' policies were too frequently self interested in the development of resources, including labour, with insufficient attention to making an adequate contribution to improving local economies and conditions.

Surprisingly a tribal war finally resulted in American and UN neo-colonial intervention in Somalia. This has been supported by millions of Americans who regarded colonialism as the "Great Satan" of the Western world and who through their influence helped end colonial rule in Africa.

Far be it from me to criticize the intervention in Somalia. Rather, it was too little too late. Similar action could have saved over half a million lives in Idi Amin's Uganda and countless millions elsewhere. It is still overdue in the Sudan, where millions are dying by starvation and a most bitter war based on religious as well as tribal issues. With the more recent incidence of intertribal genocide in Rwanda can the international community continue to stand by and let the mass slaughter of innocent people continue?

One particularly disturbing factor in independent Africa is the schismatic nature of national and tribal ambitions. This was one of my concerns in the 1950s when I stressed that larger units had the advantage of greater efficiency owing to economies of scale and were more economically stable owing to the greater diversification of economic activities. So far, the Federation of the Rhodesias and Nyasaland has come to its untimely end, and the East African community has broken up. Nigeria has been able, through the Biafran civil war, to maintain its national unity, but separatist moves are common throughout Africa. The division into smaller units has caused a major increase in the need for outside aid.

*   *   *

Except for Egypt and the Mediterranean countries, with the inception of black majority rule in South Africa, we are now at the end of white dominated government in Africa.

Unfortunately, in South Africa, we have tribal rivalries and a ruling body which has always favoured socialist and communist principles. With the divisions between the various Bantu groups, continuing intertribal violence is to be expected. Land ownership is certain to be a real problem. Some protection of white property rights has initially been accepted by the Bantu leaders. Is this likely to continue given the pressures of the masses for an equality unrelated to the individual's contribution to the economy? Based on experience elsewhere, can the inefficiency and corruption which so often follow the introduction of black government be avoided? Although it obviously should be the ultimate goal can a viable economy be maintained in the face of the likely immediate demand for equal facilities and living standards?

South Africa is a classic example of a country failing to face up to its interracial problems. Asians and coloureds were given minority representation in the national government in 1984 but negotiations to admit the Bantu people only started in 1990. A real attempt should have been made at a much earlier date to set up a multi-racial society free of the evils of apartheid, possibly along the lines proposed for the Central African Federation. A gradual transition to an integrated democratic society could have been achieved with the progressive education of the electorate and the development of mutual under-standing between all races.

I wish the new South African leaders well in solving all their problems, not the least of which will be the demands of the black electorate. At the same time, I am filled with a deep sense of sadness about the possible decline into economic ruin, anarchy and tribal warfare of this lovely, wealthy and in many ways cultured country which I knew so well. If what I fear happens one may well try to reassure oneself that the Afrikaners have only themselves to blame for any misfortunes they may now face, but what of the white section of the population which has always opposed apartheid and sought black advancement?

I have a continuing concern for the future of Malawi and its people. Dr Banda's rule has often been criticized as being autocratic to the extent of suppressing all opposition. He has, however, been pragmatic in facing up to the country's real problems. As a result Malawi is one of the few Bantu countries which can substantially feed itself and which has a supporting infrastructure.

The Banda era has now ended. Hopefully the new leadership will have the strength of purpose and the public support necessary to hold a mixed tribal society together. Dr Banda has created the Kamuzu Academy, based on the British public school concept and old school tie principle, to educate the future leaders of the society. This may well prove to be one of Dr Banda's valued legacies to the country.

*   *   *

Africa is likely to remain one of the major problem areas facing the Western world over the next few decades. Concerns are likely to be related to protecting human and property rights, introducing democratic government, insisting on accountability, developing the economies and providing economic and humanitarian aid. Within this context the framework of the more developed countries' own social and economic structures and their approach to the problems of Africa should be considered.

The disruptive influence of the USSR in Africa has ended. The former USSR is now a group of countries forced to improve the state of their own economies and the living standards of their populations and no longer interested in spreading the communist doctrine through war and subversion. The failure of the Eastern block economies is also likely to have a significant effect on the thinking of many African leaders who have blindly accepted communist/socialist doctrines because many of them were educated and indoctrinated in the USSR, China or India.

Indian policies, accompanied by the mass Indian migration into East, Central and Southern Africa, created major difficulty for colonial governments and was one of the main problems they had to face in the 1950s. As a result of my many visits to India in more recent years, I have grown to admire many aspects of Indian culture and more fully appreciate the social and other problems India faces. I have also met many cultured and intelligent Indians who have shown the highest standards of integrity and responsibility. Anyone with a sense of compassion would wish to lessen the hardship and poverty suffered by much of the Indian population. I was tempted to revise my comments about India in the main chapters of this book written in the 1950s but, after reflection, felt they should stand as an honest opinion of what a British colonial felt about Indian policies and activities at the time.

India's internal problems have always been acute, but there are signs that she is at last tackling these rather than becoming further involved in overseas interests. India has done something to stem its population growth, which was one of the main factors in her interest in African settlement. She also has had some shocks in the treatment of Indians in Africa by some Bantu governments.

It is encouraging that steps seem finally underway to end the slavery of the bonded and child labour systems. These practices should not be tolerated in any civilized society and should have been eliminated years ago. They were, however, so ingrained in the Indian social structure that complete elimination may take some time.

The changes in the USSR, India's poor relations with China and the continuing need for concessionary aid from the West are likely to be factors in India's future external policies and may substantially increase Western influence.

*   *   *

What of the present policies of the former colonial powers of France, Britain, Portugal and Belgium? Britain, to some extent, has been going it alone, through the Commonwealth, instead of combining her interests in her former colonies with those of the other former colonial powers which should, I believe, be dealt with through the European Community.

Development of the European Community has been delayed, due largely to British reserves and the wish to retain many essentially British interests. For Europe to achieve its optimum political and economic power, full federation of central government and more effective coordination of the economies is needed.

Britain still thinks Commonwealth before thinking Community. This may be due to an innate sense of responsibility to the former colonies but is against the better interests of Britain and the other European countries. The so-called Commonwealth is an anachronism which, with the inefficiencies and corruption in many of the ex-colonies and their social and economic demands, can only lead to common poverty.

I believe there is a strong case for putting the interests of the

European Community before those of the Commonwealth and withdrawing Britain's direct support for the latter. A stronger European Community would be able to provide increased aid to the developing world. I still believe that all Western aid should be limited to countries that support the democratic system and the full rights of their nationals, and are prepared to accept full accountability including opening their governmental systems to an examination of corruption and graft.

In Great Britain, there is a doubly divided community, a division between the haves and have-nots and between the ethnic Caucasian population and the ex-colonial coloured immigrants. Despite the windfall of oil revenues, the economy is not as strong as it should be. There is widespread depression in the north of the country, with a geographical and political division between the haves and have-nots.

The outdated, inefficient and divided Commonwealth, with the need for continuing aid to, and writing off the debt of, former colonies, is undoubtedly contributing to Britain's economic problems. There is a pressing need to develop the home economy and to provide additional employment and a better standard of living for the population, rather than providing aid to ex-colonies which are frequently ruled by dictators and communists who have often sequestered the assets of Britain and its nationals.

Britain has done too little too late in restricting immigration to an already overcrowded island. It is now a multi-racial state, with all the concurrent problems. However, it should face the facts as they now are and do its best to integrate all residents fairly into a truly multi-racial society.

*   *   *

A factor in the ability to provide aid to the developing countries is the economic well-being of donor countries. As a result of the strength of its economy, the USA has been the world's major donor of aid, with the Japanese now approaching parity and the various European countries making major contributions, particularly when considered on a *per capita* basis. The actual amount contributed is not, however, a true assessment of a country's contribution but should be related to the return to the donor's economy resulting from purchases paid for out of the aid. This is particularly important in an era of unfair trading practices.

Unfair trading practices have become a major problem in world trade and, despite the efforts made through GATT, one wonders if free trade, however desirable, is a realistic aim. Japan, which has consistently underbid almost everyone in world markets, has the advantages of cheap money through national savings, high productivity, and low management and litigation costs. It has every right to take advantage of these factors in a free trade system. Japan has, however, taken the unfair trading advantage of increasing production, with consequent economies of scale, and exporting the increased production at marginal cost, plus profit margin, while maintaining home prices by restricting imports. Japan's Achilles heel is that it cannot maintain home prices in a completely open market. Japan's trading partners and competitors are not unaware of this position, and there are increasing pressures for Japan to open its home market or face import restrictions elsewhere.

It is also suggested by other countries' manufacturers that Japanese suppliers, working as a cartel, are exporting at below production cost to put the competition out of business and then take over the market. And to protect its trading advantage, Japan is now directing major overseas investments into areas in which they can take part in, or control, exports to Japan if the home market is opened.

In an attempt to find an effective means of competing internationally, the USA has encouraged a fall in the value of the dollar. The USA could do this without major inflation, because imports only account for about 25 per cent of total home consumption. Is the dollar undervalued? I only know that at present rates of exchange one can buy most items required for personal consumption for considerably less in the USA than in Europe or Japan. An under-valued dollar may be the biggest "no confidence" scam of all time. However, it also may prove to have been dangerous to encourage the loss of confidence in the dollar when there are serious budget deficits and trading imbalances caused by high consumption levels, profligate use of raw materials and inadequate national savings. These create a need for major foreign funding to meet the cost of defence, health and welfare services. An undervalued dollar can restrict the availability and increase the cost of these funds. It is to be hoped that the American government will continue to face up to its budget problems, and an increase in the value of the dollar may follow.

Foreign countries have now discovered that, at the dollar's present level, real assets such as property, stocks and even American companies can be purchased at fire-sale prices. Foreign investment is pouring in, encouraged by the ever increasing budget deficit. There are real dangers in this. Major foreign ownership can influence national, economic, production, marketing and trading policies; sometimes against the best interests of America. To those Americans who do not accept these conclusions I recommend Shintaro Ishihara's book *The Japan Which Can Say No.*

The USA has carried an almost intolerable burden in meeting a major part of the cost of defending the free world. The Western Alliance, Japan and the developed Asian countries should shoulder a greater part of what one hopes will be a reduced defence burden.

When will the Western industrial countries and communities start considering their own populations' interests? It is counter-productive for a country, or an economic group, efficiently producing an item within its own economy, to provide concessionary aid to allow a developing country to buy that item from elsewhere because internationally bid prices are lower (and frequently not directly related to overall production costs). This way, the countries providing aid are unable to efficiently use their productive resources and expand employment opportunities.

Most countries could provide aid at an increased level if their resources and labour capacity were more fully used. Furthermore, uneconomically low prices, often subsidized by the suppliers' home market, can create an uneconomic expansion of facilities and an imbalance in the development programmes of the developing countries themselves. The economic evaluation of projects should always stand on true rather than subsidized costs.

Tied aid and procurement is not favoured by the international lending agencies, although often accepted where co-financing is involved. While it may present problems in allocation of aid funds, these are not insurmountable. They may be less contentious and time-consuming than international competitive bidding, where awards are frequently the subject of dispute and suppliers take short cuts to obtain advantage. Tied aid would also end much of the bribery and corruption which may be a problem when the developing countries are involved in the procurement process.

There is a need for massive American and European aid to the USSR and other Eastern Bloc countries to revitalize their economies. I believe this aid is essential if market economy practices are to be followed and democratic governments are to survive. The position is similar to that existing in Western Europe after the war, which was dealt with by providing aid under the Marshall Plan. Leaving aside the humanitarian needs of the developing countries, which obviously should have a high priority, a strong case can be made for urgent aid to the Eastern Bloc countries. This would expedite development, with a prosperous Eastern Europe, perhaps within an extended common market, being able to increase the European aid contribution for the less developed countries.

* * *

There has to be an equitable accommodation in every country between all races making up the population. In particular there is need for rethinking on interracial relations in Britain and the USA, with their large coloured populations, which seem to worsen rather than improve. It applies to a lesser extent in Western Europe. The Russian republics and the Eastern European nations are fortunate in being substantially free of this problem, although they have localized difficulties with their ethnic pockets. The West Indies have probably achieved more than anyone else in this respect.

The rights of all nationals must be respected in any interracial society. We should follow the principle of equal opportunity for all races and persons, with advancement based on merit and ability. Quota systems are undemocratic and result in inefficiency and bad feeling between the races concerned. Such systems are also against the better interests of the minorities themselves in reducing the need for self-improvement. Equal opportunity is true democracy, and preference based on colour, or bleeding heart propaganda, is against national, racial and personal interests.

It should now be obvious to the Negro peoples, amongst whom many in Africa have espoused communism, that their friends in the Soviet Union were imposing neo-colonial rule and influence over Eastern Europe by force. They were also limiting personal freedom, failing to respect human rights and ruining the economies of the USSR and Eastern Bloc countries. The African countries should compare this with the good things resulting from colonial rule in Africa.

Must the record of slavery always remain a bar to satisfactory interracial relations? All the nations involved in the eighteenth- and nineteenth-century African slave trade now regret following the practices of earlier conquerors and taking economic advantage of the enslavement of fellow human beings. Remember that the slave raiders and purveyors were largely the Africans themselves. Also accept that slavery, by placing a commodity value on the captives, prevented many deaths during tribal raids and wars. Would there have been the mountains of skulls in Idi Amin's Uganda if there had been a market for the unfortunate victims?

This is no excuse for the human misery slave trading created and the development of organized slave raiding activities. The white populations finally came to realize how evil slavery was, and many of them, such as the missionaries and colonials, fought bravely to end it. It is now time to forget the guilt complex. The Italians have no such feelings about the slaves taken by the Romans throughout Europe. They are instead proud of the civilization their colonial empire brought to Europe in the wake of conquest.

With emancipation and the development of humanitarian measures and equal rights, the ex-slaves' descendants are now far more advanced and better off than their kinfolk who remained in Africa. The Caribbean countries have been taken over by the coloured population. Brazil has large and increasingly influential black communities in most major cities, although serious poverty continues to exist in many areas. The USA has black Americans in all walks of life and all sections of society. A similar trend is taking place in the United Kingdom.

B. Tell it like it is

At the time I wrote the original chapters of this book, in the late 1950s, I stressed the need for better publicity about the British position in Africa. Sadly, over the last three decades, the position has deteriorated rather than improved, and we appear to have failed completely in explaining the good aspects of colonial rule. Colonialism has become a dirty word and is blamed for most of the evils which exist in the now independent countries of Africa.

Almost everything about Africa I read today, hear on radio or see on TV paints the whites who have served or settled in Africa as black as possible. This despite the fact that they brought a measure of civilization, an interim peace, reasonable social services and, at least, some development of most economies. At best, the Europeans are depicted as exploiters; at worst, destroyers of older civilizations and flourishing economies.

There are Europeans who for reasons of their own, or through lack of adequate background, support these contentions. Some of these people, who often masquerade as experts on African history and sociology, have established a platform and are frequently believed. An opposing view is likely to be unpopular, and I fear I may be accused of racism in trying to restore a proper perspective in this matter. What particularly concerns me is that the pro-black African propaganda, which is largely based on biased information and part-truths, is accepted, owing to the abysmal lack of knowledge about the continent and its history, including, in particular, the colonial period. Hopefully, this book may help to redress the situation.

There were, of course, earlier civilizations in Africa, but these were almost wholly in the northern half of the continent, and many owed their development to outside influence. Some were also based on mixtures of races. This is shown by the languages in those areas which developed the more advanced civilizations. These are frequently descended from, or mixed with, Amharic, Arabic, Berber, Hamitic, Nilitic and Semitic. (For example, amongst the more developed Bantu peoples are the Hausa and Swahili. Their languages are in part related to Hamitic and Arabic.)

Because of the easier access, the more advanced black civilizations have developed in the areas adjoining the Mediterranean, near Arabia, or along the coast on the north west and north east of the continent. These included the West Sudanese, Hausa and Yoruba to the west and the East Sudanese, Ethiopian and Swahili to the east (the Swahilis settled coastal areas as far south as Kilwa).

Few traces of earlier civilizations pre-date the arrival of the Arabs and Europeans in the southern and central parts of the continent, where first the Bushmen and later the Bantus were mainly concentrated. I have travelled widely throughout this area, and the only signs of any earlier civilization I have seen are the cave paintings and the yet-to-be-identified stone ruins in Zimbabwe.

The absence of more advanced cultures is, however, not surprising considering the almost continuous tribal wars, endemic tropical diseases and famine. A further factor was the nomadic existence of the people, who practised subsistence agriculture which impoverished the soil, after which the family, or tribe moved on.

As Dean Swift has perhaps pointedly put it:

So geographers in Afric-maps,
With savage-pictures fill their gaps;
And o'er unhabitable downs
Place elephants for want of towns.

There have been great achievements in art and civilization in the northern and coastal regions of Africa. The heritage is a far more open question. Egypt, which was a predominantly white-ruled Mediterranean country, had its own peculiar funerary culture which, with a substantial contribution from slave and indentured labour, achieved advanced processes, unprecedented civil works and unique works of art. Many experts trace the methods used in the production of the bronzes of Benin, in West Africa, to the Egyptian heritage.

During the period prior to colonization Africa had a low and relatively stable population density. Many critics of Western activities have ascribed this to the slave trade. It has been estimated that Africa had a population of about 100 million in the mid-seventeenth century. This fell to about 95 million in the mid-nineteenth century. Undoubtedly this fall in population was partly due to the slave trade, with the number of slaves taken estimated as 15 million. The tribal wars, the effects of famine and the absence of tropical medicine were, however, the major factors in limiting population growth. With the suppression of tribal wars and the related slave trade during the colonial period and, most importantly, since the introduction of health services, tropical medicine and humanitarian aid, the population has grown to more than 650 million. The population is now doubling every twenty-five to thirty years. As I have indicated in the preceding section this is likely to become one of the major problems facing the African states

Much has been written and said about the morality and effects of European settlement of large parts of southern Africa. Even the missionaries, who gave up their material comforts and frequently their lives in bringing Christianity, peace, improved health services and education to the Bantu, have been criticized as fifth columnists.

Frequently the loss of the witch doctors, with their bestial practices, human sacrifices and necromancy, is bemoaned as a loss to civilization. Obviously, the critics do not know of many of the practices of witchcraft, and the Mau Mau atrocities.

The missionaries and colonials were responsible for recording the written languages on which Bantu society is based (English, French and Portuguese are, of course, still in common usage in the ex-colonies). (My friend Doc compiled the present standard Chiyao dictionary.) As a result, most Bantu languages use the Roman alphabet despite the associations with Arabic. Nearly all Central African politicians and government officials received their initial education in mission schools. Where it exists, responsible Bantu government has substantially evolved through the education of leaders under the system established by the missionaries.

How did the European settlers arrive? Generally, the missionaries came first. Frequently in their efforts to pacify, install Christian principles, end slavery and bring about progress, they supported the extension of European government, trading and, where they thought it might help, European settlement. They sometimes did this by encouraging local tribal chiefs to seek extended European interest in their tribal areas. The settlers were able to take over substantial areas, largely because of the way of life of the indigenous population, their lack of respect for the land and the low population density.

Free (what a misnomer) Africa inherited the advantages of established government structures, civil and social services, basic infrastructure, cities and towns, public utilities and developing economies. Nothing comparable had existed in black Central Africa before colonization.

There has been considerable denigration of that great Englishman Cecil Rhodes who contributed so much to the pacification and development of Central Africa, including the elimination of inter-tribal wars and the suppression of slave-raiding. It is a credit to the government of Zimbabwe that Rhodes' last resting place in the Matopas has been left undisturbed. How long this will continue remains to be seen when ill-informed, irresponsible individuals, mainly European, publicly suggest that the grave is an insult to the people of Zimbabwe.

In Malawi, European and Asian settlement was restricted owing to the high population density – another sign of the responsible position adopted by the Colonial Office and British Government. European trading activities, which were encouraged, were an integral part of the process of getting rid of slavery – a fact that David Livingstone realized when he made his famous pronouncement, criticized so often by his detractors, of bringing Christianity *and trade* to Central Africa.

Unless one wishes to redevelop a nation based on the pathetic remnants of the Bushmen, there is some justice in the Afrikaner claim that the ownership of the Cape Province of South Africa should rightly be vested in the European settlers. The Afrikaners also can argue that they arrived in the other provinces contemporaneously with the Bantu and have made the greater contribution to development of the country and the economy. They have also done more than many Western nations in improving standards of living and social services for both indigenous and migrant Bantus. Nevertheless, apartheid was an indefensible system, and full acceptance of the Bantu into the society, with equal opportunity, was essential to the future of South Africa.

I feel the ex-colonial powers can justifiably reject most of today's criticism of the claimed evils of colonialism and of all the Europeans are stated to have done to destroy earlier civilizations and economies. Most of the present-day evils, and the deteriorating economic and social position, result from intertribal wars and misgovernment by many African leaders. Placing the blame on colonialism is against the better interest of independent Africa, as it discourages real responsibility. If one can blame conditions which are outside one's control, one is well along the way to excusing one's own shortcomings and inefficiency.

* * *

There is an increasing sense of objectivity and realism amongst African writers and leaders. A remarkable African writer, who is both factual and constructive, is the Nigerian chief, Areoye Oyebola. In his book

Black Man's Dilemma, published in 1976 in Nigeria but as far as I can trace not generally available in the West, Chief Oyeobola has made some of the most realistic and objective analyses of the problems of black Africa and the Negro race to be found anywhere.

I disagree with much of what Chief Oyebola has written, including his comments on colonialism, Russia and China and his suggested solutions to the problems existing in South Africa. Later events, such as the failure of communism in Russia and the human rights problems in China, have shown the shortcomings of the Russian and Chinese systems. The end of apartheid, and introduction of black majority rule in South Africa, has been achieved, but are the remaining problems, including tribalism, any closer to solution?

Chief Oyebola would undoubtedly also disagree with much that I have written from my European and right wing standpoint. However, there is a surprising commonality about many of our opinions on the problems of independent Africa and the Negro race.

The coincidence of many of our views led me to get in touch with Chief Oyebola. We have corresponded by letter and telephone but have yet to meet. He, and his publishers, have agreed that I may quote freely from his book. Although I have hesitated about quoting him out of context, I feel that the following excerpts stand largely on their own and need no qualification:

> There are three intriguing facts about the black race. They are facts which most black and "coloured" peoples and some liberal whites would prefer not to face honestly and squarely. One such fact is that no black country has ever made a breakthrough to modernity . . . The second intriguing fact about the black race is that it was the only race in history which had between 14.6 million and 20 million of its members physically transported as slaves from Africa to a completely new area . . . Equally strange was the active support which the African chiefs and middle class gave to the capturing and transportation of their fellow blacks to America. . . . The third perplexing fact will undoubtedly arouse the resentment

of my black and coloured brothers and sisters. Relying on the fact that the different races of the world came into existence at the same time I have come to the sad, but valid conclusion that the black man has made little or no contribution to world civilization . . . I have become fully convinced that the much vaunted black civilizations of ancient Ghana, Shonghai, Mali, Zimbabwe, Hausa/Fulani, Yoruba, Benin and other areas were quite inferior to the civilizations of other races . . . I regard the writings of Western liberal scholars and black historians on the greatness, glory and achievements of ancient African kingdoms, empires and emirates as a deliberate morale booster for the dehumanized black race . . .

Many Western liberals are aware of the fact that the white countries have a lot to lose if the black man faces the reality of his situation and if he accepts the fact that he hadn't a past that he can be proud of. The whites have a lot to lose if the blacks henceforth work hard to place their membership of human family on the basis of genuine equality. White experts publish books about our past glory, grandeur and achievements. They've got willing disciples among black intelligentsia who have lost the candour of any critical self-searching . . . The absurd view has been expressed that colonialism and slavery led to the death of black Africa's cultural heritage. A culture can only die if a whole people can be exterminated as the Romans did in the annihilation of Carthage . . . Malcolm X was right to say that the Egyptian civilization was African. But the ancient Egyptians were white and not "black" African . . .

One major problem of the black man is that he is today not aware of his basic human weaknesses and problems . . . Some of my fellow blacks are too frightened to talk about our basic problems . . . Others blame the slave trade, the kindness of nature, colonialism and neo colonialism for our underdog position in the world. They look for scapegoats. But unfortunately we have never realized that there was hardly any problem the black man faces or has faced – slavery, colonialism, neo-colonialism – which other racial groups like the Chinese, Japanese and even the Europeans did not face in the past . . .

One of our greatest weaknesses is our lack of self discipline both as individuals and as a society. I believe that if we must make it as a race it is discipline we must foster and cling to. It is with discipline that the black man can achieve the much needed colossal re-orientation of social attitudes and a new way of life . . . Our poor attitude to work and indiscipline also affect our attitude to our countries. We have never learnt how to subjugate self to the good of our country. We can't put our nation before self . . . One other glaring weakness of the black man is that he is very selfish and individualistic . . . The best people are either destroyed, subjugated or at best merely tolerated.

But very poor leadership appears to me as the black man's greatest problem. It is sad to admit that with only a few exceptions the black race is ill-served by all sorts of poor leaders who have emerged since the attainment of independence by many black states . . . Many black political leaders have a narrow concept of what constitutes a life of fulfilment. They have no lofty dream of leaving their country better than they found it. Above all our leaders are corrupt. They abuse their official positions and corruptly enrich themselves.

I find an almost uncanny closeness between these extracts from *The Black Man's Dilemma* and what I had written earlier in my original and these later chapters. In fairness, the extracts do not include much of the comment on dehumanization and the negative attitudes adopted by the Western powers and societies toward the Negro race.

Chief Oyebola is concerned about continuing foreign domination, even after independence, and feels there is white conspiracy, imperialistic influence and sabotage at work designed to maintain white supremacy on a neo-colonial basis. Although I question this conclusion, I support the idea that, given the basic freedoms and rights of individual members of the population, independent African states should be free of outside influence and should learn from their own mistakes. However, where humanitarian or economic aid is required, there should be full accountability. One of my contentions in this book has been that the Commonwealth, which might be regarded as a neo-colonial system, should be disbanded.

I have been particularly impressed by the repeated plea for increased discipline and responsibility at all levels. I was reminded of my problems resulting from lack of social responsibility on the part of many of our Bantu staff in Nyasaland. I also thought of the vocation of my friend the bishop, who worked so hard to develop this sense. He was probably the most farseeing and wisest of us all in realizing that this was the major problem developing countries faced in introducing a modern and responsible social structure and economy.

In considering this weakness in Africa, we should not overlook the failures and materialism of our present Western civilizations, where an "I'm all right Jack" attitude exists amongst many people. There is also a lack of pride in honest workmanship and a failure to accept responsibility. Selfishness predominates everywhere; people live to the maximum extent of their means with little thought of the future – "Social Security will always look after us." Lack of responsibility extends beyond the individual level to the national level, and our politicians, with a few exceptions, fail to face our national problems and, to remain popular, give us the leadership we unfortunately deserve.

Few people today read Gibbon's *The Decline and Fall of the Roman Empire*. If they did, they would realize that even great civilizations can decay and destroy themselves from within if there is an emphasis on materialism with a lack of responsibility, both in leadership and amongst the people.

The plea for responsibility amongst the black people of Africa in order to develop modern civilizations should also be urgently directed to our own people if we are to preserve the civilizations we already have and help underdeveloped and poorer countries advance into a modern, civilized and democratic world.

At the time I worked in Nyasaland, the coat of arms consisted of a leopard rampant in front of the rising sun, with the phrase "Lux In Tenebris". I take some pride that, following the work of the early missionaries and of my fellow colonial officers, I had some small part in continuing to bring light into darkest Africa.

Despite the propaganda of the African nationalists, and some Europeans and Americans, I still honestly believe that European colonization of Central Africa was the best thing that ever happened to that area. The alternative would have been continuing tribal wars; exploitation of the weak and defenceless; high mortality; few, if any, health, welfare, education or cultural facilities; and the rule of the witch doctor with its related cruel and bestial practices. Life would still be based on subsistence agriculture, with destruction of fertility and frequent famine.

The truth of these conclusions is supported by the state of Africa today and the present conditions in many countries compared to those at the time colonial rule ended. One should not overlook the re-emergence of many of the pre-colonial evils of tribal war, terrorism, famine, deteriorating social services and lack of freedom which now exist in many of the ex-colonies.

We cannot go back, but one hopes the free countries of Africa can go forward with the help of the developed countries and international agencies, and will learn the lessons the so often despised missionaries and colonial system taught.

Bantu terms used in this book

Bantu	Tribes using the Bantu group of languages.
Boma	District Headquarters.
Bwana	Lord or master.
Chabi	Inferior, poor quality.
Chewa (Nyanja)	A leading tribe.
Chimbuzi	Toilet.
Chi-	Language.
Cipyela	Witchcraft burning place.
Donah	Lady.
Katundu	Baggage, items.
Lobola	Bride price.
Mau Mau	Kikuyu rebels in Kenya. Given to atrocities.
Mfiti	Magic, witchcraft.
Mfiti niumba	House of witchcraft. House of black magic.
Mkuku	Chicken.
Msanga (msanga)	Quickly.
Mwabui	Trial by poison.
Mwera	The storm wind of Lake Nyasa.
Ngoni (Nguni)	An invading tribe from the south.
Nguru	A tribe from Portuguese East Africa widely settled in Malawi.
Panga	A machete. Used for clearing bush or admonishing one's wife.
Poli (poli)	Slowly.

Posho	Food or food allowance.
Tiki	Small silver coin equivalent to three pence.
Tumbuku	A tribe in the north of the country.
Wa chabe ndithu	The worthless ones.
Yao	Another leading tribe.

Some Notes on the Post Office

The records available relating to the history of the Post Office were not very complete owing to an invasion of termites, which, before their presence was discovered in one of the strong rooms, destroyed most of the early records. We did, however, have some documents stored elsewhere including the official stamp collection and these are extant today.

One very interesting document held in the Central African Archives, with a photostat copy kept in my office in Zomba, was a notice signed by Mr Alfred Sharpe, later as Sir Alfred Sharpe to become the first Governor of the Protectorate, but at the time titling himself Acting Postmaster. This announced the commencement of mail services from Tshilomo on 20 July 1891. By 1894 the number of post offices in Nyasaland had grown to fourteen.

In 1895, the British Africa Company assumed authority for operating the postal services. In the same year Cecil Rhodes' conception of the Cape to Cairo telegraph line was carried further when the existing line to Salisbury was extended to Blantyre. This line was next extended in 1901 to link Nyasaland with Tanganyika. The line was again extended in 1904 to Abercorn in Northern Rhodesia. This line continued for many years to be the only international telecommunications facility available in Nyasaland.

Radio telegraph service to the outside world was introduced in the 1940s. It was not until 1950 that high frequency radio telephone service was introduced to other countries. This was followed in 1953 by the better quality very high frequency service. This system also provided teleprinter service via Salisbury in Southern Rhodesia.

Mail in the early days took about three months to reach the UK. Following the opening of the Blantyre–Beira railway link in 1923 this was reduced to something less than one month. The next improvement took place in 1932 when air service from the UK to Salisbury was introduced with a total transit time in the region of thirteen days. The first direct air mail flights into Nyasaland were introduced in 1933. In the 1950s airmail from and to the UK took 2½ days with a twice-weekly service in operation.

In 1956 there were some seventy post offices and thirty postal agencies operating in Nyasaland. Internal services were good by any standards and first-class mail was given air transport where this offered any time advantage. A twenty-four-hour service operated to all main centres with maximum transit times to minor centres of two to three days.

Comparatively primitive means of transport continued up to recent times. Mail carriers were the normal means of transport between main centres until the late 1920s with carrier service to the old provincial headquarters at Mzimba continuing until 1936 and to Karonga until 1950. I saw the end of the last carrier service, to any main post office, in 1956 when we replaced female mail carriers to Chinteche by a Land Rover service. Some carrier services were still operating to postal agencies operated largely by the native authorities.

Although an internal telephone network existed, consisting of some small, mainly isolated, manual telephone exchanges, introduction of a modern interconnected automatic telephone system dated from the early 1950s when, as a result of our development programme, the number of telephone subscribers increased by about 500 per cent and the number of telephone calls by 1,500 per cent.

One other note of some interest relates to the high power very high frequency radio equipment used on the link between Nyasaland and Southern Rhodesia.

Before the war, the British Post Office was experimenting with the use of high power very high frequency radio equipment for systems which were beyond the line of sight to which the range of higher frequency transmission is normally restricted. Such a system was installed in the late 1930s between the UK and Channel Islands. In the early days of the war, I was responsible for communications through the Channel Islands to Pirou, near Granville on the French coast. This provided the rear line of communications for our forces in France.

When we evacuated from Guernsey, some ten days after Dunkirk, we recovered what equipment was possible and amongst this was the Channel Island terminal of the experimental link. Later, after the occupation of Germany and when the Russians tried to isolate Berlin by cutting all cables, we had this equipment brought to Germany and installed between the British Zone and Berlin where it provided the main line of communications until the Germans were able to manufacture and install high power equipment of their own. The equipment was then returned to the British Post Office and stored until we again requested its use in Central Africa. It was, I believe, finally recovered in the 1980s and returned to the British Telecommunications Authority for their museum.

Countries in which the author has worked:

Argentina	Kenya	Singapore
Bangladesh	Lebanon	South Korea
Britain	Malawi/Nyssaland	Switzerland
Burmah	Malaysia/Sabah/Sarawak	Taiwan
Curacao	Mauritius	Tanzania
Egypt	Mexico	Thailand
Ethiopia	Nepal	Turkey
Fiji	Nigeria	Uganda
Germany	Pakistan	USA
Indonesia	Papua/NG	Zambia
Iran	Saudi Arabia	Zimbabwe
Jamaica	Seychelles	

Additional countries to which visits were made for discussions, meetings etc.

Barbados	Hong Kong	Portugal
Belgium	India	Sri Lanka
Bermuda	Japan	South Africa
Ecuador	Luxemburg	Trinidad
France	Mozambique	Venezuela
Holland	Peru	